Bitesize
AQA GCSE (9-1)
MATHEMATICS
REVISION GUIDE
FOUNDATION

Series Consultant:
Harry Smith

Author:
Navtej Marwaha

Contents

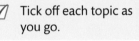 Tick off each topic as
you go.

How to use this book

Use the features in this book to focus your revision, track your progress through the topics and practise your exam skills.

② Features to help you revise

Scan the **QR codes** to visit the BBC Bitesize website. It will link straight through to more revision resources on that subject.

Questions that test **problem-solving** skills are explained in callouts and in the *Problem solving* section at the back.

Test yourself with **exam-style practice** at the end of each page and check your answers at the back of the book.

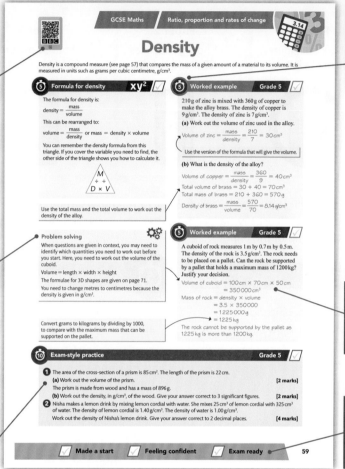

Each bite-sized chunk has a **timer** to indicate how long it will take. Use them to plan your revision sessions.

Complete **worked examples** demonstrate how to approach exam-style questions.

Tick boxes allow you to track the sections you've revised. Revisit each page to embed your knowledge.

② Exam focus features

The *About your exam* section at the start of the book gives you all the key information about your exams, as well as showing you how to identify the different questions.

Throughout the topic pages you will also find green *Exam skills* pages. These work through an extended exam-style question and provide further opportunities to practise your skills.

② ActiveBook and app

This Revision Guide comes with a **free online edition**. Follow the instructions from inside the front cover to access your ActiveBook.

You can also download the **free BBC Bitesize app** to access revision flash cards and quizzes.

If you do not have a QR code scanner, you can access all the links in this book from your ActiveBook or visit **www.pearsonschools.co.uk/BBCBitesizeLinks**.

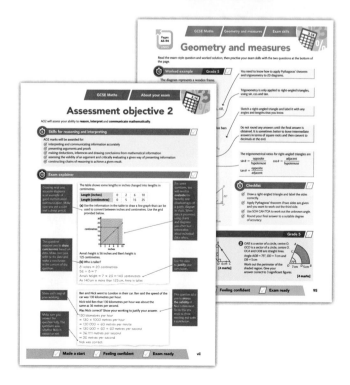

Your Maths GCSE

This page will tell you everything you need to know about the structure of your upcoming AQA Foundation GCSE Maths exam.

⑤ About the exam papers

You will have to take **three papers** as part of your GCSE Maths qualification.

Paper 1
1 hour 30 minutes
80 marks in total

Paper 2
1 hour 30 minutes
80 marks in total

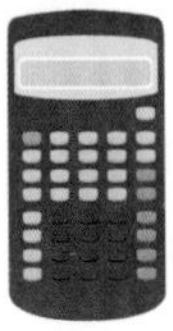

Paper 3
1 hour 30 minutes
80 marks in total

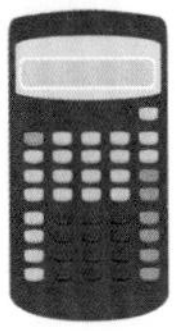

You could be tested on any of the topics you have studied in any of the three written papers. There will be a mixture of question styles on each paper. Papers will usually start with shorter and easier questions and will progress towards harder questions worth more marks at the end of the paper.

⑤ Topics

Your AQA GCSE Maths Foundation specification is divided into five topics. This pie chart shows the five topics and the average proportion of marks that will be allocated to each one:

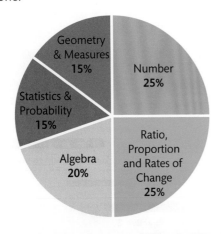

Geometry & Measures 15%
Number 25%
Statistics & Probability 15%
Ratio, Proportion and Rates of Change 25%
Algebra 20%

⑤ Assessment objectives

In your exams, marks will be allocated based on three assessment objectives.

Assessment objective 1 (AO1) is about applying and using standard mathematical techniques. About 50% of the marks in your exam will be AO1 marks.

Assessment objective 2 (AO2) is about reasoning, interpreting and communicating mathematically. About 25% of the marks in your exam will be AO2 marks.

Assessment objective 3 (AO3) is about solving unfamiliar problems, and solving problems involving real-life contexts. About 25% of the marks in your exam will be AO3 marks.

You can see some examples of the different assessment objectives on pages vi, vii and viii.

② My exam dates

Find out the date and time of each of your GCSE Maths papers and write them in this table.

	Date	AM or PM?
Paper 1		
Paper 2		
Paper 3		

Watch out – no calculators allowed on this paper.

sharp pencil
protractor
sharpener
ruler
eraser
black pen
pair of compasses

Made a start | Feeling confident | Exam ready

Exam strategies

In your exam you will need to demonstrate your **problem-solving skills**. This page gives some top tips for answering problem-solving questions and how to approach your exam.

 ## Problem solving

Lots of questions in your GCSE Maths exam will have a problem-solving element. In your exam, marks will be awarded specifically for:

- following through mathematical processes clearly and correctly
- mathematical proofs
- showing your methods clearly
- solving problems in unfamiliar contexts
- combining techniques in an unfamiliar way.

The **top tip** here is **don't be scared** if a question doesn't look familiar, or if it looks like it requires a lot of steps. You will definitely have covered the techniques needed in your course, so take a deep breath and have a go!

Revision advice

☑ Make a list of all the topics you need to revise.

☑ Create a realistic schedule – you can work backwards from the date of your exam!

☑ Start early – don't wait until a few days before your exam!

☑ Revise in small chunks and plan to revisit topics again later.

☑ Take regular short breaks.

☑ Drink plenty of water and eat healthy snacks like fruit or vegetables.

☑ Make sure your notes are easy to read – but remember, they don't have to be works of art.

☑ Don't work too late at night.

☑ Minimise TV and video game time in the run-up to your exams – it will help with concentration.

 ## Exam advice

Exam top tips

- Read all the instructions carefully.
- Check that you haven't missed any pages or questions at the end.
- Answer all the questions on each paper.
- Keep explanations short and use correct mathematical language.
- Make sure your answers look sensible.
- Show all your working.

- Read each question carefully before starting to answer it.
- Check your working if you have any spare time at the end.
- Write down some working even if you can't finish a question.
- 1 mark = about 1 minute.
- Write down an answer even if you're not sure it's right.
- Write down all the figures from your calculator display before rounding your answer.

 ## Exam language

Sometimes the wording of a question gives you a clue about how to tackle it:

You **must** show your working.

This means you **have** to show your method and working clearly. If you just write down the correct answer, you might not get the marks.

Explain…

You need to give a **written** answer. Make sure you use the correct mathematical language. You can back your answer up with data or calculations.

Give a reason for your answer.

Either explain your answer in words, or make sure you have **shown enough working** to justify how you reached the conclusion. Or both!

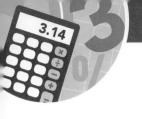

Assessment objective 1

AO1 will assess your ability to **use and apply standard techniques**.

5 Standard mathematical techniques

AO1 marks will be awarded for:

- accurately recalling facts, terminology and definitions
- using and interpreting notation correctly
- accurately carrying out routine procedures or set tasks requiring multi-step solutions.

10 Exam explainer

Multiplying out brackets is an example of a **routine** task. Questions like this should be familiar from your course and your revision.

Expand $4(x + 5)$ **[1 mark]**

$= 4 \times x + 4 \times 5$

$= 4x + 20$

'Write down' questions can usually be answered quickly, using familiar techniques. You don't necessarily need to show a lot of working for these questions.

1 Write down the inequality shown on the number line.

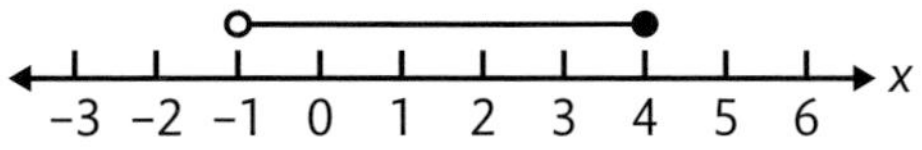

[2 marks]

2 Write down the mathematical name of each of these quadrilaterals.

(a) 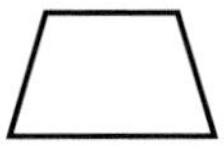 **[1 mark]**

(b) 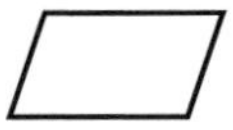 **[1 mark]**

10 Exam explainer

CDE is an equilateral triangle.
F lies on *DE*. *CF* is perpendicular to *DE*.
Show that triangle *CFD* is congruent to triangle *CFE*.

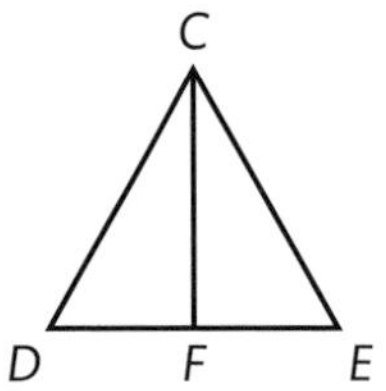

CD = *CE* (triangle *CDE* is equilateral)
CD is the hypotenuse of triangle *CDF*
CE is the hypotenuse of triangle *CEF*
CF is common to triangle *CDF* and triangle *CEF*
Angle *CFD* = angle *CFE* = 90°
Triangle *CDF* is congruent to triangle *CEF* by the RHS rule.

This is a harder question, but you still need to be able to **recall** standard facts and information, such as angle facts.

Make sure you are confident with standard techniques and processes.

3 Solve these simultaneous equations.

$2x + 5y = 16$

$2x + 3y = 8$ **[4 marks]**

Your exam will begin with **multiple choice questions**. Read them really carefully. Here you have to circle the correct value. If you want to change your answer, cross it out then circle the correct answer.

Circle the value of the digit 4 in 6.458.

$\frac{1}{40}$ $\frac{1}{4}$ ~~$\frac{4}{100}$~~ $\frac{4}{10}$ **[1 mark]**

Made a start | Feeling confident | Exam ready

3.14

Assessment objective 2

AO2 will assess your ability to **reason**, **interpret** and **communicate mathematically**.

(5) Skills for reasoning and interpreting

AO2 marks will be awarded for:
- ☑ interpreting and communicating information accurately
- ☑ presenting arguments and proofs
- ☑ making deductions, inferences and drawing conclusions from mathematical information
- ☑ assessing the validity of an argument and critically evaluating a given way of presenting information
- ☑ constructing chains of reasoning to achieve a given result.

(10) Exam explainer

Drawing neat and accurate diagrams is an example of good mathematical communication. Make sure you use a ruler and a sharp pencil.

The table shows some lengths in inches changed into lengths in centimetres.

Length (inches)	0	2	6	10
Length (centimetres)	0	5	15	25

(a) Use the information in the table to draw a line graph that can be used to convert between inches and centimetres. Use the grid provided below.

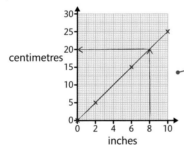

For some questions, you will need to **evaluate** the benefits and disadvantages of a graph, diagram or chart. When data is presented using charts and diagrams you often lose information about individual data values.

This question requires you to **draw conclusions** based on data. Make sure you refer to the data and make a conclusion in the context of the question.

Anna's height is 56 inches and Ben's height is 125 centimetres.

(b) Who is taller?

8 inches = 20 centimetres
56 ÷ 8 = 7
Anna's height = 7 × 20 = 140 centimetres
As 140 cm is more than 125 cm, Anna is taller.

Use the data to **justify** your conclusion.

Show each step of your working.

Ben and Nick went to London in their car. Ben said the speed of the car was 130 kilometres per hour.

Nick told Ben that 130 kilometres per hour was about the same as 36 metres per second.

Was Nick correct? Show your working to justify your answer.

130 kilometres per hour
= 130 × 1000 metres per hour
= 130 000 ÷ 60 metres per minute
= 130 000 ÷ 60 ÷ 60 metres per second
= 36.1111 metres per second
≈ 36 metres per second
Nick was correct.

This question asks you to **assess the validity** of Nick's statement. To do this you need to show working and write a conclusion.

Make sure you answer the question fully. The questions asks whether Nick is correct or not.

Assessment objective 3

AO3 will assess your ability to **solve problems within mathematics and in other contexts**.

 Skills for problem solving

AO3 marks will be awarded for:
- ✓ interpreting results in the context of the given problem
- ✓ translating problems in mathematical or non-mathematical contexts into a process or a series of mathematical processes
- ✓ evaluating methods used and results obtained
- ✓ making and using connections between different parts of mathematics
- ✓ evaluating solutions to identify how they may have been affected by assumptions made.

 Exam explainer

Asha made some ginger biscuits, which she sold at a charity event. She started with:
- 6 kg flour
- 3.75 kg butter
- 2.4 kg sugar
- 355 g ginger.

Here is the list of ingredients for making a batch of 18 ginger biscuits.

125 g flour

100 g butter

80 g sugar

10 g ginger

(a) Asha made as many batches of ginger biscuits as she could, using the ingredients she had.

Work out how many batches of ginger biscuits she made.

Flour: 6000 ÷ 125 = 48
Butter: 3750 ÷ 100 = 37.5
Sugar: 2400 ÷ 80 = 30
Ginger: 355 ÷ 10 = 35.5

Asha made 30 batches of biscuits.

(b) How many biscuits did Asha make in total?

Number of biscuits = 30 × 18 = 540

*This question is given in a **non-mathematical context**. You need to select the most appropriate mathematical techniques to solve the real-life problem.*

Questions that require you to work through a long answer will probably award you marks for using a correct method, so show all of your working.

When there are a lot of steps in a question it is a good idea to write down your working at each stage.

*You need to **evaluate** your solution and give an appropriate answer in context. Having enough ginger for 35 batches does not mean Asha can make 35 batches – she does not have enough sugar for that.*

*Your answer should make sense in the context of the question. Part **(a)** asks how many batches Asha made, not how many biscuits.*

Place value

The value of a digit in a number depends on its position or place within that number.

 Values of digits

Place value of digits					
10 000 Ten thousands (TTh)	1000 Thousands (Th)	100 Hundreds (H)	10 Tens (T)	1 Units (U)	Number in words
				4	four
			5	7	fifty-seven
		3	6	2	three hundred and sixty-two
	7	3	2	7	seven thousand, three hundred and twenty-seven
3	5	8	9	6	thirty-five thousand, eight hundred and ninety-six

The table can be extended to hundred thousands, millions, ten millions and higher values. Every digit in a number has a value that depends on its place in the number (its place value), however big or small the number is.

 Worked example — **Grade 1**

(a) Write the number 7860 in words.

1000	100	10	1
7	8	6	0

Seven thousand, eight hundred and sixty

(b) Write, in figures, the number twenty-five thousand and fourteen.

10 000	1000	100	10	1
2	5	0	1	4

25 014

(c) Write down the place value of the digit 6 in the number 6315.

1000	100	10	1
6	3	1	5

6 is in the thousands column, so it represents 6000

> You can draw a table and fill in the digits so you know the place value of each digit.

> If there is no digit for a particular place value, write 0 in that column.

 Worked example — **Grade 1**

(a) Write these numbers in order of size. Start with the smallest.

3081   1308   3801   1803   3108

1000	100	10	1
3	0	8	1
1	3	0	8
3	8	0	1
1	8	0	3
3	1	0	8

1308   1803   3081   3108   3801

> If you need to compare the size of very large numbers or very small numbers, write them in a table to make the place values easier to see.

 Exam-style practice — **Grade 1**

1 There were 9520 spectators at a football match.

(a) Write the number 9520 in words. **[1 mark]**

There were 3851 club members at the football match.

(b) Write down the place value of the digit 8 in the number 3851. **[1 mark]**

2 The table gives information about the prices of five luxury cars.

Cars	A	B	C	D	E
Price	£50 142	£50 058	£51 042	£52 014	£50 241

Write down the prices of the cars in order of value, starting with the cheapest. **[1 mark]**

 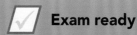

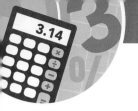

Negative numbers

Negative numbers are less than zero. You should be able to add, subtract, multiply and divide using negative numbers.

5 Using number lines

You can use number lines to work out calculations involving negative numbers.

The diagram shows an example of a number line from −10 on the left to +10 on the right.

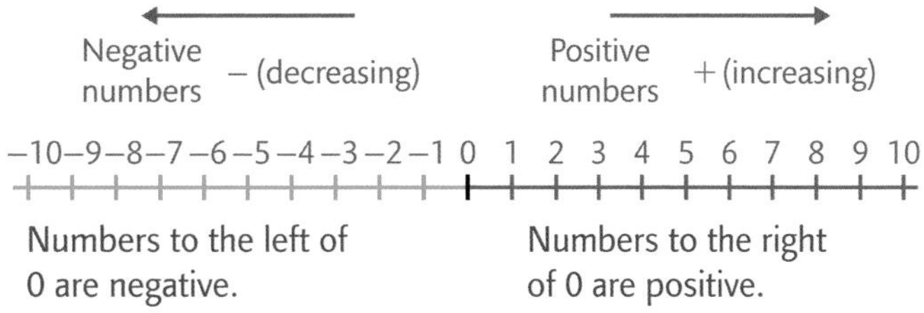

Negative numbers
− (decreasing)
Positive numbers
+ (increasing)
−10 −9 −8 −7 −6 −5 −4 −3 −2 −1 0 1 2 3 4 5 6 7 8 9 10
Numbers to the left of 0 are negative.
Numbers to the right of 0 are positive.

To add a positive number, count the places to the right of your starting value.

To subtract a positive number, count the places to the left.

> Start at 4 and count 6 places to the left on the number line. The value you land on, −2, is the answer.

> The temperature increases by 12 degrees, so you need to add 12. Start at −5 and count 12 places to the right.

Exam focus

- Subtracting a negative number is the same as adding a positive number.
- Adding a negative number is the same as subtracting a positive number.

2 Multiplying and dividing

- When both numbers are negative or both numbers are positive, the answer is positive.

  4 × 2 = 8 −4 × −2 = 8 −4 ÷ −2 = 2
- When one number is negative and one is positive, the answer is negative.

  4 × −2 = −8 4 ÷ −2 = −2

2 Worked example — Grade 1

1 Circle the number that is 10 less than −4.

14 [−14] −6.6

2 Work out −40 ÷ 5

40 ÷ 5 = 8

(One number is negative.)

−40 ÷ 5 = −8

> One number is negative and one number is positive, so the answer is negative.

2 Worked example — Grade 1

Write the following numbers in order.
Start with the lowest number.

−4 0 7 −9 −6

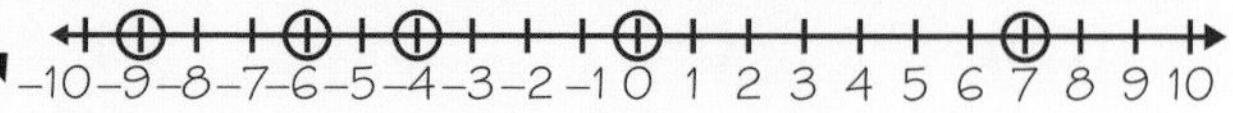

−10 −9 −8 −7 −6 −5 −4 −3 −2 −1 0 1 2 3 4 5 6 7 8 9 10

−9 −6 −4 0 7

> Place all the numbers you are given on a number line. Write down each number in the order that they appear on the number line, from left to right.

5 Worked example — Grade 1

1 Work out 4 − 6

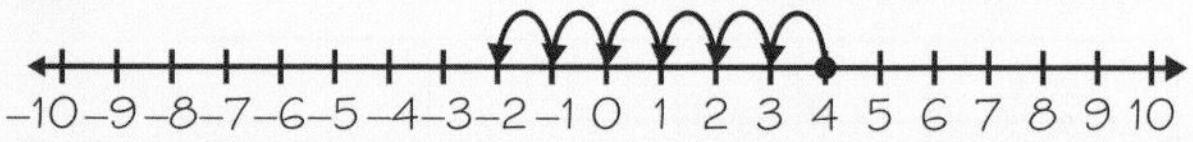

−10 −9 −8 −7 −6 −5 −4 −3 −2 −1 0 1 2 3 4 5 6 7 8 9 10

4 − 6 = −2

2 At 6 a.m. the temperature was −5 °C. By 2 p.m. the temperature had increased by 12 degrees. Write down the temperature at 2 p.m.

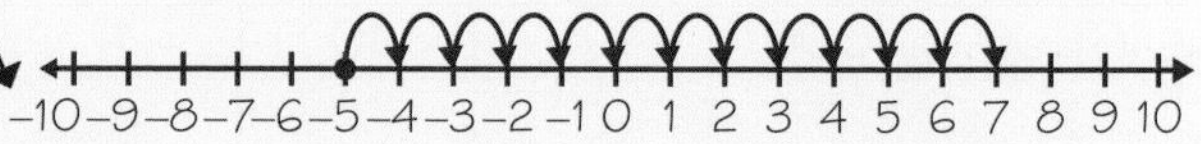

−10 −9 −8 −7 −6 −5 −4 −3 −2 −1 0 1 2 3 4 5 6 7 8 9 10

−5 + 12 = 7 The temperature was 7 °C.

3 Work out 8 − (−6)

8 − (−6) = 8 + 6 = 14

10 Exam-style practice — Grade 1

1 Work out

(a) 8 − (−7) **[1 mark]** **(b)** −5 − (−11) **[1 mark]**

(c) −4 × −8 **[1 mark]** **(d)** −30 ÷ 5 **[1 mark]**

2 Write the following numbers in order.
Start with the lowest number. **[1 mark]**

7 −8 −10 −2 8

3 Charlotte is going on holiday. The temperature in London when she leaves is −3 °C.
When she arrives in Morocco, the temperature is 19 °C. By how much has the temperature increased? Give your answer in degrees. **[1 mark]**

Adding and subtracting

You need to be able to add and subtract whole numbers without using a calculator.

(5) Column addition and subtraction

To add or subtract large numbers, write out their digits in columns according to place value. Then work through each column from right to left, adding or subtracting the units, then the tens, then the hundreds and so on.

Addition

If the answer for one column is higher than 9, carry the 1 across to the bottom of the next column on the left.

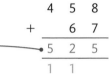

```
      4  5  8
   +     6  7
   ─────────────
      5  2  5
      1  1
```

Draw lines above and below your answer space. If any digits are carried into the next place value, write them underneath the bottom line.

Add the units first.
$8 + 7 = 15 \rightarrow$ write 5 and carry the 1. Then add all the digits in the tens column, including the 1.
$5 + 6 + 1 = 12 \rightarrow$ write 2 and carry the 1.
$4 + 1 = 5 \rightarrow$ write 5

You can use the column methods with decimal numbers as well. Revise this on page 7.

Problem solving

To work out the total population, you need to add the populations of Penn and Compton together.

(2) Mental methods

You can break down sums to quickly add or subtract in your head.

First add or subtract the tens, then the units.

For example, to work out $689 - 54$, subtract 50 and then 4.

```
     −4              −50
   635   639                 689
```

Subtraction

If you have to take a bigger number away from a smaller number, 'borrow' from the column on the left.

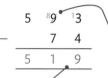

```
      5  ⁸9̶ ¹3
   −     7  4
   ─────────────
      5  1  9
```

Subtract the right-hand column first. 4 is bigger than 3, so borrow 1 from the tens column to give $13 - 4 = 9 \rightarrow$ write 9 in the answer space.

You have borrowed a 1 from the tens column, so cross out 9 and write 8.
$8 - 7 = 1 \rightarrow$ write 1
$5 - 0 = 5 \rightarrow$ write 5

(5) Worked example   Grade 1

1 The village of Penn has a population of 3148 and the village of Compton has a population of 4863. Work out the total population of Penn and Compton.

```
      3  1  4  8
   +  4  8  6  3
   ─────────────
      8  0  1  1
      1  1  1
```
The total population is 8011.

2 Javed has £2156 in his bank account. He spends £348 on some clothes. How much money does he have left in his bank account?

```
    ¹2̶  ¹1  ⁴5̶  ¹6
   −        3   4   8
   ──────────────────
      1   8   0   8
```
Javed has £1808 left in his bank account.

(15) Exam-style practice   Grades 1–2

1 Work out
   (a) $45 + 68$ **[1 mark]**   **(b)** $128 - 49$ **[1 mark]**

2 Alan travels a distance of 3158 miles and Bob travels a distance of 2366 miles.
   (a) Work out the total distance Alan and Bob travel.   **[1 mark]**
   (b) How many more miles does Alan travel than Bob?   **[1 mark]**

3 The table shows the numbers of medals won by the United States and Great Britain in the 2016 Olympics.

	Gold	Silver	Bronze
United States	46	37	38
Great Britain	27	23	17

Which country won more medals and by how many?
You must show your working.   **[3 marks]**

Multiplying and dividing

You need to be able to multiply and divide whole numbers without using a calculator.

To multiply a whole number by a power of 10, count the number of zeros. Using a place value diagram, move all the digits that number of places to the left. The resulting number is bigger.

To divide a whole number by a power of 10, count the number of zeros and then, using a place value diagram, move all the digits that number of places to the right. The resulting number is smaller.

You can think of this as repeated multiplication or division by 10. You can write it using **indices**.
$\times 1000$ is the same as $\times 10 \times 10 \times 10$, which is the same as $\times 10^3$.
$48 \times 1000 = 48 \times 10^3 = 48\,000$
Go to page 15 to revise indices.

1 Work out

(a) 48×10

$= 480$

(b) 48×1000 ◄

$= 48\,000$

2 Work out

(a) $52\,000 \div 100$

$= 520$

(b) $52\,000 \div 1000$

$= 52$

If you are multiplying a whole number by a power of 10, you can check your answer by counting the number of zeros at the end of the number. For example, if you have multiplied a whole number by 1000 then you should have written three extra zeros on the end of the original number.

To multiply two- and three-digit numbers, break the numbers into their place values and use long multiplication to multiply them together. Write down the two numbers in columns according to their place value.

Write the larger number on top.

2. Then multiply 248 by 60. To do this, write down 0 in the units column and then multiply each digit in 248 by 6.

```
        2   4   8
    ×       6   3
        ₁7  ₂4   4
    1 ₂4 ₄8   8   0
    1   5   6   2   4
        ₁       ₁
```

1. Multiply 248 by 3. Break it into hundreds, tens and units, multiplying each by 3, and then add them together.

3. Add the two rows together using column addition to get the final answer.

To work out $768 \div 8$, write the digits in columns like this:

The number on top is the answer.

3. Bring down the 8 from the units so that you have 48. Work out how many times 8 goes into 48: $8 \times 6 = 48$

4. Write 6 on the answer line in the units column and 48 underneath 48.

```
          9   6
    8 | 7  6   8
        7  2
           4   8
           4   8
               0
```

1. Work out how many 8s are in each digit in 768. 8 does not go into 7, so leave the space above 7 blank.

2. Work out how many times 8 goes into 76. Using the 8 times table, you know that $8 \times 9 = 72$ so write 9 on the answer line above the 6. Subtract 72 from 76 to get 4 and write the 4 under the tens column.

5. Subtract the numbers. If there is a remainder, repeat the process.

1 (a) Work out 36×24 [2 marks]

(b) Work out $4571 \div 7$ [2 marks]

2 The cost of a calculator is £14. Work out the cost of 49 of these calculators. [2 marks]

3 A school buys some books. The school pays £784. Each book costs £8
Work out how many books the school bought. [2 marks]

Made a start | Feeling confident | Exam ready

Order of operations

When a calculation involves more than one operation, you must carry it out in a particular order.

5 BIDMAS

You need to remember this order for all your calculations.

If your calculation has brackets with more than one operation in, you still need to use the BIDMAS order of operations for everything inside the brackets. Substitute the value back into the original expression.

B	I	D	M	A	S
Brackets	Indices	Division	Multiplication	Addition	Subtraction
(...)	$\sqrt{x}$ x^2	÷	×	+	−

The I in BIDMAS stands for 'indices', but remember that this includes square roots as well.

10 Worked example — Grades 2–3

Work out

(a) $5 + 6 \times 2$

$6 \times 2 = 12$

So $5 + 6 \times 2 = 5 + 12 = 17$

(b) $16 \div (2 \times 4)$

$2 \times 4 = 8$

$16 \div (2 \times 4) = 16 \div 8 = 2$

(c) $3^2 \times (8 + 2) - 6$

$8 + 2 = 10$

$3^2 = 9$

So $3^2 \times (8 + 2) - 6 = 9 \times 10 - 6$

$\qquad = 90 - 6$

$\qquad = 84$

Exam focus

Jot down BIDMAS in pencil on your exam paper so that you can refer to it during the exam.

You have a multiplication and an addition. Work out the multiplication first: $6 \times 2 = 12$. Then substitute 12 into the addition calculation: $5 + 12 = 17$

According to BIDMAS, brackets are first, so work out (2×4). Then substitute that answer into the original calculation:

$16 \div (2 \times 4)$ becomes $16 \div 8 = 2$

Substitute the values for the bracketed expression and the index. You still need to use BIDMAS, so carry out the multiplication before the subtraction.

Problem solving

The order of operations is the same order that each stage happens in.

1 The discount is applied: £90 − £30

2 Adam and Bobby buy four jackets: × 4

3 Adam and Bobby split the cost: ÷ 2

Work out the calculation in the brackets first and then the division and multiplication. Leave your answer in £.

5 Worked example — Grade 3

The price of a jacket is £90. The manager gives Adam and Bobby a discount of £30 per jacket. They buy 4 jackets and share the cost equally.

Work out how much they each pay for the jackets.

They each pay $(90 - 30) \times 4 \div 2$

£90 − £30 = £60

£60 × 4 = £240

£240 ÷ 2 = £120

Adam and Bobby each pay £120 for the jackets.

10 Exam-style practice — Grades 2–3

1 Work out

(a) $4 + 5 \times 6$ **(b)** $25 - 3 \times 7$ **(c)** $(18 \div 3) - 1 + 7$ **(d)** $4^2 - 24 \div 4$ **[4 marks]**

2 Mira has a length of pipe 8 m long. She wants to cut off three lengths, each of 1.75 m. How much will she have left? Write down the calculation that Mira needs to carry out. You can only use three numbers. **[2 marks]**

Decimals

You need to understand place value for decimals and be able to compare the size of decimals.

 Place value

Every digit in a decimal number has a value depending on its place in the number (its place value). The table below is an extension of the table on page 1.

100 Hundreds (H)	10 Tens (T)	1 Units (U)	.	$\frac{1}{10}$ Tenths	$\frac{1}{100}$ Hundredths	$\frac{1}{1000}$ Thousandths
		0	.	0	4	8
		0	.	0	5	0
		0	.	4	3	7

0.05 is the same as 0.050

0.05 is bigger than 0.048 because 5 hundredths is more than 4 hundredths.

0.437 is bigger than 0.05 because 4 tenths is more than 5 hundredths.

 Comparing decimals

When asked to order decimals in terms of their size, start with the lowest number. For example:

0.56   0.067   0.6   0.65   0.605

1 Write your numbers down in a place value table.

2 Write each decimal with the same number of decimal places by writing zeros at the end.

						Size order
0	.	5	6	0		2
0	.	0	6	7		1
0	.	6	0	0		3
0	.	6	5	0		5
0	.	6	0	5		4

3 Ignoring the decimal points, compare the whole numbers 560, 67, 600, 650, 605

4 Write out the decimals, starting with the smallest number: 0.067, 0.56, 0.6, 0.605, 0.65

 Worked example — **Grade 1**

1 Write these numbers in order of size. Start with the smallest number.

0.301   0.36   0.27   0.329

					Size order
0	.	3	0	1	2
0	.	3	6	0	4
0	.	2	7	0	1
0	.	3	2	9	3

0.27   0.301   0.329   0.36

2 Which is larger, 0.012 or 0.12?

					Size order
0	.	0	1	2	2
0	.	1	2	0	1

0.012 < 0.12 so 0.12 is the larger number.

 Worked example — **Grade 1**

Write down the value of

(a) the 3 in 10.4534

$$\frac{3}{1000}$$

You could write 3 thousandths.

(b) the 2 in 0.026 34

$$\frac{2}{100}$$

You could write 2 hundredths.

 Checklist

☑ Digits after the decimal point have place value

☑ 0.5 = 0.50 = 0.500

☑ Compare numbers using the symbols < (is less than), ≤ (is less than or equal to), > (is greater than) or ≥ (is greater than or equal to). For example: 0.05 > 0.048

Write the numbers, aligning the decimal points, so that the digits align in columns.

Always write out the final answer, using the decimals as they are given in the question.

 Exam-style practice — **Grade 1**

1 (a) Circle the value of the digit 3 in 7.436

$\frac{1}{30}$ $\frac{1}{3}$ $\frac{3}{10}$ $\frac{3}{100}$ **[1 mark]**

(b) What is the place value of the 9 in 0.000 922 2?   **[1 mark]**

2 Write each set of five numbers in order of size. Start with the smallest number.

(a) 0.502   0.5   0.52   0.55   0.505   **[1 mark]**

(b) 0.82   0.814   0.8   0.87   0.869   **[1 mark]**

 Made a start **Feeling confident** **Exam ready**

Operations with decimals

You need to be able to add, subtract, multiply and divide decimals.

⑤ Addition and subtraction

To add or subtract decimals, use the column method on page 3.

1 Write the decimals in a column, with the decimal points aligned.

2 Make sure that the digits in the decimal places are aligned according to their place value. Write in extra zeros to fill in any spaces.

3 Add or subtract each column, starting from the right, making sure the decimal point is in the final answer.

⑩ Worked example   Grade 2

Work out

(a) 3.48 + 2.7

```
  3 . 4 8
+ 2 . 7 0
---------
  6 . 1 8
    1
```

(b) 6.5 − 2.34

```
  6 . ⁴5̶ ¹0
− 2 . 3  4
-----------
  4 . 1  6
```

(c) 6.37 × 4.6

```
        6  3  7
    ×      4  6
  -------------
    3 ₂8 ₄2  2
  ₂2 ₁5 ₂4  8  0
  -------------
    2  9  3  0  2
       1     1
```

6.37 × 4.6 = 29.302

(d) 0.27 ÷ 0.3

0.3 × 10 = 3 and 0.27 × 10 = 2.7

```
      0 . 9
   -------
 3 | 2 . 7
     2   7
   -------
         0
```

0.27 ÷ 0.3 = 0.9

When dealing with money, you always need to write your answer to 2 decimal places, even if the second digit is 0.

⑤ Multiplication and division

Multiplying decimals

1 Write out the calculation without the decimal points.

2 Multiply the numbers by the long multiplication method. See page 4 for more about multiplying.

3 Place the decimal point in the answer by adding the numbers of decimal places in the numbers being multiplied.

Dividing decimals

1 Multiply the divisor by 10 or 100 or 1000 to remove the decimal point.

2 Multiply the number you are dividing by the same number, 10 or 100 or 1000.

3 Carry out the division. See page 4 to revise dividing.

Make sure the decimal points are lined up. Write 0 at the end of 2.7 to write it to 2 decimal places.

2.34 is written to 2 decimal places so 6.5 must be written to 2 decimal places. Write 0 at the end (to make it 6.50).

Write the calculation out in columns according to their place value.

Count the decimal places in 6.37 (2) and 4.6 (1). There are a total of 3 decimal places in the final answer.

If you multiply both numbers in a division by the same number the answer stays the same. Multiply 0.27 and 0.3 by 10 so you are dividing by a whole number.

⑮ Exam-style practice   Grade 2

1 Work out
   (a) 1.3 + 0.45 + 12.368   **[1 mark]**
   (b) 10.36 − 4.987   **[1 mark]**
   (c) 7.86 × 4.7   **[2 marks]**
   (d) 8.47 ÷ 0.7   **[2 marks]**

2 The cost of a hat is £5.65. Work out the cost of 36 of these hats.   **[2 marks]**

3 Andy bought 2 CDs. One cost £10.95 and the other cost £6.89. He paid with a £20 note. How much change did he receive?   **[3 marks]**

4 It costs £34.65 to buy nine identical books. How much would it cost to buy eight of these books?   **[3 marks]**

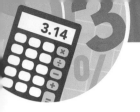

Rounding

You can round numbers to different levels of accuracy. This helps with making approximations and estimating.

5 Rounding numbers

To round to a particular place value, look at the digit to the right of the place value.

For example, to round to the nearest 100, look at the digit in the tens column.

If the tens digit is less than 5 (so 0, 1, 2, 3 or 4), leave the hundreds digit as it is and write zeros in the tens and units columns. This is called **rounding down**.

If the tens digit is 5 or above (so 5, 6, 7, 8 or 9), then add 1 to the hundreds digit and write zeros in the tens and units columns. This is called **rounding up**.

140 rounded to the nearest 100 is 100, but 150 rounded to the nearest 100 is 200

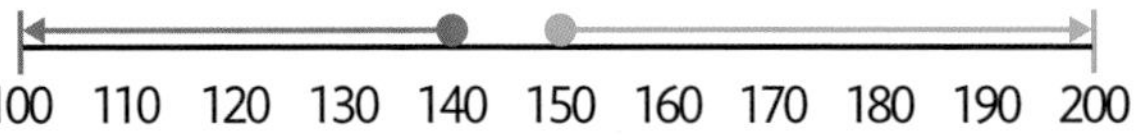
100 110 120 130 140 150 160 170 180 190 200

5 Rounding decimals

You might be asked to give your answer to a certain number of decimal places (d.p.). This works in the same way as rounding whole numbers.

4.5272 to 1 decimal place is 4.5

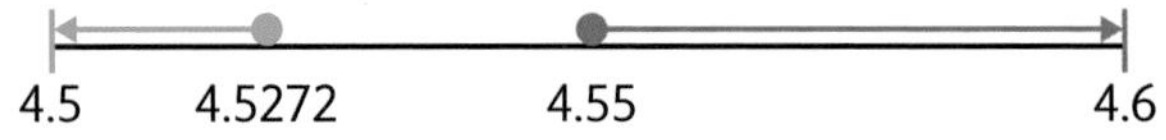
4.5
4.5272
4.55
4.6

4.5272 to 2 decimal places is 4.53

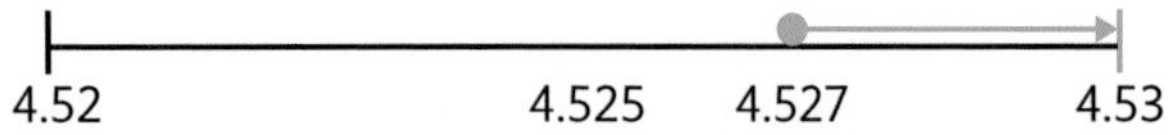
4.52
4.525
4.527
4.53

5 Worked example — Grade 1

1 Round 8.7625

(a) to 1 decimal place

8.7625 ← Underline the first decimal place. Look at the digit to its right.

8.8

(b) to 3 decimal places.

8.7625

5 rounds up, so 8.763

2 **(a)** Round 7549 to 2 significant figures.

7549

4 is less than 5 so round down to get 7500

(b) Round 0.001 385 to 3 significant figures.

0.001385

5 rounds up, so 0.00139

To round numbers that are less than 1, apply the same rules but start counting the significant figures from the first non-zero digit.

5 Worked example — Grade 1

There are 17 892 people at a football match. Round 17 892 to the nearest

(a) 10

17 892 ← Underline the digit in the tens, 9. The digit after that is a 2 so you round down.

17 890

(b) 100

17 892 ← The digit after 8 is 9 so round up.

17 900

(c) 1000

17 892

18 000

You could draw a number line to work this out. 17 892 is closer to 18 000 than to 17 000.

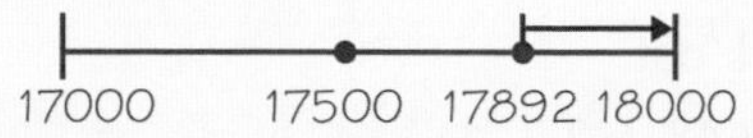
17000
17500
17892
18000

5 Significant figures

The first significant figure in any number is the first non-zero digit. This could be either to the left or the right of the decimal point.

4.7232 rounded to 1 significant figure is 5

40 502 rounded to 1 significant figure is 40 000

0.0375 rounded to 1 significant figure is 0.04

The first significant figure is 4, so you look at the digit to its right.

Write zeros to show the place value of a significant figure.

Remember to write the zeros in your answer to show the place value of the significant figures.

10 Exam-style practice — Grades 1–2

1 Round 5462 to the nearest

(a) 10 **(b)** 100 **(c)** 1000 **[3 marks]**

2 Round 653.015 02 to the following degrees of accuracy:

(a) 1 decimal place **(b)** 3 decimal places **[3 marks]**

3 **(a)** Round 13.582 34 to 1 significant figure. **[1 mark]**

(b) Round 0.005 632 148 to 2 significant figures. **[1 mark]**

(c) Round 217 504 to 3 significant figures. **[1 mark]**

Made a start | Feeling confident | Exam ready

Fractions

A fraction is a part of a whole. Words in everyday use, such as a quarter and a half, are used to describe fractions.

(5) Simple fractions ✓

An object can be divided into equal parts or fractions.

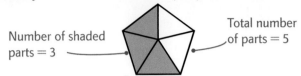

Number of shaded parts = 3

Total number of parts = 5

The fraction of the whole that is shaded is 3 out of the 5 parts. This can be written as $\frac{3}{5}$

The top number is the **numerator**.
The bottom number is the **denominator**.

(5) Equivalent fractions ✓

Equivalent fractions are different fractions that have the same value.

The diagram shows that these fractions are equivalent:

$$\frac{4}{12} = \frac{2}{6} = \frac{1}{3}$$

$\frac{1}{3}$
$\frac{2}{6}$
$\frac{4}{12}$

(5) Finding a fraction of an amount ✓

To work out a fraction of an amount, divide the amount by the **denominator** and multiply the answer by the **numerator**. For example, to work out $\frac{2}{5}$ of 35:

1 $35 \div 5 \times 2 = 7 \times 2$

2 $7 \times 2 = 14$

3 $\frac{2}{5}$ of 35 is 14

Remember to use BIDMAS. Go to page 5 to revise the order of operations.

(5) Worked example Grade 1 ✓

1 Circle the fraction that is **not** in its simplest form.

$\frac{3}{7}$ $\boxed{\frac{15}{27}}$ $\frac{2}{3}$ $\frac{8}{15}$

2 Liam has £540. He spends $\frac{5}{9}$ of this.
Work out how much money Liam has left.

$\frac{5}{9}$ of 540 = 540 ÷ 9 × 5 = 60 × 5 = £300

Money left = £540 − £300 = £240

(10) Worked example Grade 1 ✓

1 What fraction of this shape is shaded?

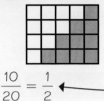

$\frac{10}{20} = \frac{1}{2}$

The number of shaded squares is the numerator. Simplify your fraction if possible.

2 Write down two different fractions that are equivalent to $\frac{1}{3}$

$\frac{3}{9}$ and $\frac{5}{15}$

To work out equivalent fractions, multiply or divide the numerator and the denominator by the same number.

(5) Cancelling fractions ✓

To cancel a fraction to its simplest form, divide the numerator and the denominator by the same number.

$\frac{18}{24} \xrightarrow[\div 2]{\div 2} \frac{9}{12} \xrightarrow[\div 3]{\div 3} \frac{3}{4}$

When you cannot cancel the fraction any more, it is in its **simplest form** or **lowest terms**.

If the numerator and the denominator have a common factor (other than 1) then the fraction is not in simplest form.

(15) Exam-style practice Grades 1–2 ✓

1 (a) Shade $\frac{3}{4}$ of the shape below. **[1 mark]**

(b) Circle the fraction that is in its simplest form.

$\frac{8}{12}$ $\frac{2}{10}$ $\frac{3}{9}$ $\frac{3}{4}$ **[1 mark]**

2 There are 800 students in a college. All of the students are 16, 17 or 18 years old. $\frac{3}{10}$ of the students are 16 years old. $\frac{2}{5}$ of the students are 18 years old. Work out how many of the students are 17 years old. **[3 marks]**

Operations with fractions

You should be able to add, subtract, divide and multiply fractions without using a calculator.

⑤ Adding and subtracting fractions

To add or subtract fractions, you need to find equivalent fractions with the same denominator. Then, add or subtract the fractions by adding or subtracting the numerators.

For adding and subtracting improper fractions, see page 11.

⑤ Multiplying and dividing fractions

When **multiplying** fractions, multiply the numerators and multiply the denominators. Cancel if you can.

$$\frac{3}{4} \times \frac{2}{3} = \frac{6}{12} = \frac{1}{2}$$
$\div 6$ (top) $\div 6$ (bottom)

To **divide** one fraction by another fraction, turn the second fraction upside down and then multiply.

$$\frac{2}{5} \div \frac{4}{6} = \frac{2}{5} \times \frac{6}{4} = \frac{12}{20} = \frac{3}{5}$$
$\div 4$ (top) $\div 4$ (bottom)

⑤ Worked example   Grades 3–5

1 Work out

Multiply the denominators and multiply the numerators.

(a) $\frac{4}{5} \times \frac{5}{6}$

If it is possible, simplify the fraction.

$$\frac{4}{5} \times \frac{5}{6} = \frac{20}{30} = \frac{2}{3}$$

(b) $\frac{2}{5} \div \frac{3}{4}$

$$\frac{2}{5} \div \frac{3}{4} = \frac{2}{5} \times \frac{4}{3}$$

$$= \frac{8}{15}$$

You can't simplify this answer any further.

2 Yesterday a canteen used 120 potatoes.
$\frac{1}{4}$ of them were used for jacket potatoes.
$\frac{1}{3}$ of them were used for roast potatoes.
The rest of them were made into chips.
How many potatoes were used for chips?

Number of jacket potatoes $= \frac{1}{4} \times 120 = 30$

Number of roast potatoes $= \frac{1}{3} \times 120 = 40$

Potatoes used so far: $30 + 40 = 70$

Number of potatoes left for chips: $120 - 70 = 50$

⑤ Worked example   Grades 3–5

Work out

(a) $\frac{1}{3} + \frac{1}{4}$

$$\frac{1}{3} + \frac{1}{4} = \frac{1}{3} \times \frac{4}{4} + \frac{1}{4} \times \frac{3}{3}$$

$$= \frac{4}{12} + \frac{3}{12}$$

The denominators are the same, so you can add the numerators.

$$= \frac{7}{12}$$

(b) $\frac{5}{6} - \frac{2}{3}$

The lowest common multiple of 6 and 3 is 6. Write equivalent fractions with 6 as the denominator.

$$\frac{5}{6} - \frac{2}{3} = \frac{5}{6} \times \frac{1}{1} - \frac{2}{3} \times \frac{2}{2}$$

$$= \frac{5}{6} - \frac{4}{6} = \frac{1}{6}$$

To find equivalent fractions with the same denominator, work out the lowest common multiple of 3 and 4.

Multiples of 3 are 3, 6, 9, 12

Multiples of 4 are 4, 8, 12

12 is the lowest common multiple.

Flip the second fraction and change the operation to multiplication. Then multiply the numerators and multiply the denominators.

Problem solving

Write down the information you are given.

1 Work out $\frac{1}{4}$ of 120 and $\frac{1}{3}$ of 120

2 Add the quantities together.

3 Then subtract that from the total number.

⑩ Exam-style practice   Grades 3–5

1 Work out

(a) $\frac{1}{3} + \frac{2}{5}$ **(b)** $\frac{4}{5} - \frac{1}{4}$ **(c)** $\frac{3}{8} \div \frac{5}{6}$ **(d)** $\frac{9}{10} \times \frac{3}{5}$

[4 marks]

2 There are 240 counters in a box. The counters are black, red or green. $\frac{3}{8}$ of the counters are black and $\frac{2}{5}$ of the counters are red. Work out the number of green counters in the box.   **[4 marks]**

Mixed numbers and improper fractions

You should be able to add, subtract, multiply and divide fractions and mixed numbers without using a calculator.

2 Improper fractions

In an improper fraction, the numerator is higher than the denominator. For example, $\frac{13}{8}$ is an improper fraction. It shows you that the fraction represents a quantity that is bigger than 1.

$\frac{13}{8} = \frac{8}{8} + \frac{5}{8} = 1\frac{5}{8}$

Improper fractions can be written as mixed numbers. Write down the whole numbers and the remaining fraction.

$\frac{31}{8} = 3 \times \frac{8}{8} + \frac{7}{8} = 3\frac{7}{8}$

2 Using improper fractions

When calculating with mixed numbers you can either:

- treat the whole number parts and fraction parts separately
- convert both mixed numbers to **improper fractions** before you add, subtract, divide or multiply.

10 Worked example — Grade 5

1 Work out

(a) $3\frac{1}{4} \times 1\frac{1}{5}$

$= \frac{13}{{}_2\not{4}} \times \frac{{}^3\not{6}}{5} = \frac{39}{10} = 3\frac{9}{10}$

(b) $3\frac{3}{5} \div 2\frac{1}{4}$

$= \frac{18}{5} \div \frac{9}{4} = \frac{{}^2\not{18}}{5} \times \frac{4}{{}_1\not{9}} = \frac{8}{5} = 1\frac{3}{5}$

Turn $\frac{9}{4}$ upside down to get $\frac{4}{9}$, swap the ÷ sign for a × sign and multiply.

Convert each mixed number into an improper fraction and cancel where possible. Cancelling as soon as you can makes the final multiplication much easier.

2 The pattern for a dress requires $2\frac{1}{4}$ m of fabric. How many dresses could be made from a 12 m roll of fabric?

$12 \div 2\frac{1}{4} = \frac{12}{1} \div \frac{9}{4}$

$= \frac{12}{1} \times \frac{4}{9}$

$= \frac{48}{9}$

$= 5\frac{3}{9} = 5\frac{1}{3}$

So 5 complete dresses can be made.

Write down the calculation you need to perform.

5 Worked example — Grade 4

Work out $4\frac{1}{3} - 2\frac{4}{5}$

$= \frac{13}{3} - \frac{14}{5}$

In this case, $\frac{4}{5} > \frac{1}{3}$ so it will be easier to change the mixed numbers into improper fractions first.

$= \frac{13}{3} \times \frac{5}{5} - \frac{14}{5} \times \frac{3}{3}$

$= \frac{65}{15} - \frac{42}{15}$

$= \frac{23}{15}$

$= 1\frac{8}{15}$

For your final answer, remember to convert the improper fraction to a mixed number.

10 Exam-style practice — Grades 4–5

1 Work out

(a) $2\frac{3}{5} \times \frac{2}{5}$ **(b)** $7\frac{1}{2} \div 1\frac{1}{2}$

(c) $1\frac{3}{4} \times 1\frac{1}{3}$ **(d)** $2\frac{3}{5} \div \frac{3}{4}$ **[4 marks]**

2 A rope is $12\frac{3}{4}$ m long. How many lengths of rope, each of $2\frac{1}{8}$ m, can be cut from this rope? **[3 marks]**

Factors, multiples and prime numbers

The factors of a number are any integers that divide into it exactly. The multiples of a number are all the numbers in its times table. A **prime number** has exactly two factors, 1 and itself.

5 Factors

A factor is a whole number that can divide into another whole number.

$$10 \times 8 = 80$$

8 and 10 are factors of 80. They multiply together to make 80, so they are a **factor pair**.

To find factors of a number, write the pairs of factors in a systematic way.

For example, to work out the factors of 80, start with the factor pairs. List all the whole numbers that go into 80 and the number that you need to multiply them by.

$80 = 1 \times 80$ $80 = 2 \times 40$

$80 = 4 \times 20$ $80 = 5 \times 16$

$80 = 8 \times 10$

The next pair would be 10×8 but that is the same as 8×10 so stop at this point.

This shows that the factors of 80 are:
1, 2, 4, 5, 8, 10, 16, 20, 40 and 80

5 Worked example   Grades 1–2

❶ Work out the factors of

  (a) 12

$12 = 1 \times 12$, $12 = 2 \times 6$, $12 = 3 \times 4$

Factors of 12 are 1, 2, 3, 4, 6 and 12

  (b) 42

$42 = 1 \times 42$, $42 = 2 \times 21$, $42 = 3 \times 14$, $42 = 6 \times 7$

Factors of 42 are 1, 2, 3, 6, 7, 14, 21 and 42

❷ Write down the first 12 prime numbers.

2, 3, 5, 7, 11, 13, 17, 19, 23, 29, 31 and 37

❸ Write down the first five multiples of

  (a) 9

9, 18, 27, 36 and 45

  (b) 15

15, 30, 45, 60 and 75

2 Checklist

☑ Factors are integers that divide exactly into whole numbers.

☑ Multiples are the numbers in the times tables.

☑ Prime numbers have only two factors.

5 Prime numbers

Number	Factors
1	1
2	1 and 2
3	1 and 3
4	1, 2 and 4
5	1 and 5
6	1, 2, 3 and 6
7	1 and 7
8	1, 2, 4 and 8
9	1, 3 and 9
10	1, 2, 5 and 10

In the table, the numbers in the shaded rows have exactly two factors. These are examples of prime numbers.

A prime number can only be divided by 1 and itself.

The numbers 2, 3, 5, 7, 11, 13, 17, 19, 23 and 29 are the first ten prime numbers.

5 Multiples

The multiples of a number are the products that appear in the times tables for that number.

Multiples of 3 are 3, 6, 9, 12, 15 and so on.

| Always look for factor pairs when finding factors. |

| 1 is not a prime number because it only has one factor. |

| 2 is the only prime number that is even. |

15 Exam-style practice   Grades 1–2

❶ Here is a list of numbers.

  5   15   17   30   50   60   90   100   125

From the numbers in the list, write down

(a) a multiple of 20   **(b)** a factor of 45

(c) a prime number.   **[3 marks]**

❷ Here is a list of numbers.

  4   5   30   31   39   49   72   100

From the list, write down

(a) a multiple of 8   **(b)** a factor of 50

(c) a prime number.   **[3 marks]**

❸ Circle the number that has exactly two factors.

  6   12   15   23   **[1 mark]**

Prime factors, HCF and LCM

The highest common factor (HCF) of two or more numbers is the largest number that is a factor of all of them. The lowest common multiple (LCM) of two or more numbers is the smallest number that appears in the times tables of all of them. For example, 18 is the LCM of 9 and 6 and 3 is the HCF.

 Prime factors

A prime factor of a number is a factor that is a prime number.

You can use factor trees to work out prime factors.

Writing a number as the product of its prime factors uniquely defines the number. This means that the given set of prime factors defines only that number.

> You can write your final answer in **index form**, like this. This is called expressing the number as the product of powers (or indices) of its prime factors.
> Revise **indices** on page 15.

 Highest common factor (HCF)

The highest common factor of two numbers is the largest number that is a factor of both numbers.

Here are the numbers 36 and 84 expressed as products of their prime factors:

$36 = 2 \times 2 \times 3 \times 3$ and $84 = 2 \times 2 \times 3 \times 7$

Circle the numbers that are in both lists.

$36 = ②\times②\times③\times 3$ and $84 = ②\times②\times③\times 7$

Multiply them together to work out the HCF.

$HCF = 2 \times 2 \times 3 = 12$

 Worked example Grades 3–5

❶ Work out the highest common factor of 16 and 40.

$16 = ②\times②\times②\times 2 \qquad 40 = ②\times②\times②\times 5$

Highest common factor $= 2 \times 2 \times 2 = 8$

❷ Work out the lowest common multiple of 3 and 4.

Multiples of 3: 3, 6, 9,⑫, 15, 18, 21, …

Multiples of 4: 4, 8,⑫, 16, 20, …

Lowest common multiple $= 12$

❸ Give as a product of powers of its prime factors
   (a) 120

$120 = 2 \times 2 \times 2 \times 3 \times 5 = 2^3 \times 3 \times 5$

   (b) 150

$150 = 2 \times 3 \times 5 \times 5 = 2 \times 3 \times 5^2$

   (c) Work out the highest common factor of 120 and 150.

$HCF = 2 \times 3 \times 5 = 30$

 Worked example Grade 5

Give, as products of their prime factors:

(a) 60   **(b)** 132

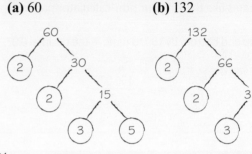

$60 = 2 \times 2 \times 3 \times 5$ $132 = 2 \times 2 \times 3 \times 11$
$60 = 2^2 \times 3 \times 5$ $132 = 2^2 \times 3 \times 11$

 Lowest common multiple (LCM)

The lowest common multiple of two numbers is the smallest number that is a multiple of both numbers.

To identify the LCM, write out the multiples of each number, until you reach a multiple that is the same for both.

Multiples of 36 are: 36, 72, 108, 144, 180, 216, ㉕㉒

Multiples of 84 are: 84, 168, ㉕㉒, 336

$LCM = 252$

> List the **factors** in order so they are easy to compare.

> List the **multiples** in order so they are easy to compare.

 Exam-style practice Grades 3–5

❶ **(a)** Write 108 as a product of powers of its prime factors. **[3 marks]**

   (b) Work out the highest common factor (HCF) of 108 and 24 **[1 mark]**

   (c) Work out the lowest common multiple (LCM) of 108 and 24 **[1 mark]**

❷ **(a)** Give 56 as the product of powers of its prime factors. **[3 marks]**

   (b) Work out the highest common factor (HCF) of 56 and 98 **[1 mark]**

   (c) Work out the lowest common multiple (LCM) of 56 and 98 **[1 mark]**

Estimation and outcomes

You need to be able to estimate answers by rounding each number to 1 significant figure and to list outcomes in a systematic way.

(2) Estimation

Round all the numbers to 1 significant figure, then write out the calculation with the rounded values and work out your estimate.

$5.36 \times 19.47 \approx 5 \times 20 = 100$

$\approx$ is the symbol for approximately equal.

The answer is approximately equal to 100. You might have to make estimates like this on your non-calculator paper.

Multiply top and bottom by 100 to remove the decimal 0.02.

$$\frac{3500}{0.02} = \frac{350\,000}{2}$$

$\times 100$

(5) Worked example — Grade 5

Work out an estimate for

Round each number to 1 significant figure.

(a) $\dfrac{67 \times 402}{197}$

$$\frac{67 \times 402}{197} \approx \frac{70 \times 400}{200} = \frac{28\,000}{200} = 140$$

(b) $\dfrac{509 \times 6.89}{0.021}$

$$\frac{509 \times 6.89}{0.021} \approx \frac{500 \times 7}{0.02} = \frac{3500}{0.02} = \frac{350\,000}{2}$$
$$= 175\,000$$

(2) Estimation checklist

- ☑ Always round each number to 1 significant figure.
- ☑ To remove a decimal from the denominator, multiply numerator and denominator by 10 or 100 or 1000.
- ☑ Estimate square roots or cube roots by working out the nearest square number or cube number.

(5) Listing strategies

When listing all possible outcomes, you need to take a logical approach.

For example, the drinks machine at the local leisure centre sells tea (T), coffee (C) and hot chocolate (H). Heidi buys two drinks at random.

List all the possible pairs of drinks that she could buy.

She could buy TT, TC, TH, CT, CC, CH, HT, HC and HH.

	T	C	H
T	TT	TC	TH
C	CT	CC	CH
H	HT	HC	HH

However, the order that the drinks come in does not matter.

TH is the same as HT, so remove all the repeats.

The possible pairs are TT, TC, TH, CC, CH, HH.

(5) Worked example — Grade 2

Bilal has a box with a red crayon (R), a blue crayon (B), a green crayon (G) and a purple crayon (P).

He is going to take two crayons from the box at random.

Write down all the possible combinations of colours he can take.

RB, RG, RP, B̶R̶, BG, BP, G̶R̶, G̶B̶, GP, P̶R̶, P̶B̶, P̶G̶

The possible combinations are RB, RG, RP, BG, BP, GP

The order in which the crayons are chosen doesn't matter, so cross out any repeated pairs.

(10) Exam-style practice — Grades 4–5

1. Estimate

   (a) $\dfrac{765}{3.9 \times 9.7}$ [2 marks]

   (b) $\dfrac{5.78 \times 324}{0.521}$ [2 marks]

   (c) $\dfrac{9.82 \times 19.54}{0.183}$ [2 marks]

2. Ravina is going to spin an ordinary fair coin and roll an ordinary fair 6-sided dice.
   List all the possible outcomes she could get. One has been done for you.

   (Heads, 1) [2 marks]

Made a start Feeling confident Exam ready

Indices and roots

Indices, or powers, are a short way of writing repeated multiplications. Square and cube numbers can be written as indices. A number multiplied by itself once is a square and a number multiplied by itself twice is a cube. The inverse operations of squares and cubes are square roots and cube roots.

5 Square and cube numbers

When a number is multiplied by itself, the product is a square number. This is normally written as an **index**, or power.

4 is a square number because $2 \times 2 = 2^2 = 4$

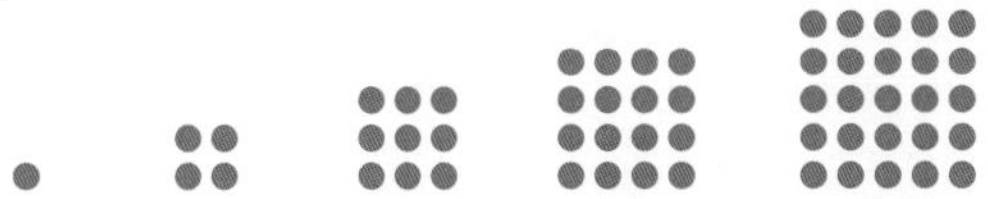

1 1×1 | 4 2×2 | 9 3×3 | 16 4×4 | 25 5×5

When a number is multiplied by itself and then multiplied by itself again, the product is a cube number.

8 is a cube number because $2 \times 2 \times 2 = 2^3 = 8$

1 $1 \times 1 \times 1$ | 8 $2 \times 2 \times 2$ | 27 $3 \times 3 \times 3$ | 64 $4 \times 4 \times 4$

2 Indices with whole numbers

Indices tell you how many instances of a number have been multiplied together.

$6^3 = 6 \times 6 \times 6$ three 6s are multiplied

$4^7 = 4 \times 4 \times 4 \times 4 \times 4 \times 4 \times 4$ seven 4s are multiplied

To work out the values of powers, either write out the full multiplication or use [$x^\square$] on your calculator.

$9^4 =$ [9] [$x^\square$] [4] [=] 6561

A number to the power 1 is always equal to the number itself. $17^1 = 17$

A number to the power 0 is always equal to 1. So for example $17^0 = 1$

You need to be able to use the laws of indices with algebra. Revise the laws on page 25.

You also need to know how to use powers of 10 (written as 10^2, 10^3, 10^4). Revise this with standard form on page 16.

5 Worked example Grade 1

1 Write down the first 10 square numbers.

$1^2 = 1$, $2^2 = 4$, $3^2 = 9$, $4^2 = 16$, $5^2 = 25$, $6^2 = 36$, $7^2 = 49$, $8^2 = 64$, $9^2 = 81$ and $10^2 = 100$

1, 4, 9, 16, 25, 36, 49, 64, 81 and 100

2 Work out the value of $3^3 - 3^2$.

$3^3 - 3^2 = 27 - 9 = 18$

3 Work out $\sqrt[3]{64}$.

$4 \times 4 \times 4 = 64$

so $\sqrt[3]{64} = 4$

You should recognise that 64 is a cube number.

4 Work out $\sqrt{240}$ to 2 decimal places.

$\sqrt{240} = 15.491933$

$= 15.49$ (2 d.p.)

Use BIDMAS. Indices come before subtraction.

Learn the square and cube numbers to help you work out square and cube roots.

If you don't recognise a square number and the question specifies a degree of accuracy, you will probably need to use your calculator.

5 Roots

A square root $\sqrt{x}$ is the inverse operation of squaring a number.

A cube root $\sqrt[3]{x}$ is the inverse operation of cubing a number.

If you know the first ten square numbers, you should know their square roots as well. $8^2 = 64$ and $\sqrt{64} = 8$

To work out the square root of a number on your calculator, use [$\sqrt{\square}$].

$\sqrt{1600} =$ [$\sqrt{\square}$] [1] [6] [0] [0] [=] 40

15 Exam-style practice Grade 1

1 Write down the value of the square root of 144 **[1 mark]**

2 Circle the power of 3 that is 243 **[1 mark]**

3^4 3^5 3^6 3^7

3 Work out the value of $5^2 + 2^3$ **[2 marks]**

4 Alan's age is a square number.
Beth's age is a cube number.
Alan is 2 years younger than Beth.
How old are Alan and Beth? **[2 marks]**

5 Work out $\sqrt{144} + \sqrt{289}$ **[2 marks]**

Made a start | Feeling confident | Exam ready

Standard form

You can use standard form to write very small and very large numbers by using powers of 10 to express the size of the number.

(5) Numbers in standard form

Notation

A number in standard form is written as:

$A \times 10^n$

where $1 \leqslant A < 10$ and n is an integer.

Standard form is used for writing very small and very large numbers.

$856\,000\,000 = 8.56 \times 10^8$

$0.000\,000\,321 = 3.21 \times 10^{-7}$ — For numbers less than 1, n is negative.

Writing numbers in standard form

Think of the number as two parts: a number, A, multiplied by a power of 10, 10^n

$34\,500\,000 = 3.45 \times 10\,000\,000$

$\qquad = 3.45 \times (10 \times 10 \times 10 \times 10 \times 10 \times 10 \times 10)$

$\qquad = 3.45 \times 10^7$

Changing from standard form

To convert the number from standard form, work out the calculation.

$6.34 \times 10^6 = 6.34 \times 1\,000\,000$

$\qquad = 6\,340\,000$

(5) Multiplying and dividing

Multiplying standard form numbers

Rearrange so that the powers of 10 are together.

$(6.4 \times 10^7) \times (2 \times 10^{-3})$

$= (6.4 \times 2) \times (10^7 \times 10^{-3})$

Multiply the number parts and **add** the powers.

$= 12.8 \times 10^4$

Rewrite your answer in standard form if necessary.

$= 1.28 \times 10^5$

Dividing standard form numbers

Rearrange so that the powers of 10 are together.

$(3 \times 10^{-8}) \div (6 \times 10^5)$

$= (3 \div 6) \times (10^{-8} \div 10^5)$

Divide the number parts and **subtract** the powers.

$= 0.5 \times 10^{-13}$

Rewrite your answer in standard form if necessary.

$= 5 \times 10^{-14}$

See page 25 for the laws of indices. You need to learn them.

See page 58 for more about speed, distance and time.

(5) Worked example | Grade 5

1 Write these numbers in standard form.

Divide by a power of 10 to leave a number between 1 and 10.

(a) $562\,000$

$562\,000 = 5.62 \times 100\,000$

$\qquad = 5.62 \times 10 \times 10 \times 10 \times 10 \times 10$

$\qquad = 5.62 \times 10^5$

(b) $0.000\,326$

$0.000\,326 = 3.26 \times 0.0001$

$\qquad = 3.26 \times 10^{-4}$

Write as a number between 1 and 10 multiplied by a power of 10.

2 Write 8.29×10^{-5} as an ordinary number.

$8.29 \times 10^{-5} = 8.29 \times 0.00001 = 0.000\,082\,9$

Work out the calculation.

(2) Use of a calculator

Standard form can be entered into a calculator using the $\boxed{\times 10^x}$ button.

Suppose you want to enter 3.2×10^{12} into the calculator.

Enter $\boxed{3}$ $\boxed{.}$ $\boxed{2}$ and then press $\boxed{\times 10^x}$ followed by $\boxed{1}$ $\boxed{2}$

It will show 3.2×10^{12}

Then add, subtract, multiply or divide the number as usual.

(5) Worked example | Grade 5

Work out

(a) $(4.5 \times 10^8) \times (3 \times 10^{-6})$

$(4.5 \times 3) \times (10^8 \times 10^{-6}) = 13.5 \times 10^2$

$\qquad\qquad\qquad\qquad\qquad = 1.35 \times 10^3$

(b) $(3 \times 10^9) \div (4 \times 10^{12})$

$(3 \div 4) \times (10^9 \div 10^{12}) = 0.75 \times 10^{-3} = 7.5 \times 10^{-4}$

(5) Exam-style practice | Grade 5

A satellite travels for 5×10^2 hours at a speed of 9×10^4 km/h.

(a) Use distance $=$ speed $\times$ time to calculate the distance travelled by the satellite. Give your answer in standard form. **[2 marks]**

A second satellite travels 3×10^4 km one month and 4×10^3 km the next month.

(b) Work out the distance travelled by the satellite in the two months. Give your answer in standard form. **[2 marks]**

Error intervals

Error intervals give a possible range of values when numbers are rounded.

 Smallest and greatest numbers

When a number is rounded, its actual value can be up to half the rounded unit above and half the rounded unit below.

If the mass of an egg is 50 g to the nearest ten grams:

- the lowest actual mass could be 50 – 5 = 45 g
- the greatest actual mass could be up to but not including 50 + 5 = 55 g

The actual mass could be anywhere between 45 g and 55 g, but not 55 g because at this point you would round the mass up.

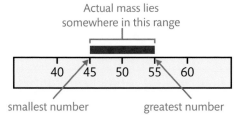

Actual mass lies somewhere in this range

smallest number   greatest number

The **greatest number** it could be is the maximum value or upper limit for a measurement.

The **smallest number** it could be is the minimum value or lower limit of the measurement.

Error interval

An error interval is a way of writing the smallest and greatest possible values as an inequality.

smallest number $\leqslant$ actual value $<$ greatest number

If the value is 50 g rounded to the nearest ten grams, the error interval can be written as

$$45 \leqslant \text{actual value} < 55$$

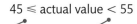

This means greater than or equal to.

This means less than but not equal to. It shows that 55 cannot be the actual value.

 Truncation

Instead of rounding a number, it can be **truncated**. This is where some of the digits are taken off the end without rounding. For example, 3.141 59 can be truncated to 3.141. If it was **rounded** to 3 decimal places, it would be 3.142.

The error interval for a truncated number is different from the error interval for a rounded number.

If a number was truncated to 3.141, the error interval would be $3.141 \leqslant x < 3.142$. The extra decimal places mean it has to be larger than or equal to 3.141, but smaller than 3.142

Worked example | **Grade 4**

1 Kim's watch cost £200 correct to 2 significant figures.

Write down an error interval for the actual cost of Kim's watch.

10 ÷ 2 = 5 so the value is £200 ± 5
200 − 5 = £195
200 + 5 = £205
The error interval is £195 ≤ actual value < £205

2 The mass, m, of an apple is 34 g to the nearest gram.

Complete the following statement to show the range of possible values of m.

1 ÷ 2 = 0.5 so the mass is 34 ± 0.5 g
Smallest possible value = 34 − 0.5 = 33.5 g
Greatest possible value = 34 + 0.5 = 34.5 g

$$\underset{\text{33.5 g}}{\ldots\ldots\ldots} \leqslant m < \underset{\text{34.5 g}}{\ldots\ldots\ldots}$$

3 Jonathan calculated a value, x, for a science experiment, but only wrote down the first four digits from his calculator display. Write an error interval for the actual value.

6.167

6.167 ≤ x < 6.168

 Exam-style practice | **Grade 4**

1 The volume, V, of a box is 39 cm³ to the nearest integer.

Complete this statement to show the range of possible values of V.

.... $\leqslant V <$ .... **[2 marks]**

2 The width, w, of a laptop is 45.6 cm to 1 decimal place.

Complete the following statement to show the range of possible values of w.

.... $\leqslant w <$ .... **[2 marks]**

3 A length, l, is given as 54.86 cm to 2 decimal places.

Give the error interval for the range of possible values for l. **[2 marks]**

4 The height, h, of a toy is 83.58 cm to 2 decimal places. Complete the following statement to show the range of possible values of h.

.... $\leqslant h <$ .... **[2 marks]**

 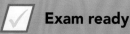

Number

Read the exam-style question and worked solution, then practise your exam skills with the questions at the bottom of the page.

 Worked example · 10 · · **Grades 4–5**

Ravina measured the length and the width of her rectangular patio.

16 m

10.25 m

She measured the length to be 16 m correct to the nearest metre and the width to be 10.25 m correct to the nearest centimetre.

> The smallest possible value is the smallest value that an amount can have when the number is written to a specified degree of accuracy.

> The greatest possible value is the largest value that an amount can have when the number is written to a specified degree of accuracy.

(a) Write down the error interval for the length, l m.

The smallest possible value is 15.5 m
The greatest possible value is 16.5 m
The error interval is $15.5 \leqslant l < 16.5$

(b) Write down the error interval for the width, w m.

The smallest possible value is 10.245 m
The greatest possible value is 10.255 m
The error interval is $10.245 \leqslant w < 10.255$

> An error interval for a number, x, can be written as smallest possible value $\leqslant x <$ greatest possible value

> For any number, written correct to a specified degree of accuracy, the exact value lies in a range from half a unit below to half a unit above the rounded number.

 Exam-style practice · 15 · **Grades 4–5**

1 The table shows some temperatures at midnight in Scotland.

City	Temperature at midnight
Aberdeen	$-8\,°C$
Dundee	$-3\,°C$
Edinburgh	$6\,°C$
Glasgow	$-1\,°C$

(a) What is the difference in temperatures between:

   (i) Aberdeen and Dundee **[1 mark]**

   (ii) Aberdeen and Glasgow? **[1 mark]**

In Edinburgh, the temperature drops by 8 degrees from midnight to 6 a.m.

(b) What is the temperature in Edinburgh at 6 a.m.? **[1 mark]**

2 Joe and Libby set the alarms on their phones to sound at 7.45 a.m.

Both alarms sound together at 7.45 a.m.
Joe's alarm then sounds every 8 minutes.
Libby's alarm then sounds every 9 minutes.
At what time will both alarms next sound together? **[3 marks]**

> You need to work out the lowest common multiple of 8 and 9, then add that number of minutes to the starting time.

3 **(a)** Work out

   (i) $1\frac{3}{4} + 2\frac{4}{5}$ **[3 marks]** **(ii)** $\frac{4}{7} \times £42$ **[1 mark]**

   (b) Estimate the value of 19.84×302.67 **[2 marks]**

4 3 chairs cost a total of £47.82.
Work out the total cost of 7 chairs. **[2 marks]**

5 Zoe is selling books and magazines to raise money for charity. She wants to raise a total of £175.
Zoe sells 86 hardback books for 90p each.
She sells 112 paperback books for 75p each.
She sells magazines for 30p each.
Zoe has 36 magazines to sell.

Work out if she has enough magazines to sell to reach her £175 target. **[5 marks]**

6 **(a)** Write the following numbers as products of their prime factors.

   (i) 60   **(ii)** 96 **[3 marks]**

   (b) Work out the highest common factor of 60 and 96. **[1 mark]**

   (c) Work out the lowest common multiple of 60 and 96. **[1 mark]**

Function machines

You can use function machines when you need to find a relationship between two variables.

A **function machine** is a diagram that represents an operation (or a set of operations) that takes an **input**, applies a rule and delivers the answer as an **output**.

input ⟶ | function machine | ⟶ output

This is an example of a function machine with two operations.

x ⟶ | $+3$ | ⟶ | $\times 4$ | ⟶ y
5 ⟶ ⟶ 32

You can work backwards through a function machine using **inverse** or opposite operations. To work out the value of x, given the value of y, you would need to $\div 4$ and then -3.

When you use function machines, the order matters. Multiply by 3 first and **then** add 1.

(a) Write one operation in each box so that $y = 3x + 1$

x ⟶ | $\times 3$ | ⟶ | $+1$ | ⟶ y

(b) Write one operation in each box so that $y = 3(x + 1)$

x ⟶ | $+1$ | ⟶ | $\times 3$ | ⟶ y

Remember BIDMAS: you need to apply the operation inside the brackets first.

1 x ⟶ | $+4$ | ⟶ | $\times 2$ | ⟶ y

Use the function machine to work out

(a) the value of y when $x = 2$

$2 + 4 = 6$
$6 \times 2 = 12$
$y = 12$

(b) the value of x when $y = 10$.

$10 \div 2 = 5$
$5 - 4 = 1$
$x = 1$ ⟵

Work backwards through the function machine, using inverse operations, to work out x.

2 An approximate rule for changing from degrees Celsius (C) to degrees Fahrenheit (F) is:

Double C and add 30

Draw a function machine to convert a temperature in degrees Fahrenheit (F) to one in degrees Celsius (C).

F ⟶ | -30 | ⟶ | $\div 2$ | ⟶ C

Multiplying a number by 2 is the same as doubling it. You will need the inverse function: $\div 2$

1 Here is a function machine.

x ⟶ | square | ⟶ | -5 | ⟶ y

Complete the table, using positive values for x.

x	y
3	
4	
	20
	-1

[4 marks]

2 When the numbers 4, 5, 6, 7 are inputs, the outputs are 15, 17, 19, 21. Draw a 2-step function machine for these inputs and outputs. **[3 marks]**

Algebraic substitution

Algebraic expressions use letters to represent numbers. When you replace the letters with numbers, this is known as algebraic substitution.

 5 Algebraic expressions

Algebra replaces the numbers in a calculation with letters. The same operations are used as in a numerical calculation ($+$, $-$, $\times$, $\div$). However, these calculations, or algebraic expressions, can look slightly different:

- $4 \times x$ is written as $4x$
- $x \times y$ is written as xy
- $4 \div y$ is written as $\frac{4}{y}$
- $y \times y$ is written as y^2

 5 Substituting numbers

You can **evaluate** an algebraic expression by substituting a number for each letter.

For example, if $n = 5$ then $2n = 2 \times 5 = 10$

If the expression has more than one term make sure you use the correct **order of operations**.

Go to page 5 to revise BIDMAS.

 10 Worked example — **Grades 2–3**

1 $k = 3$ and $m = 7$

Work out the value of $3k + 4m$.

$3k + 4m = 3 \times 3 + 4 \times 7$
$= 9 + 28$
$= 37$

> Make sure you follow the order of operations. Use BIDMAS: <u>M</u>ultiplication is carried out before <u>A</u>ddition.

2 $P = 2x + 5y$

$x = 7$

$y = -4$

Work out the value of P.

$P = 2x + 5y$
$= 2 \times 7 + 5 \times -4$
$= 14 - 20$
$= -6$

> Substitute the values of x and y into the formula.

> Formula and equation are the names for algebraic statements with an equals sign.
> $x + 3y^2$ is an expression.
> $x + 3y^2 = 12$ is an equation or a formula.
> Go to page 24 to revise formulae.

3 A person's body mass index (BMI) is given by the following formula:

$$B = \frac{m}{h^2}$$

where B is body mass index
m is mass in kilograms
and h is height in metres.

Robert has a mass of 60 kg. He has a height of 1.68 m. If his BMI is more than 25, he is considered overweight.

Is Robert overweight?
You must show your working.

$B = \frac{m}{h^2}$
$m = 60, h = 1.68$
$B = 60 \div 1.68^2$
$= 21.2585034$
$= 21.3$ (1 d.p.)
Robert is not overweight because 21.3 is less than 25

Problem solving

Read the question carefully and write down the values you have been given. The question gives the values for m and h, so you just need to substitute these numbers into the formula to work out the value of B. Make sure you write a short conclusion to answer the question.

 **10 Exam-style practice** — **Grades 2–3**

1 $p = 7u + 0.4t$

Work out the value of p when $u = -4$ and $t = 18$

[2 marks]

2 $x = -5$

$y = 2$

Work out the value of $3x^2 + 4y$ **[2 marks]**

Collecting like terms

Expressions can be simplified by collecting together any terms that are made up of the same letters.

⑤ Simplifying expressions

Like terms are terms that have the same letter(s) with the same powers but can have different numerical coefficients.

Terms with $+$ or $-$ in front of them can be simplified by collecting like terms.

$t + 3t$ can be combined to give $4t$

$t^2 + 3t^2$ can be combined to give $4t^2$

$t + 3t^2$ cannot be combined as t and t^2 are not like terms even though they have the same letter. They have different powers.

> Combine the like terms. There are four ts so write this as $4t$.

> Add or subtract the coefficients on like terms.
> $2 + 4 - 3 = 3$

> There are two different sets of like terms in this expression. Collect all the d terms together and all the c terms together.

> Combine x^2 terms in the same way you would combine x. Add or subtract the coefficients on the like terms.

② Expressions with different terms

Sometimes expressions have two or more terms which are not like terms. Arrange the expression so that all of the like terms are next to each other. Then you can collect together all the like terms to give a simplified expression.

For example, to simplify the expression $r + 4p + 2r - 9p$:

① Rearrange the expression so the like terms are together:
$r + 2r + 4p - 9p$

② Add or subtract the coefficients to combine the terms.
r terms: $1 + 2 = 3$
p terms: $4 - 9 = -5$

③ Collect the like terms: $3r - 5p$

② Checklist

- ☑ Keep each term together with the $+$ or $-$ in front of it.
- ☑ Like terms have the same letter(s) and the same power.
- ☑ x by itself is same as $1x$.

⑩ Worked example   Grades 1–2

① Circle the expression that can be written as $3a$.

$a^3 \qquad a \times a \times a \qquad 3 + a \qquad \boxed{a + a + a}$

② Simplify

(a) $t + t + t + t$

$= 4t$

(b) $u + u + u - u$

$= 2u$

③ Simplify

(a) $2a + 4a - 3a$

$= 3a$

(b) $d + 6d - 4c$

$= 7d - 4c$

④ Simplify

(a) $4x^2 + 2x^2 + 6x^2$

$= 12x^2$

(b) $7y^2 - 9y^2 + z - y^2$

$= -3y^2 + z$

> Collect the like terms and then combine them. Combine the terms for y^2 and then add z.

⑤ Simplify

(a) $5e + 7f - 6e + 4f$

$= 5e - 6e + 7f + 4f$

$= -e + 11f$

(b) $x + 4x^2 + 3x - 5x^2$

$= x + 3x + 4x^2 - 5x^2$

$= 4x - x^2$

> Collect the x and the x^2 terms separately. x and $4x^2$ are not like terms because the powers of x are different.

⑩ Exam-style practice   Grades 1–2

① Simplify

(a) $m + m + m - m + m + m - m$ **[1 mark]**

(b) $5x - 3y + 4x - 2y$ **[2 marks]**

② Simplify

(a) $3c^2 + 5c^2 - c^2$ **[1 mark]**

(b) $9x - 3y - 6x - 7y$ **[2 marks]**

③ Simplify $6t - 3 - 8t + 7$ **[2 marks]**

④ Simplify $7a + 5b - 2a - 9b$ **[2 marks]**

Simplifying expressions

You need to be able to simplify algebraic expressions that include multiplication signs and division signs.

② Multiplying expressions

To simplify an algebraic expression that includes a multiplication sign, follow these rules.

1 Multiply all the numbers, including coefficients.

2 Use the laws of indices to simplify the powers of the letters. Go to page 25 to revise laws of indices.

A **coefficient** is the number in front of a letter in an algebraic expression. It means how many lots of that letter there are. For example: $3c$ means $3 \times c$

a is multiplied by itself 6 times so, using the laws of indices ($a^m \times a^n = a^{m+n}$), you can write it as a^6

$5x$ means $5 \times x$. You can multiply in any order and get the same answer, so multiply the numbers and then the letters.

Write the division as a fraction.

Divide the numbers as much as possible, then cancel any common letters on the top and bottom of the fractions.

Letters in algebra can be simplified so that they are written next to each other in alphabetical order.

② Dividing expressions

To simplify an algebraic expression that includes a division sign, follow these rules.

1 Write the expression as a fraction.

2 Cancel the numbers. Write any numbers that are not whole as fractions instead of decimals.

3 Use index rules (page 25) to simplify the powers of the letters.

⑤ Worked example | Grade 2

Simplify $\dfrac{5x^2 \times 4x^4}{6x^3}$

$= \dfrac{5 \times x^2 \times 4 \times x^4}{6 \times x^3} = \dfrac{5 \times 4 \times x^2 \times x^4}{6 \times x^3}$

$= \dfrac{20x^6}{6x^3}$

$= \dfrac{10x^3}{3}$

⑩ Worked example | Grades 1–2

1 Simplify

(a) $a \times a \times a \times a \times a \times a$

$= a^6$

(b) $5x \times 3x$

$= 5 \times x \times 3 \times x$

$= 5 \times 3 \times x \times x = 15x^2$

2 Simplify

(a) $10x \div 2$

$= \dfrac{10 \times x}{2} = 5x$

(b) $20xy \div y$

$= \dfrac{20 \times x \times \cancel{y}}{\cancel{y}} = 20x$

3 Simplify

(a) $3b \times 4b \times 2b$

$= 3 \times b \times 4 \times b \times 2 \times b$

$= 3 \times 4 \times 2 \times b \times b \times b = 24b^3$

(b) $4x \times 5y$

$= 4 \times x \times 5 \times y$

$= 4 \times 5 \times x \times y = 20xy$

4 Simplify $25x^3 \div 5x$.

$= \dfrac{25 \times x^{\cancel{3}2}}{5 \times \cancel{x}}$

$= 5 \times x^2 = 5x^2$

Remember that x is the same as x^1. Use the rule $a^m \div a^n = a^{m-n}$ to simplify the expression.

② Checklist

- ☑ $a \times a = a^2$ (not $2a$)
- ☑ $a \times b = ab$ or ba
- ☑ $a \times a \times a = a^3$ (not $3a$)
- ☑ $1a = a$

Simplify the expression in the numerator as much as possible. Then cancel a factor of 2 and a factor of x^3 from the top and bottom of the fraction.

⑩ Exam-style practice | Grades 1–2

1 Simplify $c \times d \times 5$ **[1 mark]**

2 Simplify $3 \times w \times 2$ **[1 mark]**

3 Simplify $3g \times 5h$ **[1 mark]**

4 Simplify $24x \div 6$ **[1 mark]**

5 Simplify $48xy \div 8y$ **[1 mark]**

Writing expressions

It is important to be able to interpret information and then write it in terms of algebraic expressions.

⑤ Interpreting information

Instructions or rules can be written as algebraic expressions.

Jess wants to put an advert for her school play in the local paper.

The cost is £2 for each line of text, plus a £10 fee.

To write this as an expression, use a letter to represent the number of lines of text.

For example, the cost is:

$$£2 \times \text{number of lines} + £10$$

Or $\qquad 2n + 10$

where n is the number of lines of text.

> If there are 25 crayons in the tub to start with, then the number left must be p crayons less than this.

> Remember that $5 \times x$ is written as $5x$.

> The order of operations means that multiplication comes before addition.
>
> In order for this expression to be correct, $d + 4$ must happen before $\times 15$. Place brackets around the $d + 4$ expression to make sure this part of the formula is calculated first.

⑤ Worked example Grade 3

Sandeep, Pavan and Jake sell toy cars.

Sandeep sells x cars. Pavan sells 6 more cars than Sandeep. Jake sells twice as many cars as Sandeep.

Write an expression, in terms of x, for the total number of toy cars sold by Sandeep, Pavan and Jake.

Sandeep	Pavan	Jake
x	$x + 6$	$2x$

The total number of toy cars is $x + x + 6 + 2x$

$$= x + x + 2x + 6$$
$$= 4x + 6$$

⑩ Worked example Grade 3

1 Crayons are sold in cartons and in tubs.
There are 5 crayons in a carton.
There are 25 crayons in a tub.
Asha buys one tub of crayons.
She takes p crayons out of the tub.

   (a) Write down an expression, in terms of p, for the number of crayons left in the tub.

➤ $25 - p$

   Poppy buys x cartons of crayons and y tubs of crayons.

   (b) Write down an expression, in terms of x and y, for the total number of crayons Poppy buys.

$5x + 25y$

2 The cost of hiring a bike for d days can be worked out using this rule.

   Add 4 to the number of days' hire.

   Multiply your answer by 15.

   Write down an expression, in terms of d, for the total cost for hiring a bike for d days.

$(d + 4) \times 15$

$15(d + 4)$ ◄

Exam focus 📌

When you have finished working out an expression, make sure that you have collected all of the like terms and cancelled the number parts or the indices to simplify the equation.

'6 more than' means adding 6 and 'twice as many' means multiply by 2, or double it.

⑩ Exam-style practice Grade 3

1 Ben has x cats.
Jenny has twice as many cats as Ben.
Kathy has 2 more cats than Ben.

Write an expression, in terms of x, for the total number of pets that Ben, Jenny and Kathy have. **[2 marks]**

2 Blank revision cards are sold in packets and in boxes.
There are 8 revision cards in a packet.
There are 27 revision cards in a box.

Avi buys p packets of revision cards and b boxes of revision cards.

Write an expression for the number of revision cards Avi buys, in terms of p and b. **[3 marks]**

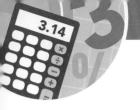

Algebraic formulae

A formula is a mathematical rule. You use algebra to write a formula (the plural of formula is formulae). A formula is similar to an algebraic expression, but it has an equals sign, and more than one variable. You need to be able to substitute numbers into formulae to solve them.

5 Writing a formula

Peter advertises his business in the local magazine.

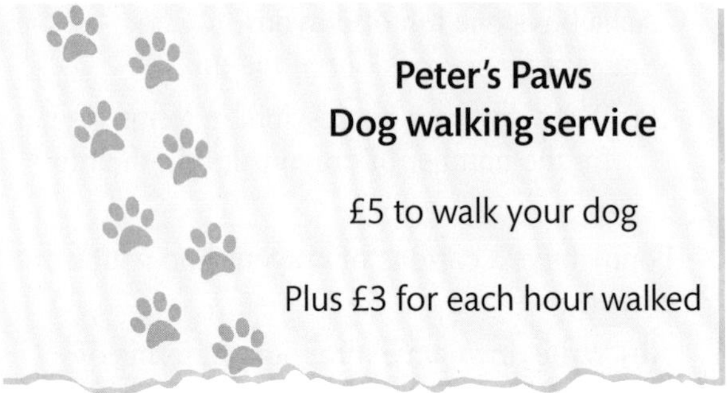
Peter's Paws
Dog walking service
£5 to walk your dog
Plus £3 for each hour walked

To write this as an algebraic formula, substitute the variables for letters.

For example, if the total cost is £T, and the number of hours is n, then the formula Peter can use is:

total cost = (number of hours × £3) + £5

$$T = 3n + 5$$

When you define your variables, you must give their units. If you have a value for n you can now solve this formula. If Peter takes his neighbour's dog on a two-hour walk, how much will he charge?

$T = 3 \times 2 + 5$

$= 6 + 5 = 11$

He will charge £11

5 Worked example Grade 5

This formula gives you the distance, s metres, travelled by an object in t seconds.

$s = 10t + 5t^2$

Work out the value of s when $t = 3$

$s = 10 \times 3 + 5 \times 3^2$ ← Substitute the value of t into the formula.

$= 30 + 5 \times 9$

$= 30 + 45$

$= 75$

When substituting, you might use brackets. You could write $10t$ as $10(t)$ or $10(3)$. If there are numbers or letters outside brackets, without an operation in between, this means that you multiply the term outside the brackets with whatever is inside the brackets.

For example: $10(3)$ means 10×3

Order of operations is very important when you are evaluating formulae. Remember to use BIDMAS.

5 Worked example Grade 3

Bulbs are sold in packets and in boxes. There are 3 bulbs in a packet. There are 12 bulbs in a box.

Kamran buys x packets of bulbs and y boxes of bulbs.

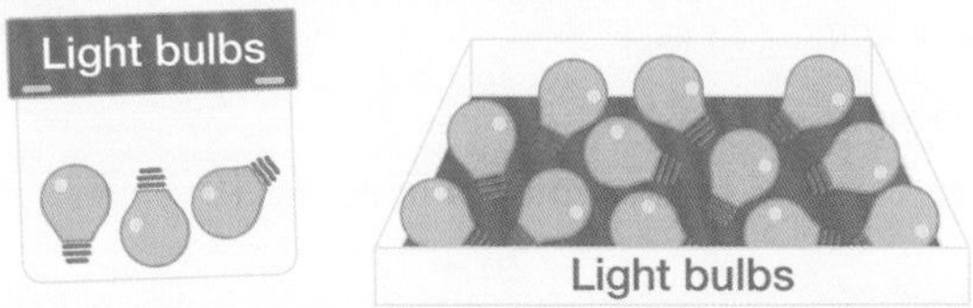
Light bulbs
Light bulbs

(a) Write down a formula, in terms of x and y, for the total number, N, of bulbs Kamran buys.

$N = 3 \times x + 12 \times y$

$= 3x + 12y$

(b) Kamran buys 4 packets and 2 boxes of bulbs. How many bulbs does he buy?

$N = 3 \times 4 + 12 \times 2$

$= 12 + 24$

$= 36$ He buys 36 bulbs.

The variables are N (the total number of bulbs), x (the number of packets) and y (the number of boxes).

Substitute the values given in the question into the formula you worked out in part **(a)**.

10 Exam-style practice Grades 4–5

1 $L = \dfrac{2x + 3y}{x}$

Work out the value of L when $x = 8$ and $y = 12$

Give your answer as a fraction in its simplest form. **[3 marks]**

2 A farmer uses 200 metres of fencing to make an enclosure divided into eight equal rectangular pens.

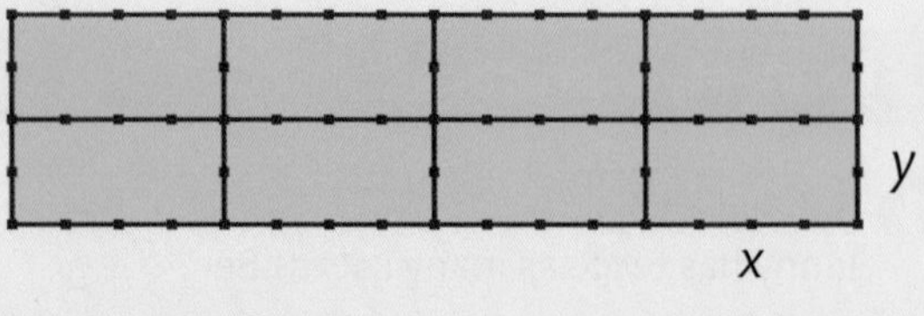
y
x

The length of each pen is x metres and the width of each pen is y metres.

(a) Show that $y = 20 - 1.2x$

The total area of the enclosure is A m^2.

(b) Show that $A = 160x - 9.6x^2$ **[3 marks]**

Algebraic indices

Indices are also called powers. They represent how many times a number has been multiplied by itself. Examples include squaring and cubing numbers.

(5) Basic rules of indices

Learn the basic rules of indices.

$a^m \times a^n = a^{m+n}$ $x^4 \times x^6 = x^{4+6} = x^{10}$

$a^m \div a^n = a^{m-n}$ $x^4 \div x^6 = x^{4-6} = x^{-2}$

$(a^m)^n = a^{mn}$ $(x^4)^6 = x^{4\times6} = x^{24}$

$a^{-n} = \dfrac{1}{a^n}$ $x^{-4} = \dfrac{1}{x^4}$

$a^0 = 1$ $x^0 = 1$

Go to page 15 to revise how indices work.

(2) Indices checklist

- ☑ Only combine powers (indices) when the base numbers are the same.
- ☑ When you multiply, add the powers.
- ☑ When you divide, subtract the powers.
- ☑ When you raise a power to a power, multiply the powers together.

(10) Worked example — Grades 4–5

1 Simplify

(a) $p^7 \times p^4$

$= p^{7+4} = p^{11}$

The base is the same, p, so you can combine the indices.

(b) $p^9 \div p^5$

$= p^{9-5} = p^4$

(c) $(p^2)^4$

$= p^{2\times4} = p^8$

2 Simplify

(a) $\dfrac{x^5 \times x^7}{x^3}$

$= \dfrac{x^{5+7}}{x^3} = \dfrac{x^{12}}{x^3} = x^9$

(b) $\left(\dfrac{x^8}{x^5}\right)^2$

$= (x^{8-5})^2 = (x^3)^2 = x^6$

3 Simplify

Deal with each base letter separately.

(a) $5x^4y^3 \times 2x^3y^2$

$= 5x^4 \times 2x^3 \times y^3 \times y^2 = 10x^7y^5$

(b) $\dfrac{24x^4y^3}{8x^2y}$

Treat the numbers and each base separately.
$24 \div 8 = 3$
$x^4 \div x^2 = x^2$
$y^3 \div y = y^2$

$= \dfrac{24x^4}{8x^2} \times \dfrac{y^3}{y} = 3x^2y^2$

4 Work out 2^{-3}

$= \dfrac{1}{2^3} = \dfrac{1}{8}$

A negative power shows that the value is a reciprocal and can be written as a fraction, $a^{-n} = \dfrac{1}{a^n}$

Substitute 2^{-3} into $a^{-n} = \dfrac{1}{a^n}$

(5) Worked example — Grade 5

1 Work out the value of n given that

$p^4 \times p^n = p^{10}$

$4 + n = 10$

$n = 6$

Add the indices then set this equal to 10.

2 Work out the value of t given that

$(5^4)^t = 5^{12}$

$4t = 12$

$t = 3$

Since the base is the same on both sides, the powers must be equal, so you can form an equation and solve it.

(10) Exam-style practice — Grades 4–5

1 Simplify

(a) $p^2 \times p^9$ **[1 mark]**

(b) $\dfrac{x^4 \times x^6}{x^2}$ **[2 marks]**

(c) $4x^2y^4 \times 3xy$ **[2 marks]**

2 Simplify

(a) $m^8 \div m^2$ **[2 marks]**

(b) $(m^5)^3$ **[2 marks]**

(c) $3w^2y^3 \times 4w^6y$ **[2 marks]**

(d) $\dfrac{32x^6y^8}{4x^2y}$ **[2 marks]**

3 Solve

$x^{15} = x^n \times x^8$ **[1 mark]**

4 $1000^a \times 100^b = 10^x$

Show that $x = 3a + 2b$ **[2 marks]**

Expanding brackets

Sometimes mathematical expressions include terms written in brackets. You can remove the brackets by expanding them.

② Removing brackets

To remove brackets, you **expand** them. 'Expand' means **multiply**.

An expression such as $2(x + 4)$ can be expanded by multiplying 2 and x, and 2 and 4. There is an invisible multiplication sign between the 2 and the $(x + 4)$.

$$2(x + 4) = 2 \times (x + 4)$$
$$= 2 \times x + 2 \times 4$$
$$= 2x + 8$$

② Negative terms

When the term outside is negative, you have to multiply the terms inside the bracket by a negative number.

For example:

$$-5(a - 2) = -5 \times (a - 2)$$
$$= -5 \times a + -5 \times -2$$
$$= -5a + 10$$

A negative multiplied by another negative gives a positive number: $-5 \times -2 = +10$.
Go to page 2 to revise multiplying negative numbers.

② Problem solving

You can be asked to use multiple skills in one question. If you are asked to expand and simplify, you need to expand all the brackets and then collect like terms and combine them.

For example, to expand and simplify $5(e + 1) - 3e(4 - 6e)$:

$$5(e + 1) - 3e(4 - 6e)$$
$$= 5 \times e + 5 \times 1 - 3e \times 4 - 3e \times -6e$$
$$= 5e + 5 - 12e + 18e^2$$
$$= 18e^2 - 7e + 5$$

⑩ Worked example — Grades 2–4

① Expand

(a) $4(x + 5)$
$$= 4 \times x + 4 \times 5$$
$$= 4x + 20$$

When multiplying out brackets, always multiply every term inside the bracket by the term outside.

(b) $3(x - 7)$
$$= 3 \times x - 3 \times 7$$
$$= 3x - 21$$

② Expand

(a) $-x(x - 3)$
$$= -x \times x - x \times -3$$
$$= -x^2 + 3x$$

Draw arrows from the term outside the brackets to each term inside, so you know which terms you need to multiply.

(b) $-3x(x + 1)$
$$= -3x \times x - 3x \times 1$$
$$= -3x^2 - 3x$$

③ Expand and simplify

(a) $5(x + 7) + 3(x - 2)$
$$= 5 \times x + 5 \times 7 + 3 \times x - 3 \times 2$$
$$= 5x + 35 + 3x - 6$$
$$= 5x + 3x + 35 - 6$$
$$= 8x + 29$$

After multiplying out the brackets, collect the like terms and combine them.

(b) $3m(m + 4) - 2m(4m + 1)$
$$= 3m \times m + 3m \times 4 - 2m \times 4m - 2m \times 1$$
$$= 3m^2 + 12m - 8m^2 - 2m$$
$$= 3m^2 - 8m^2 + 12m - 2m$$
$$= -5m^2 + 10m \text{ or } 10m - 5m^2$$

Exam focus

Write out the expression with each separate operation in it. Include any negative numbers.

This will help you make sure you haven't missed any terms or signs out.

⑩ Exam-style practice — Grades 2–4

① Expand

(a) $5(m + 2)$ **[1 mark]** **(b)** $-3(n + 6)$ **[1 mark]** **(c)** $x(x - 5)$ **[1 mark]** **(d)** $3x(x - 2)$ **[1 mark]** **(e)** $-4x(x - 1)$ **[1 mark]**

② Simplify

(a) $7a + 4(a - 2b)$ **[2 marks]** **(b)** $4(3 + 2g) + 2(5 - 3g)$ **[2 marks]**

(c) $4r(3 + 4p) + 3p(8 - r)$ **[2 marks]** **(d)** $t(3t + 4) + 3t(3 + 2t)$ **[2 marks]**

③ Expand $x(x - 5)$. Circle your answer. **[1 mark]**

$x^2 - 5$ $x^2 - 5x$ $2x - 5$ $-5x^2$

Made a start   Feeling confident   Exam ready

Expanding double brackets

Sometimes you will need to multiply out two sets of brackets and then simplify the result to work out the correct expression.

10 Double brackets

There are three different methods for multiplying out two sets of brackets to obtain a simplified expression.

Box method

The box method is a visual representation of multiplying out brackets.

×	x	$+4$
x	x^2	$4x$
$+2$	$2x$	8

Collect and simplify the terms:

$x^2 + 2x + 4x + 8 = x^2 + 6x + 8$

Expansion method

Multiply each term in the first bracket by the whole of the second bracket:

$$(x + 4)(x + 2) = x(x + 2) + 4(x + 2)$$
$$= x^2 + 2x + 4x + 8$$
$$= x^2 + 6x + 8$$

Simplify the final expression by collecting like terms.

FOIL

In the FOIL method, you multiply out the brackets in a particular order.

$(x + 4)(x + 2)$

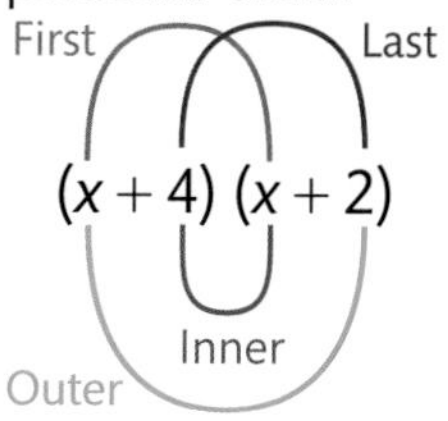

F: $x \times x = x^2$

O: $x \times 2 = 2x$

I: $4 \times x = 4x$

L: $4 \times 2 = 8$

Collect and simplify the terms:

$x^2 + 2x + 4x + 8 = x^2 + 6x + 8$

10 Worked example — Grades 4–5

1 Expand and simplify $(2x - 5)(x - 4)$

Using the box method

×	$2x$	-5
x	$2x^2$	$-5x$
-4	$-8x$	$+20$

$$(2x - 5)(x - 4) = 2x^2 - 5x - 8x + 20$$
$$= 2x^2 - 13x + 20$$

2 In this shape, all the measurements are in metres. The area of the shape is $A\,\text{m}^2$.

Write a formula for A in terms of x.

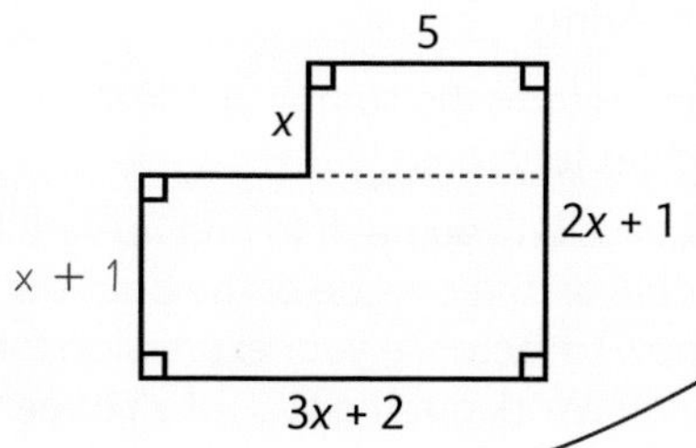

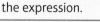

$2x + 1 - x = x + 1$

Area of small rectangle $= 5x$

Area of large rectangle $= (x + 1)(3x + 2)$

$= 3x^2 + 2x + 3x + 2$

$= 3x^2 + 5x + 2$

Total area $= 5x + 3x^2 + 5x + 2$

So $A = 3x^2 + 10x + 2$

$(x + 3)^2 = (x + 3)(x + 3)$

5 Worked example — Grade 4

Expand and simplify $(x + 2)(x - 3)$

Using the FOIL method

F: $x \times x = x^2$

O: $x \times -3 = -3x$

I: $2 \times x = 2x$

L: $2 \times -3 = -6$

$x^2 - 3x + 2x - 6$

$= x^2 - x - 6$

After you have expanded the brackets, always simplify the expression.

Problem solving

Work out the missing length, then split the shape into two parts and work out their areas.

10 Exam-style practice — Grade 4

1 Expand and simplify

(a) $(x + 3)^2$ **[2 marks]**

(b) $(x - 4)^2$ **[2 marks]**

(c) $(x - 1)^2$ **[2 marks]**

2 Expand and simplify

(a) $(x + 2)(x - 2)$ **[2 marks]**

(b) $(x - 4)(x + 7)$ **[2 marks]**

(c) $(x - 1)(x - 5)$ **[2 marks]**

(d) $(x - 3)(x - 9)$ **[2 marks]**

Factorising

Factorising is the reverse of expanding brackets. To factorise an expression, you need to work out the highest common factor of all the terms in the expression. Revise highest common factors on page 13.

 5 Factorising ✓

To factorise an expression first work out the highest common factor (HCF) of all the terms in the expression.

For example, in $4a + 8$, both terms are divisible by 2 and by 4 so 4 is the HCF. Write this on the outside of your brackets.

4( )

Then work out the terms inside the bracket by dividing the terms in the original expression by the HCF.

$4a \div 4 = a$ and $8 \div 4 = 2$

$4(a + 2)$

Factorising is the opposite of expanding brackets.

You can check your answer by expanding the brackets; it should give you the original expression.

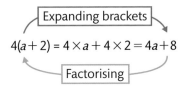

Expanding brackets

$$4(a + 2) = 4 \times a + 4 \times 2 = 4a + 8$$

Factorising

The terms $4x$ and $10xy$ have a common factor of 2. x appears in both terms, so it is also a common factor. Divide the expression by 2 first, and then by x.

Work out the common factors of both terms. 6 and p will divide into each term. t is only in one term of the expression, so it is not a factor.

Expand the brackets to check your answer.

$$6p(2p^2t - 3) = 12p^3t - 18p$$

⏱ 10 Worked example   **Grades 3–4** ✓

Factorise fully

(a) $6y + 12$

$= 6(y + 2)$

(b) $4x + 10xy$

$= 2(2x + 5xy)$

$= 2x(2 + 5y)$

(c) $12p^3t - 18p$

$= 6(2p^3t - 3p)$

$= 6(2(p \times p \times p)t - 3p)$

$= 6p(2(p \times p)t - 3)$

$= 6p(2p^2t - 3)$

2, 3 and 6 are the common factors, so the HCF is 6

The HCF is $2x$

It can help to write out p^3 as $(p \times p \times p)$

The HCF is $6p$

Problem solving

1 The perimeter is the sum of all the sides, so add the three sides together.

2 The expression you need to end up with has a multiple on the outside of the brackets, so you know to factorise your expression for the perimeter. Work out the HCF of all three terms.

3 Factorise each term fully.

4 Check your answer by expanding the brackets.

 ⏱ 5 Worked example   **Grade 5** ✓

Show that the perimeter of this triangle can be written as $3b(2a + 3c + d)$.

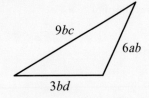

9bc

6ab

3bd

Perimeter $= 6ab + 9bc + 3bd$

To factorise, HCF is $3b$

So $6ab + 9bc + 3bd = 3b(2a + 3c + d)$

Check: $3b \times 2a + 3b \times 3c + 3b \times d$

$= 6ab + 9bc + 3bd$

 ⏱ 10 Exam-style practice   **Grades 3–5** ✓

Factorise fully

(a) $5x + 20$ **[1 mark]**   **(b)** $8a^2 + 12a$ **[2 marks]**

(c) $x^2 - 6x$ **[2 marks]**   **(d)** $3a^2b + 6ab^2$ **[2 marks]**

(e) $6y^2 - 9xy$ **[2 marks]**   **(f)** $8x^2 + 4xy$.   **[2 marks]**

✓ **Made a start**   ✓ **Feeling confident**   ✓ **Exam ready**

Linear equations

When you solve a linear equation your aim is to work out the value of the unknown. You can often do this by rearranging the equation and using inverse operations.

5 Unknown on one side

You may be asked to solve an equation that involves an unknown on one side, such as

$6x + 10 = 34$

You will often need to use **inverse operations**, which are 'opposite' calculations.

The term $+10$ can be removed from the equation by subtracting 10 from each side. This gives:

$6x + 10 - 10 = 34 - 10$

$6x = 24$

To get x by itself, divide both sides by 6

$\frac{6x}{6} = \frac{24}{6}$

$x = 4$

Every line of working should include an equals (=) sign. You should line the equals signs underneath each other.

10 Worked example — Grades 4–5

1 Solve

$5x + 7 = 11$

$5x + 7 - 7 = 11 - 7$

$5x = 4$

$x = \frac{4}{5}$

2 Solve

$7x + 8 = 2x - 3$

$7x - 2x + 8 = 2x - 2x - 3$

$5x + 8 - 8 = -3 - 8$

$5x = -11$

$x = -\frac{11}{5}$

3 Andy, Tom and Chris play hockey. Andy has scored 9 more goals than Chris, Tom has scored 6 more goals than Andy. The total number of goals scored by the three players is 90.

How many goals did they each score?

Andy	Tom	Chris
$x + 9$	$x + 9 + 6$	x

$x + 9 + x + 9 + 6 + x = 90$

$3x + 24 = 90$

$3x = 90 - 24$

$3x = 66$

$x = \frac{66}{3} = 22$

Andy	Tom	Chris
$22 + 9 = 31$	$22 + 9 + 6 = 37$	22

5 Unknown on both sides

Sometimes an equation has unknowns on both sides. To solve such an equation, rearrange it so that all the unknowns are on one side.

$3 - 4x = 15 - x$

$3 - 4x + 4x = 15 - x + 4x$

Remove the term $-4x$ from the equation by adding $4x$ to each side.

$3 = 15 + 3x$

$3 - 15 = 15 - 15 + 3x$

$-12 = 3x$

To get x by itself, divide both sides by 3.

$\frac{-12}{3} = \frac{3x}{3}$

$-4 = x$ or $x = -4$

5 Equations with brackets

Always multiply out brackets first, then collect like terms. You will be expected to solve an equation such as:

$2(2x + 5) - (3x + 4) = 9(2x + 5)$

Multiply out the brackets.

$4x + 10 - 3x - 4 = 18x + 45$

$x + 6 = 18x + 45$

Collect like terms.

$x - x + 6 = 18x - x + 45$

$6 - 45 = 17x + 45 - 45$

$-39 = 17x$

$-\frac{39}{17} = x$

$x = -\frac{39}{17}$

Problem solving

Assign a letter to the unknown value and create an algebraic equation using this letter.

Set up the equation by adding all the expressions and equating them to the total number of goals.

10 Exam-style practice — Grades 4–5

1 Solve $4x = 3$. Circle the correct answer. **[1 mark]**

$x = 1$ $x = 12$ $x = \frac{3}{4}$ $x = \frac{4}{3}$

2 Solve

(a) $3(2x - 1) = 6$ **[2 marks]**

(b) $3x + 7 = 5x - 1$ **[3 marks]**

3 Ann is x years old. Ben is twice as old as Ann. Carl is 4 years younger than Ann. The total of all three ages is 92 years.

Work out the age of each person. **[3 marks]**

Rearranging formulae

Formulae show the relationship between two or more variables. These formulae can be rearranged to make a different letter the subject.

 Changing the subject

The subject of a formula is the letter on its own on one side of the equals sign.

This is usually on the left-hand side (LHS) of the equals sign. For example, this is the formula for the area of a circle:

$$A = \pi r^2$$

In this formula, A is the subject.

Rearranging formulae is very similar to solving equations where inverse operations are used. If there is another letter or number on the same side of the equals sign as the subject, then you need to use inverse operations to remove it.

This example involves just one inverse operation. The inverse operation of $+$ is $-$, so subtract 5 from each side of the formula to get h on its own.

The inverse operation of $\times$ is $\div$, so divide both sides by 4 to make m the subject.

 Two or more inverse operations

Sometimes changing the subject of a formula involves two or more operations. For example, to make t the subject of the formula $v = u + 10t$:

$-u$ from both sides

$\div 10$ for both sides

Move the subject to the LHS

$v = u + 10t$

$v - u = 10t$

$\dfrac{v - u}{10} = t$

$t = \dfrac{v - u}{10}$

Make sure you carry out each inverse operation step by step.

For most formulae, start by adding or taking away any numbers or letters that are on the same side of the formula as the subject. Then complete any multiplication or division you need to do.

 Worked example | Grades 2–3

① Make h the subject of the formula $P = h + 5$

$P = h + 5 \qquad (-5)$

$P - 5 = h$

$h = P - 5$

② Make m the subject of the formula $n = 4m$

$n = 4m \qquad (\div 4)$

$\dfrac{n}{4} = m$

$m = \dfrac{n}{4}$

③ Make y the subject of the formula $G = 3y - 7$

$G = 3y - 7 \qquad (+7)$

$G + 7 = 3y \qquad (\div 3)$

$\dfrac{G + 7}{3} = y$

$y = \dfrac{G + 7}{3}$

There are two separate inverse operations here: $+7$ to each side, and then divide both sides by 3

Worked example | Grades 4–5

① Make W the subject of the formula $P = 2L + 2W$

$P = 2L + 2W \qquad (-2L)$

$P - 2L = 2W \qquad (\div 2)$

$\dfrac{P - 2L}{2} = W$

$W = \dfrac{P - 2L}{2}$

Here you can take $2L$ across to the LHS as part of the first inverse operation.

② Make X the subject of the formula $Y = 3\sqrt{X} - 10$

$Y = 3\sqrt{X} - 10 \qquad (+10)$

$Y + 10 = 3\sqrt{X} \qquad (\div 3)$

$\dfrac{Y + 10}{3} = \sqrt{X}$

$X = \left(\dfrac{Y + 10}{3}\right)^2$

The inverse operation of 'square root' is 'square'.

 Exam-style practice | Grades 2–4

① Rearrange $m = 3n + 8$ to make n the subject. Circle the correct answer. **[1 mark]**

$n = m - 11 \qquad n = \dfrac{3}{m + 8} \qquad n = 3m - 8 \qquad n = \dfrac{m - 8}{3}$

② Make g the subject of the formula $t = \dfrac{gh}{10}$ **[2 marks]**

③ Make a the subject of the formula $v^2 = u^2 + 2as$ **[2 marks]**

④ Rearrange $y = \frac{1}{2}x + 1$ to make x the subject. **[2 marks]**

Inequalities

You can use inequalities to compare values. Inequalities show when one value is greater than or less than another value.

⑤ Inequality symbols

You can use these symbols to describe inequalities.

Symbol	What it means
$<$	less than
$>$	greater than
$\leqslant$	less than or equal to
$\geqslant$	greater than or equal to

It is important that you learn these symbols.

⑤ Number lines

You can represent inequalities on a number line.
An **open** circle means the number is not included.

−1 0 1 2 3 4

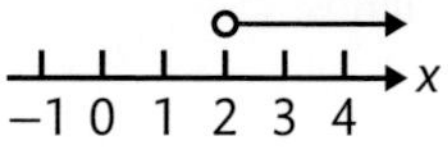

You write this as $x > 2$

A **closed** circle means the number is included.

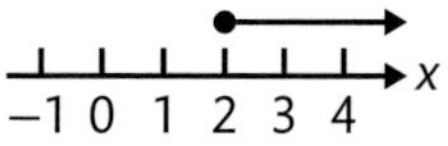

−1 0 1 2 3 4

You write this as $x \geqslant 2$

⑤ Worked example ··················· Grade 4

1 Complete the statements by writing $<$ or $>$ in the boxes.

> You can use a number line to see whether one number is less than or greater than another.

(a) 10 $\boxed{>}$ 4

(b) 9 $\boxed{<}$ 14 ◀

(c) −8 $\boxed{<}$ 4

(d) −4 $\boxed{>}$ −1

2 Write down the inequality shown in the diagram.

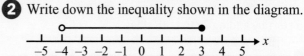
−5 −4 −3 −2 −1 0 1 2 3 4 5

$-4 < x \leqslant 3$

> −4 has an open circle so use $<$.
> 3 has a closed circle so use $\leqslant$.

⑤ Working out integer values

Sometimes an inequality may be written like this:

$2 \leqslant x < 8$

If you are asked to find all the possible **integer** values of x, you need to find all the whole numbers that make the inequalities true. You say that these numbers **satisfy** the inequalities.

You need to look carefully at the type of inequality sign used on each side of the letter. You can draw a number line to help you:

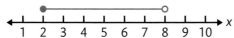
1 2 3 4 5 6 7 8 9 10

$x < 8$ means x is less than 8, so 8 is not included in the solution.

$2 \leqslant x$ means that x is greater than **or equal to** 2, so 2 is included in the solution.

The possible integers are: 2, 3, 4, 5, 6, 7.

> An integer is a whole number.

⑤ Worked example ·········· Grade 3

n is an integer such that $-4 < n \leqslant 4$

Write down all the possible values of n.

~~−4,~~ −3, −2, −1, 0, 1, 2, 3, 4

$-4 < n$ so −4 is not included in the inequality.

$n \leqslant 4$ so 4 is included.

Possible values are −3, −2, −1, 0, 1, 2, 3, 4 ◀

Integers can be positive or negative.

0 is an integer, so remember to include it.

⑩ Exam-style practice ······ Grades 3–4

1 Write down the inequality shown on the number line.

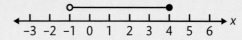
−3 −2 −1 0 1 2 3 4 5 6

[2 marks]

2 $-2 < n \leqslant 3$

n is an integer.

Write down all the possible values of n. **[2 marks]**

Solving inequalities

You can solve inequalities in a similar way as you solve equations. The difference is that equations have an equals (=) sign whereas an inequality has a <, ≤, ≥ or > sign.

 Solving inequalities

Inequalities behave in the same way as equations. The same rules are used to solve inequalities.
For example:

$x + 8 > 4$

Subtracting 8 from both sides gives

$x > 4 - 8$

$x > -4$

Never replace the inequality sign with an equals sign.

> You could write your answer as $y > \frac{3}{5}$ or as $y > 0.6$

> This inequality has unknowns on **both sides**. You need to group all the x terms together on one side to solve it, so start by adding 7x to both sides.

 Worked example | Grade 5 |

1 Solve the inequality $12 - 7x \leqslant 2x + 9$

$12 - 7x \leqslant 2x + 9$ $(+ 7x)$

$\quad 12 \leqslant 2x + 9 + 7x$ $(- 9)$

$12 - 9 \leqslant 2x + 7x$

$\quad\quad 3 \leqslant 9x$ $(\div 9)$

$\quad\quad \dfrac{3}{9} \leqslant x$

$\quad\quad x \geqslant \dfrac{1}{3}$

> Simplify $\frac{3}{9}$ by dividing the top and bottom by 3

2 (a) Solve the inequality $7 < 2x + 1 < 13$

$7 < 2x + 1$ $(- 1)$ $2x + 1 < 13$ $(- 1)$

$7 - 1 < 2x$ $2x < 13 - 1$

$6 < 2x$ $(\div 2)$ $2x < 12$ $(\div 2)$

$3 < x$ $x < 6$

$x > 3$

So $3 < x < 6$

(b) Give all the integers that satisfy the inequality.

4 and 5

> 3 and 6 are not included in the final answer.

3 $2x + 7 > 16$

x is an integer.

Work out the smallest possible value of x.

$2x + 7 > 16$ $(- 7)$

$\quad 2x > 16 - 7$

$\quad 2x > 9$ $(\div 2)$

$\quad\quad x > 4.5$

The smallest value of x is 5.

> x is an integer. The smallest integer after 4.5 is 5, so 5 is the smallest possible value of x.

 Worked example | Grade 4 |

1 Solve the inequality $4x - 7 \geqslant 17$

$4x - 7 \geqslant 17$ $(+ 7)$

$\quad 4x \geqslant 17 + 7$

$\quad 4x \geqslant 24$ $(\div 4)$

$\quad\quad x \geqslant \dfrac{24}{4}$

$\quad\quad x \geqslant 6$

2 Solve $5y + 2 > 5$

$5y + 2 > 5$ $(- 2)$

$\quad 5y > 5 - 2$

$\quad 5y > 3$ $(\div 5)$

$\quad\quad y > \dfrac{3}{5}$

 Negative numbers

To solve an inequality with a negative number in front of the unknown, add the negative term to both sides.

$6 - 3z + 3z < 4 + 3z$

$\quad 6 - 4 < 4 + 3z - 4$

$\quad\quad 2 < 3z$

$\quad\quad \dfrac{2}{3} < z$

> ÷3 to get the subject on its own.

The solution to this inequality is $z > \frac{2}{3}$.

Never multiply or divide an inequality by a negative number.

> If you change the inequality so that the subject is on the LHS, flip the inequality sign as well.

> Separate the inequalities so you have two inequalities to solve.

 Exam-style practice | Grades 4–5 |

1 Solve the inequality $3x + 8 < 35$ **[2 marks]**

2 Solve the inequality $5x + 7 \geqslant 22$ **[2 marks]**

3 Solve the inequality $6x + 7 \leqslant 2x + 21$ **[3 marks]**

4 Solve the inequalities $-6 < 4x \leqslant 12$ **[2 marks]**

5 (a) Solve the inequalities $3 < x + 4 \leqslant 7$ **[2 marks]**

     (b) x is an integer. Write down all the values of x that satisfy $3 < x + 4 \leqslant 7$ **[4 marks]**

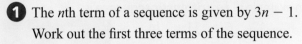
Solving sequence problems

You can use arithmetic sequences to solve mathematical problems.

 Sequences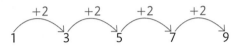

Sequences are sets of numbers that follow a rule or pattern. For example, the rule 'add 2 each time' creates the following sequence:

$$+2 \quad +2 \quad +2 \quad +2$$
$$1 \quad 3 \quad 5 \quad 7 \quad 9$$

Each number in a sequence is called a **term**.

The rule to find any term in a sequence is called the nth term formula, where n gives the position of the term you are looking for in the sequence.

A **Fibonacci sequence** is a special sequence that follows this rule:

- add two consecutive terms to get the next term.

A **geometric sequence** is a sequence where each term is found by multiplying the previous one by a fixed, non-zero number. You can find the multiplier of any geometric sequence by dividing the second term by the first term.

 Generating a sequence

You can work out the terms of a sequence by substituting the term numbers into the nth term formula.

n	$4n + 6$	$2n^2 - 5$
1	$4(1) + 6 = 10$	$2(1)^2 - 5 = -3$
2	$4(2) + 6 = 14$	$2(2)^2 - 5 = 3$
3	$4(3) + 6 = 18$	$2(3)^2 - 5 = 13$
4	$4(4) + 6 = 22$	$2(4)^2 - 5 = 27$

You should be able to recognise sequences of square, cube and triangular numbers.

Square numbers: 1, 4, 9, 16, 25...

Cube numbers: 1, 8, 27, 64, 125...

Triangular numbers: 1, 3, 6, 10, 15, 21...

1   3   6   10   15   21

 Term-to-term rule

You can use a term-to-term rule to find the next term in the sequence. You might need to work this out from a sequence of numbers, or you might be given a rule. For example:

Term-to-term rule: Add 3 then multiply by 5

First term = 4

Second term $= (4 + 3) \times 5 = 7 \times 5 = 35$

 Worked example   Grade 5

1 The nth term of a sequence is given by $3n - 1$. Work out the first three terms of the sequence.

n	$3n - 1$	Answer
1	$3(1) - 1$	2
2	$3(2) - 1$	5
3	$3(3) - 1$	8

2 Here are the first four terms of a Fibonacci sequence:

$$1 \qquad 1 \qquad 2 \qquad 3$$

Work out the next three terms of this sequence.

$2 + 3 = 5, \qquad 3 + 5 = 8, \qquad 5 + 8 = 13$

$5, 8, 13$

3 The first four terms of a geometric sequence are:

$$3 \qquad 6 \qquad 12 \qquad 24$$

Write down the next two terms of the sequence.

Multiplier = 2nd term ÷ 1st term = $6 \div 3 = 2$

5th term: $24 \times 2 = 48$; 6th term: $48 \times 2 = 96$

The sequence is geometric. Work out the multiplier.

 Exam-style practice   Grade 5

1 The rule for finding the next term in a sequence is $4n^2 - 2$

Work out the first three terms of this sequence.
[3 marks]

2 The first three terms of a Fibonacci sequence are:

$$a \qquad 4 \qquad a + 4$$

(a) Show that the 6th term of this sequence is $3a + 20$ **[2 marks]**

(b) Given that the 6th term is 35, work out the value of a.
[3 marks]

3 The term-to-term rule for a sequence is: multiply the previous term by 4 and then subtract 5. The first term is 2

(a) Write down the next four terms of the sequence. **[2 marks]**

(b) Work out whether 92 is a term in this sequence. **[1 mark]**

 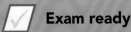

Arithmetic sequences

An arithmetic or linear sequence is a sequence of numbers in which the difference between consecutive terms is constant.

 Working out the *n*th term

An example of an **arithmetic sequence** is:

The difference between one term and the next term is always +5.

Here is another arithmetic sequence:

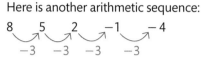

You can work out a formula to calculate any term of an arithmetic sequence. This is called the *n*th term, where *n* is an integer, and is of the form $an \pm b$, where *a* is the difference between consecutive terms.

A quick method to work out *b*

You can use this method to work out the formula for the *n*th term.

*n*th term = difference × *n* + zero term

where zero term = 1st term − difference

Using the zero term is a quick way to work out *b*, the number that needs to be added or subtracted to the first part of the formula.

 Checking a term

You may be asked to work out if a number is part of a given sequence. For example, here are the first five terms of an arithmetic sequence:

3　7　11　15　19

Is 93 is a term in the sequence?

Start with the *n*th term.

The *n*th term of this sequence is $4n - 1$

Set the *n*th term equal to 93 and solve the equation.

$4n - 1 = 93$

$4n = 94$

$n = 23.5$

If your answer is an **integer** (a whole number) then the term is in the sequence. Otherwise, it is not.

93 is not in the sequence.

 Worked example　　**Grade 5**

Here are the first four terms of an arithmetic sequence:

11　　17　　23　　29

Work out, in terms of *n*, an expression for the *n*th term of this arithmetic sequence.

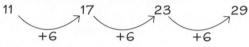

Common difference = +6
Zero term = 11 − 6 = 5
So *n*th term = 6*n* + 5

Check: 3rd term = 23　　6 × 3 + 5 = 18 + 5 = 23 ✓

 Worked example　　**Grade 5**

Here are the first five terms of an arithmetic sequence:

5　　12　　19　　26　　33

(a) Write down an expression, in terms of *n*, for the *n*th term of the sequence.

Zero term = 5 − 7 = −2
*n*th term = 7*n* − 2

(b) Is 82 a term in the sequence?
You must give a reason for your answer.

$7n - 2 = 82$

$7n = 84$

$n = 12$

Work backwards to calculate the zero term of the sequence.

Yes, 82 is in the sequence, because *n* is an integer.

Always write a conclusion.

 Exam-style practice　　**Grade 5**

1 Here are the first four terms of an arithmetic sequence:

−4　1　6　11

(a) Write down an expression, in terms of *n*, for the *n*th term of the sequence. **[2 marks]**

(b) Is 148 a term in the sequence? You must give a reason for your answer. **[1 mark]**

2 Here are the first five terms of an arithmetic sequence:

3　8　13　18　23

(a) Explain why the number 162 cannot be a term in this sequence. **[1 mark]**

(b) Write down an expression, in terms of *n*, for the *n*th term of the sequence. **[2 marks]**

Factorising quadratics

A quadratic expression contains an x^2 term. You need to be able to factorise expressions written in the form $x^2 + bx + c$ where b and c are numbers.

5 Factorising quadratic expressions

There are three types of quadratic expression that you might need to factorise.

1 When $c = 0$

Some quadratic expressions are of the form $x^2 + bx$.

For example: $x^2 - 3x$

These are factorised by taking out x as a factor; for example, in $x^2 - 3x$ the common factor of the two terms is x.

$$x^2 - 3x = x(x - 3)$$

2 When $b = 0$

For example: $x^2 - 100$

These have a special name: the **difference of two squares**.

$$x^2 - a^2 = (x - a)(x + a)$$

3 Factorising $x^2 + bx + c$

For example: $x^2 - 9x + 20$

The quadratic expression

$$x^2 - 9x + 20$$

can be factorised into the product of two brackets.

Think of two numbers that add to give −9 and multiply to give 20

$(-4) \times (-5) = 20$

$(-4) + (-5) = -9$

So $x^2 - 9x + 20 = (x - 4)(x - 5)$

Multiplying two negative numbers together gives you a positive number.

5 Worked example — Grades 3–5

Factorise

(a) $x^2 + 7x$ ← In this expression, $c = 0$

$= x(x + 7)$

(b) $x^2 - 25$

$= (x - 5)(x + 5)$

(c) $x^2 - 3x - 28$

$(-7) \times (+4) = -28$

$(-7) + (+4) = -3$

So $x^2 - 3x - 28 = (x - 7)(x + 4)$

This is the special case where $b = 0$. Find the square root of 25 and remember the rule for factorising a difference of two squares.

Write out the two brackets with the letter in each of the brackets. Then insert the two numbers you have found. Make sure you use the correct sign for each number. You could check your answer by expanding the brackets:

$(x - 7)(x + 4) = x^2 + 4x - 7x - 28$

$= x^2 - 3x - 28$ ✓

2 Checklist

- ✓ Make sure you know how to factorise the three different types of quadratic expression.
- ✓ Check your answer by expanding the brackets. You should get the original expression.

10 Exam-style practice — Grades 3–5

1 Factorise

(a) $x^2 + 9x$ **[2 marks]**

(b) $x^2 - 15x$ **[2 marks]**

(c) $x^2 - x$ **[2 marks]**

2 Factorise

(a) $x^2 - 64$ **[2 marks]**

(b) $x^2 - 9$ **[2 marks]**

(c) $x^2 - 1$ **[2 marks]**

3 Factorise

(a) $x^2 + 9x + 14$ **[2 marks]**

(b) $x^2 - 16x + 48$ **[2 marks]**

(c) $x^2 - x - 56$ **[2 marks]**

4 Factorise

(a) $x^2 - 7x + 12$ **[2 marks]**

(b) $x^2 - x - 72$ **[2 marks]**

(c) $x^2 - 13x + 42$ **[2 marks]**

Solving quadratic equations

Quadratic equations have the form $x^2 + bx + c = 0$, $a \neq 0$. You will need to know how to solve these by factorisation.

 5 $x^2 + bx = 0$

Some quadratics may be written as $x^2 + bx = 0$.
These are easy to factorise.

> The common factor on the left-hand side is x.

$x^2 - 4x = 0$
$x(x - 4) = 0$
$x = 0$ or $x - 4 = 0$, so $x = 0$ or $x = 4$

2 $x^2 + bx + c = 0$

Quadratic equations can have two different solutions.
To solve a quadratic equation:

1 Write the equation in the form $x^2 + bx + c = 0$

2 Factorise the left-hand side.

3 Find values of x that make each factor equal to 0

 5 Worked example   Grade 5

Solve $(x - 1)^2 = x + 5$

> When you are solving a quadratic equation, you need to rearrange it in the form $x^2 + bx + c = 0$ before you start to factorise it.

$(x - 1)(x - 1) = x + 5$
$x^2 - 2x + 1 = x + 5$
$x^2 - 3x - 4 = 0$
$(x - 4)(x + 1) = 0$
$x - 4 = 0$ or $x + 1 = 0$
$x = 4$ or $x = -1$

 5 Worked example   Grade 4

1 Solve $x^2 - 5x = 0$

> You can take out a factor of x from both terms. Remember there are two solutions.
> $x = 0$ or $x = 5$

$x^2 - 5x = 0$
$x(x - 5) = 0$
$x = 0$ or $x - 5 = 0$
$x = 0$ or $x = 5$

2 Solve $x^2 - 9 = 0$

> This is the **difference of two squares**.
> Use $x^2 - a^2 = (x - a)(x + a)$.

$x^2 - 9 = 0$
$(x - 3)(x + 3) = 0$
$x - 3 = 0$ or $x + 3 = 0$
$x = 3$ or $x = -3$

3 Solve $x^2 - x - 72 = 0$

$(x + 8)(x - 9) = 0$
$x + 8 = 0$ or $x - 9 = 0$
$x = -8$ or $x = 9$

 1 Key point

☑ Always rearrange quadratic equations so there is a 0 on one side:
$x^2 + bx = 0$ or $x^2 + bx + c = 0$

 5 Worked example   Grade 5

The diagram shows a rectangle.
All measurements are in cm.
The area of the rectangle is 84 cm^2.
Work out the value of x.

$x + 5$ (top), x (left side)

Area of rectangle $= x(x + 5)$
$= x^2 + 5x$
So $x^2 + 5x = 84$
$x^2 + 5x - 84 = 0$

> Always write the equation in the form $x^2 + bx = 0$ or $x^2 + bx + c = 0$

$(x + 12)(x - 7) = 0$
$x = -12$ or $x = 7$
$x = 7$ cm because it cannot be negative.

 10 Exam-style practice   Grade 5

1 Solve
 (a) $x^2 - 25 = 0$ [2 marks]
 (b) $x^2 - 4x = 5$.   [3 marks]

2 The diagram shows a rectangle.
All measurements are in centimetres.
The area of the rectangle is 44 cm^2.

$x + 3$ (top), $x - 4$ (left side)

 (a) Show that $x^2 - x - 56 = 0$ [2 marks]
 (b) Work out the value of x.   [2 marks]

Simultaneous equations

Simultaneous equations are two equations with two unknown variables. You need to be able to solve simultaneous equations to find both variables.

 Elimination method ✓

Here is a pair of simultaneous equations:

$3x + 4y = 5$ (1)

$2x - 3y = 9$ (2)

> Start by numbering each equation, so you can refer to them in your working.

If necessary, multiply one or both of the equations so that the **coefficients** of one unknown are the same.

$6x + 8y = 10$ (1) × 2

$6x - 9y = 27$ (2) × 3

Subtract equation (2) from equation (1) to eliminate the x terms.

$17y = -17$

$y = -1$

Now substitute this value into one of the original equations to work out the value of the other unknown.

$3x + 4(-1) = 5$

$3x = 9$

$x = 3$

Check the answer by substituting the values into the other (unused) original equation.

$2x - 3y = 2(3) - 3(-1)$

$= 6 + 3$

$= 9 ✓$

Problem solving

You need to convert the word problem into a pair of simultaneous equations. Let the weight of one apple be a grams, and the weight of one pear be p grams.

 Graphical method ✓

You can solve the simultaneous linear equations $3x + 4y = 5$ and $2x - 3y = 9$ by drawing a table of values and plotting a graph.

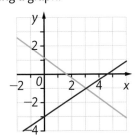

The coordinates of the point of intersection give the solution to the simultaneous equations.

The lines intersect at $(3, -1)$. The solution is $x = 3$ and $y = -1$

 Worked example   Grade 5 ✓

1 Solve the simultaneous equations.

$5x + 2y = 11$ (1)

$4x - 3y = 18$ (2)

$15x + 6y = 33$ (1) × 3

$8x - 6y = 36$ (2) × 2

> Adding will eliminate the y terms.

$23x = 69$

$x = 3$

$5(3) + 2y = 11$

$2y = -4$

$y = -2$

Always check your answer by substituting into the original equation that you did not use.

$4(3) - 3(-2) = 18 ✓$

2 Five apples and four pears together weigh 760 g, while four apples and five pears weigh 770 g. Work out how much one apple and one pear weigh together.

$5a + 4p = 760$ (1)

$4a + 5p = 770$ (2)

$25a + 20p = 3800$ (1) × 5

$16a + 20p = 3080$ (2) × 4

$9a = 720$ so $a = 80$

Substitute in (1)

$5 × 80 + 4p = 760$

$4p = 360$ so $p = 90$

$a + p = 170$

An apple and a pear together weigh 170 g.

 Exam-style practice   Grade 5 ✓

1 Use a graphical method to work out an approximate solution to the simultaneous equations $7x + 5y = 35$ and $2x - y = 2$ **[3 marks]**

2 Solve the simultaneous equations

$3x - 4y = 8$

$9x + 5y = -1.5$ **[3 marks]**

3 A theatre sells adult tickets and child tickets.

The total cost of 5 adult tickets and 1 child ticket is £40.50. The total cost of 2 adult tickets and 3 child tickets is £24. Work out the cost of an adult ticket and the cost of a child ticket.   **[4 marks]**

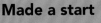 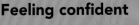

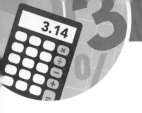

Gradients of lines

The gradient of a line is a measure of the steepness of the line.

5 Working out the gradient

To find how steep a straight line is, you need to find the gradient.

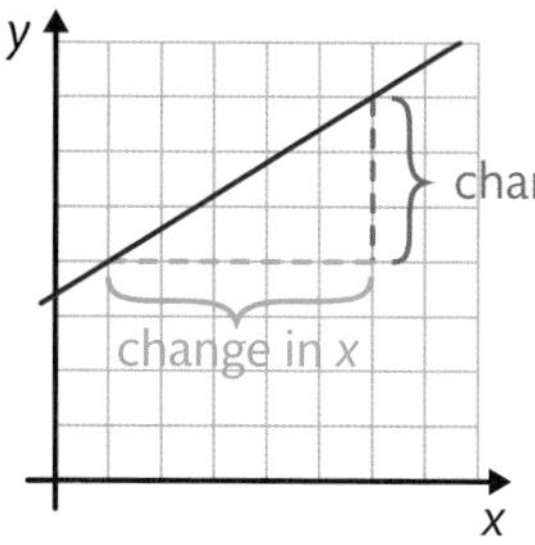

On the graph, a right-angled triangle is constructed between two points on the line.

The formula to calculate the value of the gradient is

$$\text{gradient} = \frac{\text{change in } y}{\text{change in } x}$$

The gradient of a line can be **positive** or **negative**.

Positive gradient

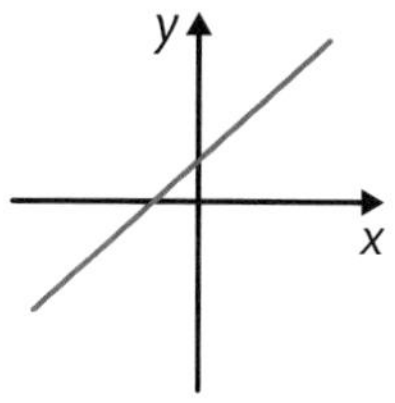

uphill slope

Negative gradient

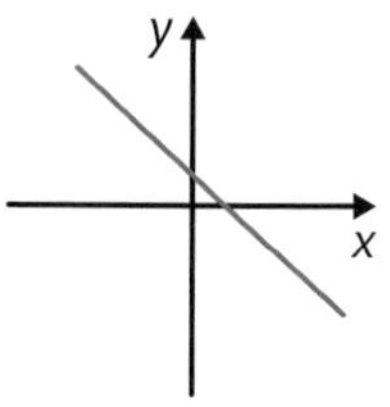

downhill slope

When the line slopes uphill, the gradient is positive. When the line slopes downhill, the gradient is negative.

10 Worked example — Grade 5

1

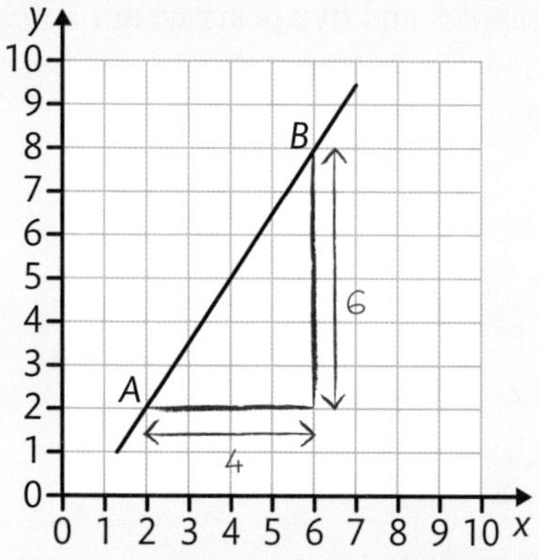

Work out the gradient of the straight line *AB*.

$$\text{gradient} = \frac{\text{change in } y}{\text{change in } x} = \frac{6}{4} = \frac{3}{2}$$

As the straight line is uphill, the gradient is positive.

2

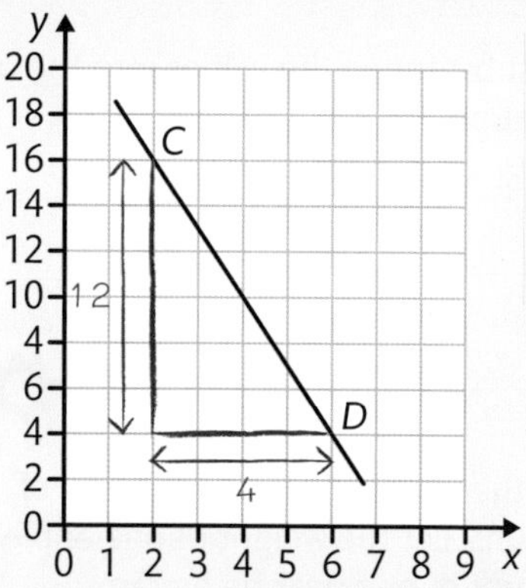

Use the scale when working out the gradient. The change in y is $16 - 4 = 12$

Work out the gradient of the straight line *CD*.

$$\text{gradient} = \frac{\text{change in } y}{\text{change in } x} = -\frac{12}{4} = -3$$

As the straight line is downhill, the gradient is negative.

15 Exam-style practice — Grade 5

1

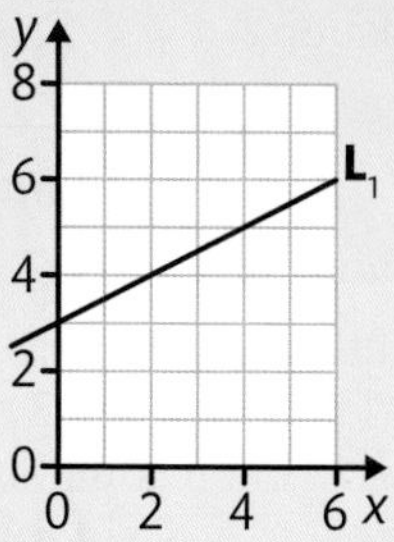

Work out the gradient of the straight line $\mathbf{L}_1$. **[2 marks]**

2

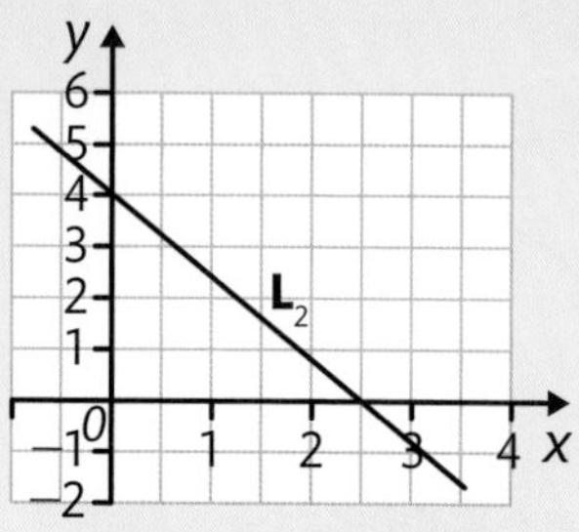

Work out the gradient of the straight line $\mathbf{L}_2$. **[2 marks]**

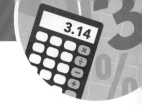

Drawing straight-line graphs

You need to know how to draw a straight-line graph.

[5] Straight-line graphs

A straight-line graph has the equation $y = mx + c$, where m is the **gradient** or slope of the line and c is the **y-intercept** (where the line cuts the y-axis).

This graph has the equation $y = -2x + 8$. This means that the gradient is -2 and the y-coordinate of the y-intercept is 8, so the y-intercept is at (0, 8).

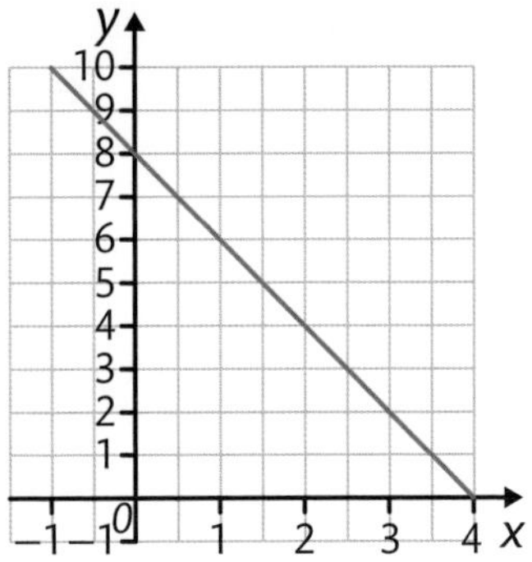

To find the y-values, substitute the x-values into the equation and then evaluate.

[5] Worked example — Grade 5

(a) Complete a table of values for $y = 2x + 3$ for values of x from 0 to 5

x	0	1	2	3	4	5
y	3	5	7	9	11	13

(b) On the grid, draw the graph of $y = 2x + 3$ for values of x from 0 to 5

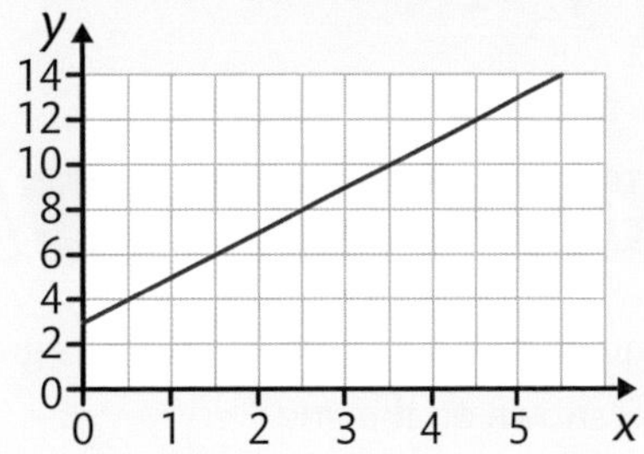

[2] Drawing straight-line graphs

You can use a table of values to draw a straight-line graph.

1. Choose three simple points as the x-values.
2. Substitute these values into the equation to find the y-values, and add to your table of values.
3. Plot the points on the graph and join them with a straight line.

[2] Straight-line graphs checklist

- ✓ Draw up a table of values.
- ✓ Work out the coordinates of at least three points.
- ✓ Plot three points and use a ruler and a sharp pencil to draw the line.

[5] Worked example — Grade 5

Draw a graph of $x + y = 5$ for values of x from -2 to 4

x	-2	0	4
$y = 5 - x$	7	5	1

Always rearrange the equation in the form $y = mx + c$ and then substitute the values of x to find the values of y.

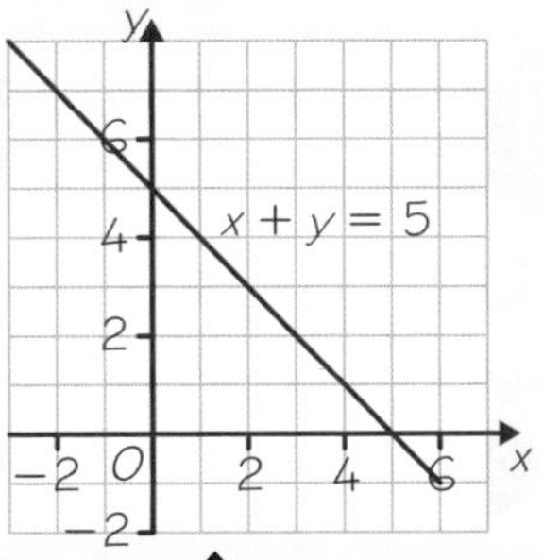

When drawing straight-line graphs always use a sharp pencil and a ruler.

[10] Exam-style practice — Grade 5

1 **(a)** Complete the table of values for $y = 8 - 2x$

x	-1	0	1	2	3	4
y		8				

(b) Draw the graph of $y = 8 - 2x$ for values of x from -1 to 4 **[2 marks]**

2 On the grid below, draw the graph with equation $y = \frac{1}{2}x + 3$ **[3 marks]**

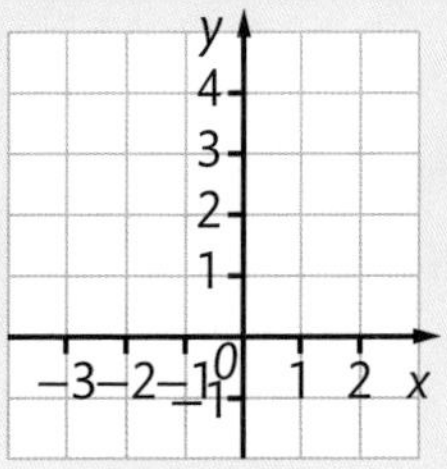

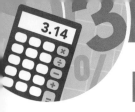

Equations of straight lines

You should be able to use algebra to work out the equation of a straight line.

5 One point and a gradient

You need to be able to use the general form $y = mx + c$, where m is the gradient and c is the y-intercept, to work out the equation of a straight line.

For example, given that a line passes through the point (3, 7) and has gradient 4, you can substitute the values of x, y and m into the equation to work out the value of c.

$y = mx + c$

$7 = 4(3) + c$

$7 = 12 + c$

Rearranging, $c = 7 - 12 = -5$

Hence, $y = 4x - 5$

5 Worked example — Grade 5

Work out the equation of the line that passes through $(4, -7)$ and has gradient $-\frac{1}{2}$

$y = mx + c$

$-7 = (-\frac{1}{2})(4) + c$

$-7 = -2 + c$

$c = -5$

So the equation is $y = -\frac{1}{2}x - 5$

Take care when you substitute the values into the equation and rearrange to find c.

5 Equations from a graph

You can find the equation of a straight line from its graph.

The straight line **L** is shown on the grid.

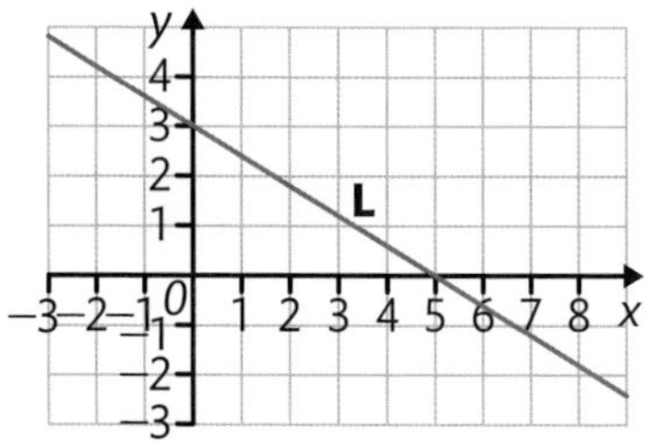

To find the equation of the straight line **L**:

1. Work out the gradient.

   Gradient $= -\frac{3}{5}$

2. Identify the intercept on the y-axis.

   The line crosses the y-axis at (0, 3) so $c = 3$

3. Use $y = mx + c$

   $y = -\frac{3}{5}x + 3$

Go to page 38 to work out the gradient of a straight line.

5 Worked example — Grade 5

Work out the equation of the line that passes through the points $(-9, 4)$ and $(-6, 2)$.

$$\text{Gradient} = \frac{\text{change in } y}{\text{change in } x}$$

$$= \frac{4 - 2}{-9 - (-6)}$$

$$= \frac{2}{-9 + 6} = -\frac{2}{3}$$

$y = mx + c$

$2 = (-\frac{2}{3})(-6) + c$

$2 = 4 + c$

$c = -2$

So the equation is $y = -\frac{2}{3}x - 2$

Use brackets when you substitute negative numbers.

2 Straight-line equation checklist

- ✓ Equation of a straight line is $y = mx + c$
- ✓ m is the gradient of the line
- ✓ The y-intercept is $(0, c)$
- ✓ To work out c substitute correctly for x, y and m.
- ✓ If two points are given, work out the gradient first.

10 Exam-style practice — Grade 5

1. Work out the equation of the line with gradient -3 that passes through the point (2, 5).

   [2 marks]

2. Work out the equation of this straight line.

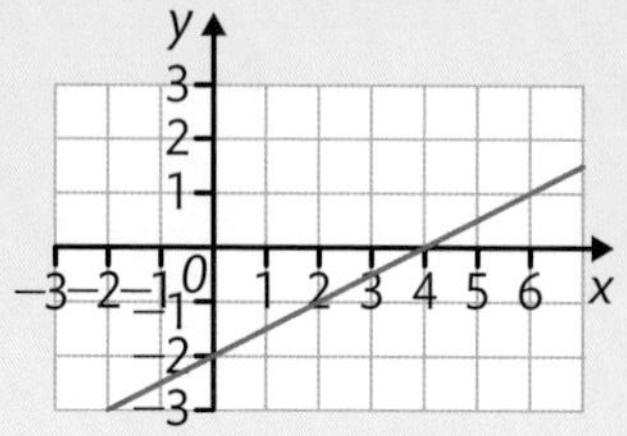

[2 marks]

Parallel lines

You should be able to use the idea of parallel lines and their gradients to work out equations of straight lines.

 Parallel lines

Parallel lines have the same gradient.

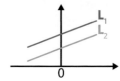

L_1 and L_2 are parallel, so they have the same gradient.

To work out the equation of L_2:

1. Work out the gradient from L_1. The lines are parallel so will have the same gradient.

2. The point $(0, 4)$ is on the line. This means that when $x = 0$, $y = 4$. Substitute these values and the gradient into the equation $y = mx + c$

3. Solve the equation to work out c:

$$4 = \frac{3}{2} \times 0 + c$$

$$4 = 0 + c$$

$$c = 4$$

4. Substitute the values you have found for m and c into $y = mx + c$

Problem solving

You might need to rearrange an equation to work out the gradient of a straight line. Write the equation in the form $y = mx + c$ and look at the value of m to find the gradient.

 Checklist

☑ Parallel lines have the same gradient.
☑ Use $y = mx + c$ to work out the equation of the straight line.

 Worked example   **Grade 5**

1 The straight line L_2 is parallel to L_1.

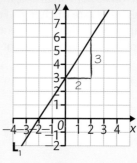

L_2 passes through $(0, 4)$.

Write down the equation of the straight line L_2.

The gradient of $L_1 = \frac{3}{2}$ so the gradient of $L_2 = \frac{3}{2}$

The intercept on the y-axis for L_2 is 4 so $c = 4$

Using $y = mx + c$, an equation of the straight line is $y = \frac{3}{2}x + 4$

2 Here are the equations of four straight lines.

Line A	Line B	Line C	Line D
$y = 3 - 2x$	$4x - 2y = 3$	$2y = 6 - 3x$	$y = 2x + 3$

Two of these lines are parallel.

Which two lines are they?

Line A	Line B	Line C	Line D
$m = -2$	$4x - 2y = 3$ $2y = 4x - 3$ $y = 2x - \frac{3}{2}$ $m = 2$	$2y = 6 - 3x$ $y = 3 - \frac{3}{2}x$ $m = -\frac{3}{2}$	$m = 2$

Lines **B** and **D** are parallel as they have the same gradient.

Rearrange the equation of line **A** to find its gradient. Then use the two points given to find the gradient of line **B**. If the gradients are not the same then the lines intersect.

 Exam-style practice   **Grade 5**

1 The straight line **L** has equation $y = 3x - 4$
Write down an equation of the straight line that passes through $(2, 5)$ and is parallel to **L**.   **[2 marks]**

2 The equation of the line L_1 is $y = 3x - 2$
The equation of the line L_2 is $3y - 9x + 5 = 0$
Show that these two lines are parallel.   **[2 marks]**

3 A and B are straight lines. Line **A** has equation $2y = 3x + 8$
Line **B** goes through the points $(-1, 2)$ and $(2, 8)$.
Do lines **A** and **B** intersect?
You must show all of your working.   **[3 marks]**

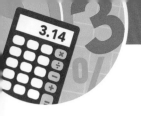

Real-life graphs

Graphs can model real-life situations and display information. You need to know about conversion graphs, distance–time graphs and speed–time graphs.

5 Rate of change

If a graph has **time** on its horizontal axis, then the gradient of the graph represents a **rate of change**. For example, on a distance–time graph, the gradient represents **speed**, and on a speed–time graph, the gradient represents **acceleration**.

Draw a triangle and use the scale when working out the lengths of its sides.

Exam focus

When a question is based on a real-life example, you should explain what any values mean in the context of the question.

10 Worked example — Grade 5

Look at this distance–time graph.

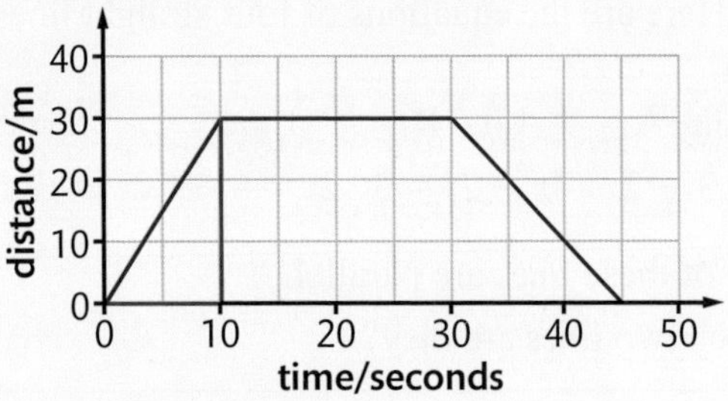

(a) (i) Work out the gradient of this distance–time graph in the first 10 seconds.

$$\text{Gradient} = \frac{30 - 0}{10 - 0} = \frac{30}{10} = 3$$

(ii) Interpret the value of the gradient.

The gradient represents speed, so the speed is 3 m/s.

(b) (i) Write down the gradient between 10 and 30 seconds.

Gradient = 0

(ii) Interpret the value of the gradient.

A zero gradient means that the object is not moving – it is stationary.

Exam focus

'Interpret' means to describe how this value relates to the motion of the object.

5 Worked example — Grade 5

Petrol is being pumped out of a tank. The graph shows the depth, d cm, of petrol in the tank after t minutes.

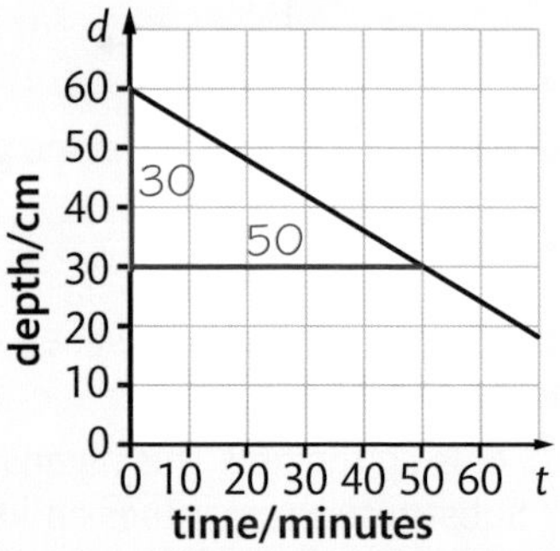

(a) Work out the gradient of this graph.

$$\text{Gradient} = \frac{\text{change in } d}{\text{change in } t} = \frac{-30}{50} = -0.6$$

(b) Give an interpretation of this gradient.

This shows that the level of petrol in the tank is falling by 0.6 cm per minute.

The gradient is negative because the slope of the line is downwards.

5 Exam-style practice — Grade 5

Water is leaking out of two containers, **A** and **B**. The water started to leak out of both containers at the same time.

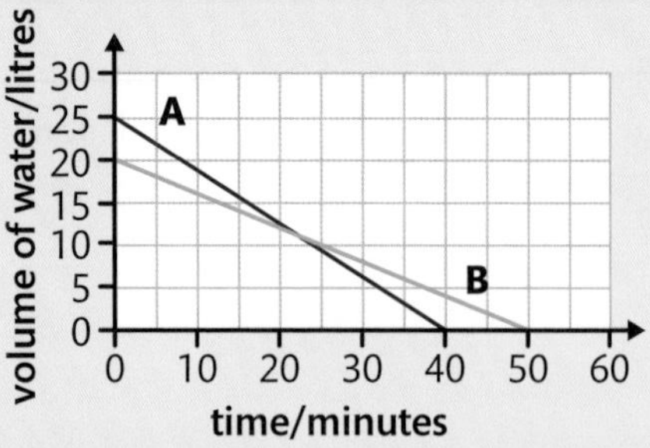

The straight line **A** shows information about the amount of water, in litres, in container **A**. The straight line **B** shows information about the amount of water, in litres, in container **B**.

(a) Work out the gradient of line **A**. **[2 marks]**

(b) State, with a reason, which container will be empty first. **[1 mark]**

Quadratic graphs

A graph with a quadratic equation has an x^2 term in it. Quadratic graphs are curved – you can draw them using a table of values.

Shapes of quadratic graphs

A quadratic graph always has the same basic shape, but it can curve upwards or downwards.

minimum point   maximum point

A quadratic graph has a **line of symmetry** through its turning point, which is its minimum or maximum point.

Worked example   Grade 5

1 The graph of $y = f(x)$ is shown on the grid. Write down the coordinates of the turning point of the graph.

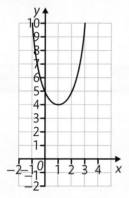

$(1, 4)$

2 (a) Complete the table of values for $y = x^2 - 4$

x	-2	-1	0	1	2
y	0	-3	-4	-3	0

(b) Draw the graph of $y = x^2 - 4$ for $x = -2$ to $x = 2$

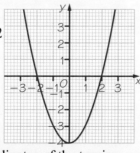

(c) Write down the coordinates of the turning point on the graph of $y = x^2 - 4$

$(0, -4)$

Worked example   Grade 5

(a) Complete the table of values for $y = x^2 - 5x + 3$

x	-1	0	1	2	3	4	5
y	9	3	-1	-3	-3	-1	3

(b) Draw the graph of $y = x^2 - 5x + 3$ for values of x from $x = 0$ to $x = 5$

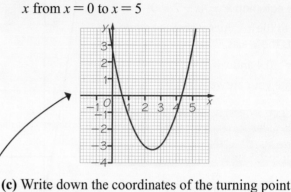

(c) Write down the coordinates of the turning point on the graph of $y = x^2 - 5x + 3$

$(2.5, -3.25)$

Exam focus

Plot the points from the table of values.

Always plot the points accurately.

Try to draw a smooth curve going through all the points.

Your graph should look symmetrical.

The square of a negative number is always positive.

Checklist

☑ Always plot the points accurately.

☑ Make sure you draw a smooth curve going through all the points.

☑ Recognise the turning points of a quadratic curve.

Exam-style practice   Grade 5

(a) Draw a table of values for $y = x^2 - 3x + 2$ from $x = -1$ to $x = 4$ **[2 marks]**

(b) On a grid, draw the graph of $y = x^2 - 3x + 2$ for values of x from -1 to 4 **[2 marks]**

(c) Write down the coordinates of the turning point of the graph.   **[2 marks]**

Using quadratic graphs

You can use quadratic graphs to find points of intersection and solve simultaneous equations graphically.

 10 Using quadratic graphs

You can use quadratic graphs to find where the curve crosses the x-axis. The points where the curve crosses the x-axis are called roots. The diagram shows the graph of $y = x^2 - 4x - 2$

You can use the graph to find estimates for the solutions to the equation $x^2 - 4x - 2 = 0$:

Read the x-values where the graph cuts the x-axis.

$x = -0.4$ and $x = 4.4$

Write your answers to 1 decimal place.

> The points where the graph crosses the x-axis are called the **roots** of the graph. **Roots** are the values of x when $y = 0$

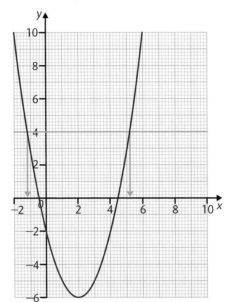

You can also use the graph to find estimates for the values of x for a given value of y, for example, when $y = 4$:

Draw a horizontal line at $y = 4$

Read down to the axis where the line crosses the curve.

$x = -1.2$ and $x = 5.2$

Write your answers to 1 decimal place.

---

10 Worked example Grade 5

(a) Complete the table of values for $y = x^2 - 3x - 1$

x	-1	0	1	2	3	4
y	3	-1	-3	-3	-1	3

(b) Draw the graph of $y = x^2 - 3x - 1$ for values of x from $x = -1$ to $x = 4$

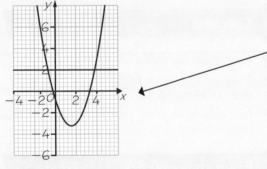

(c) Use your graph to estimate the values of x when $y = 2$

$x = -0.8$ and $x = 3.8$

(d) Write down estimates for the solutions to the equation $x^2 - 3x - 1 = 0$

$x = -0.3$ and $x = 3.3$

---

2 Quadratic graphs checklist

✓ The turning point is the maximum or minimum point on the graph.

✓ The values of x where the graph crosses the x-axis are called roots.

✓ Read values off graphs to the nearest small square.

✓ Use a table of values to draw quadratic graphs.

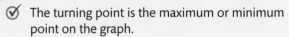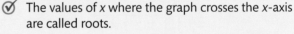
> Look at the x-values where the curve crosses the horizontal line $y = 2$

10 Exam-style practice Grade 5

(a) Complete the table of values for $y = x^2 - 2x - 2$
[2 marks]

x	-2	-1	0	1	2	3	4
y		1	-2		-2		

(b) Draw the graph of $y = x^2 - 2x - 2$ for values of x from $x = -2$ to $x = 4$ **[2 marks]**

(c) Use your graph to estimate the values of x when $y = 3$ **[1 mark]**

(d) Use your graph to write down the estimates of the solutions to $x^2 - 2x - 2 = 0$ **[1 mark]**

✓ **Made a start**   ✓ **Feeling confident**   ✓ **Exam ready**

Cubic and reciprocal graphs

You should be able to recognise, draw and interpret the shapes of cubic and reciprocal graphs.

② Cubic graphs ✓

In a cubic expression, the highest power of x is x^3. Here are two examples of cubic graphs.

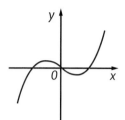 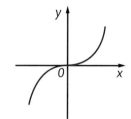

② Reciprocal graphs ✓

The graph of $y = \frac{1}{x}$ is called a reciprocal graph. Reciprocal graphs are symmetrical curves that approach but never meet the axes, as shown in this example.

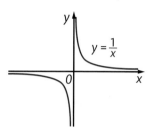

⑩ Worked example Grade 5 ✓

① **(a)** Complete the table of values for $y = x^3 - 3x + 1$

x	-2	-1	0	1	2
y	-1	3	1	-1	3

(b) Draw the graph of $y = x^3 - 3x + 1$ for values of x from -2 to 2

(c) Give estimates for the solutions of the equation $x^3 - 3x + 1 = 0$

Roots are where the curve crosses the x-axis.

$x = -1.9$, $x = 0.3$, $x = 1.5$

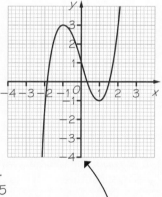

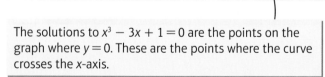

The solutions to $x^3 - 3x + 1 = 0$ are the points on the graph where $y = 0$. These are the points where the curve crosses the x-axis.

② **(a)** Complete the table of values for $y = \frac{1}{x}$

x	0.5	1	2	4	5	8
y	2	1	0.5	0.25	0.2	0.125

(b) Draw the graph of $y = \frac{1}{x}$ for $0.5 \leqslant x \leqslant 8$

(c) Give an estimate for the solution to the equation $\frac{1}{x} = 1.5$

$x = 0.6$

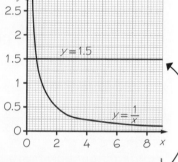

Draw the line $y = 1.5$ on the graph, to find the required value.

Exam focus 📌

In your exam you should try to read answers from graphs to the nearest small square.

⑩ Exam-style practice Grade 5 ✓

① **(a)** Draw a table of values for $y = x^3 + 2x - 1$ from $x = -2$ to $x = 2$ **[2 marks]**
(b) Draw the graph of $y = x^3 + 2x - 1$ **[2 marks]**
(c) Give an estimate for the solution to the equation $x^3 + 2x - 1 = 0$ **[2 marks]**

② **(a)** Complete the table of values for $y = \frac{1}{x}$

x	0.125	0.25	0.5	1	2	4
$y = \frac{1}{x}$						

[2 marks]

(b) Draw the graph of $y = \frac{1}{x}$ for $0.125 \leqslant x \leqslant 4$ **[2 marks]**

Recognising graphs

You should be able to recognise straight-line graphs, quadratic graphs, cubic and reciprocal graphs.

 Recognising different graphs

You need to be able to recognise the shapes of the different types of graph.

Straight line	Quadratic	Cubic	Reciprocal

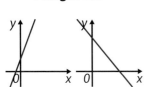 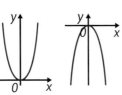 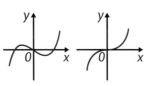 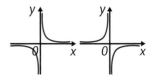

 Worked example **Grade 5**

A	B	C	D	E

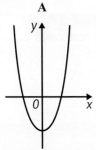 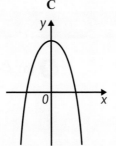 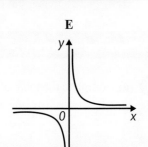

Write down the letter of the graph that could match each equation.

(a) $y = 2x + 1$ **(b)** $y = x^2 - 4$ **(c)** $y = \dfrac{1}{x}$

........D........   ....A........   ....E........

For straight-line graphs, look at the gradient and where it crosses the y-axis.

For quadratic graphs, look at the shape of the graph and where it crosses the axes.

To work out the value of y where the graph crosses the y-axis, substitute $x = 0$ into the equation.

 Exam-style practice **Grade 5**

Write down the letter of the graph that could match each equation.

A	B	C	D	E

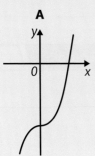 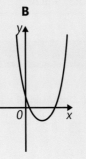 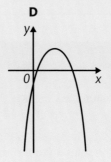 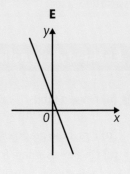

(a) $y = x^2 - 3x + 1$ **(b)** $y = 1 - 3x$ **(c)** $y = x^3 - 4$

....

Made a start   Feeling confident   Exam ready

Algebraic reasoning

You need to be able to distinguish between expressions, formulae, equations and identities.

5 Language used in algebra

You need to know these definitions.

Expressions	Formulae	Equations	Identities
An **expression** is a group of mathematical symbols representing a number or quantity. It does not have an equals sign, but it can contain more than one **term**.	A **formula** is a rule, written using symbols, that describes a relationship between different quantities.	An **equation** is a mathematical statement that shows that two expressions are equal. It always includes an equals (=) sign.	An **identity** is an equation that is always true, no matter what values are chosen. In identities, the symbol ≡ is used instead of an equals sign.
Examples	**Examples**	**Examples**	**Examples**
$2a$ $3xy + 5x$	$A = \pi r^2$ $C = \pi D$	$x^2 = 25$ $(x - 2)(x + 4) = 0$	$2x + 4x \equiv 6x$ $x^2 + 2x - 3 \equiv (x - 1)(x + 3)$

10 Worked example — Grades 2–4

1 Write expression, formula, equation or identity next to each statement:

$7x + 3x \equiv 10x$ ....Identity....

$A = L \times W$ ....Formula....

$4x + 3 = 7$ ....Equation....

$7x + 3xy$ ....Expression....

An expression does not have an equals sign in it.

$7x + 3x$ will **always** be equal to $10x$, no matter the value of x.

2 a and b are integers.

(a) Give a value of a and a value of b so that $3(a + b)$ is a multiple of 6

$a = 1$ and $b = 3$

$3(1 + 3) = 3(4)$

$3 \times 4 = 12$, and 12 is a multiple of 6

(b) Show that, if a and b are odd numbers, the value of $3(a + b)$ will always be a multiple of 6

The sum of two odd numbers must be an even number, so $(a + b)$ can be represented as $2n$, where n is an integer.

$3(a + b) = 3(2n) = 6n$

So if a and b are both odd numbers, $3(a + b)$ must be a multiple of 6

Problem solving

You need $a + b$ to be an even number. This means that a and b must either be both even, or both odd. Make sure you show enough working to show that when you substitute your values into $3(a + b)$ you get a multiple of 6

Read the question and see if you can replace any of the information in it with expressions. An even number could be written as $2n$, where n is an integer, so an odd number could be written as $2n - 1$ or $2n + 1$

10 Exam-style practice — Grades 2–5

1 Write expression, formula, equation or identity next to each statement:

$7x + 3x$ ....

$9a - 5a \equiv 4a$ ....

$A = 0.5(a + b)h$ ....

$5x + 7 = 2x$ .... **[3 marks]**

2 Show that $(x - 2)^2 \equiv x^2 - 4x + 4$ **[2 marks]**

3 Show that $(n + 1)^2 - n(n + 2) = 1$ for all positive integer values of n. **[4 marks]**

4 Show that the sum of two consecutive odd numbers is always a multiple of 4. **[4 marks]**

You can write two consecutive odd numbers as $2n + 1$ and $2n + 3$

Algebra

Pages 19–47 LINKS

Read the exam-style question and worked solution, then practise your exam skills with the questions at the bottom of the page.

10 Worked example — Grade 5

(a) Complete the table of values for $y = x^2 + 2x - 2$

x	-4	-3	-2	-1	0	1	2
y	6	1	-2	-3	-2	1	6

(b) On the grid below, draw the graph of $y = x^2 + 2x - 2$ for values of x from $x = -4$ to $x = 2$

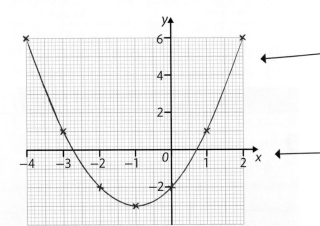

(c) Give estimates for the solutions to the equation $x^2 + 2x - 2 = 0$

$x = -2.7$ and $x = 0.7$

(d) Using the graph, write down the turning point on the graph of $y = x^2 + 2x - 2$

$(-1, -3)$

2 Checklist

✓ Make sure you substitute the values of x into $y = x^2 + 2x - 2$ correctly.

✓ Plot the points and draw a curve passing through every point plotted on the grid.

✓ Make sure that values are read off the graph to 1 decimal place.

If a question asks you to draw a graph then you must mark each plotted point clearly and then join the points, in order.

An x^2 graph has a U-shape and a $-x^2$ graph has a ∩-shape.

To give estimates for the solutions to the equation, read the x values where the graph crosses the x-axis.

The turning points are the lowest or highest points on quadratic graphs.

10 Exam-style practice — Grade 5

1 The diagram shows shape **A**.
All the measurements are in centimetres.

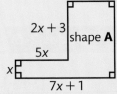

(a) Write an expression, in terms of x, for the perimeter of shape **A**. **[2 marks]**

A square has the same perimeter as shape **A**.

(b) Write an expression, in terms of x, for the length of one side of this square. **[1 mark]**

2 Solve these simultaneous equations.
$2x + 5y = 16$
$2x + 3y = 8$ **[4 marks]**

3 Here are the first four terms of an arithmetic sequence:

5   11   17   23

(a) Write, in terms of n, an expression for the nth term of this arithmetic sequence. **[2 marks]**

(b) Is 119 a term in this arithmetic sequence? You must explain your answer. **[1 mark]**

Made a start   Feeling confident   Exam ready

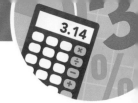

Ratio

Ratios are used to describe how two or more quantities are related.

2 Ratio and fractions

A ratio shows the relationship between two numbers. The parts of the ratio are separated by colons.

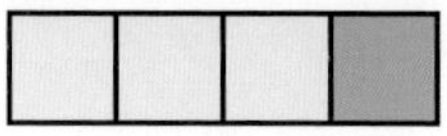

The ratio of the yellow tiles to green tiles is 3 : 1

The ratio of the green tiles to yellow tiles is 1 : 3

Ratios can be written as fractions.

Yellow tiles	Green tiles
$\frac{3}{4}$	$\frac{1}{4}$

The denominator is the sum of the parts in the ratio.

2 Dividing a quantity in a ratio

To divide a quantity in a given ratio:

1. Work out the total number of parts.
2. Divide the quantity by the total number of parts to work out what one part represents.
3. Multiply each part of the ratio by this amount.

2 Simplifying ratios

You can simplify a ratio to an equivalent ratio if you divide both of the numbers by a common factor.

24 : 12 → 12 : 6 → 6 : 3 → 2 : 1

The ratio 2 : 1 cannot be simplified any further and it is said to be in its lowest terms.

5 Worked example — Grade 3

1. Write the ratio 32 : 48 in its simplest form.

   ÷16 (32 : 48 → 2 : 3) ÷16

2. Write 45p to £2 as a ratio.

   ÷5 (45 : 200 → 9 : 40) ÷5

3. David and Mike share 35 apples in the ratio 3 : 4

   How many apples does each person get?

Total number of parts = 3 + 4 = 7

7 parts = 35 apples

1 part = 5 apples

David = 3 × 5 = 15 apples

Mike = 4 × 5 = 20 apples

When you use ratios they must be in the same units. Change £2.00 to 200p.

5 Worked example — Grades 2–4

1. Here is a tile pattern.

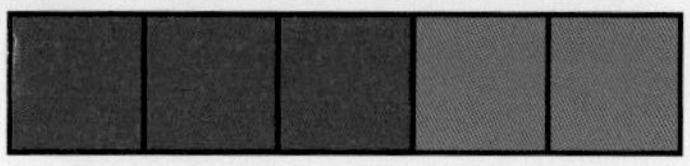

(a) Write down the ratio of the red tiles to blue tiles.

3 : 2

(b) What fraction of the tiles are blue?

$\frac{2}{5}$

2. Anjali, Ravina and Sandeep shared some money in the ratio 7 : 5 : 3, respectively.
   Anjali got £60 more than Sandeep.

   How much money did Ravina get?

Difference in Anjali's and Sandeep's amounts
= 7 parts − 3 parts = 4 parts

4 parts = £60

1 part = £60 ÷ 4 = £15

Ravina receives 5 × £15 = £75

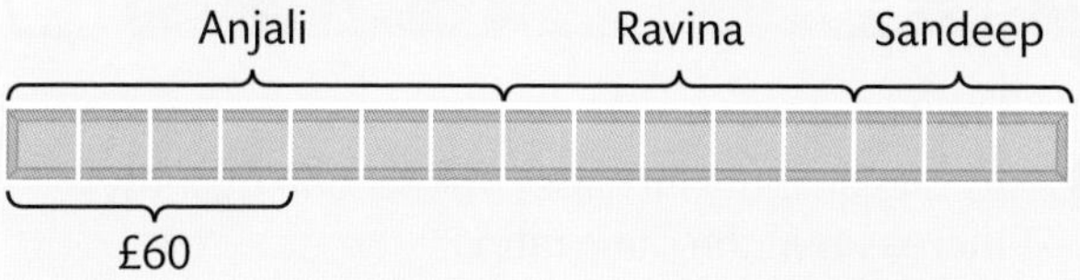

Always work out 1 part when working with ratios.

15 Exam-style practice — Grades 2–4

1. Write these ratios in their simplest form.
   (a) 3 : 6 **[1 mark]** **(b)** 3 : 18 **[1 mark]**
   (c) 6 : 24 **[1 mark]** **(d)** 15 : 9 **[1 mark]**
2. Tom and Leena receive money in the ratio 7 : 3
   Write the fraction that is received by
   (a) Tom **[1 mark]** **(b)** Leena **[1 mark]**
3. Angela and Brenda share £360 in the ratio 5 : 4
   How much should they each receive? **[2 marks]**
4. Vijay, Mia and Niamh share £960 in the ratio 4 : 5 : 3. How much more does Mia receive than Niamh receives? **[2 marks]**
5. A bag contains some black discs and 40 white discs.
   The ratio of black discs to white discs is 2 : 5
   How many black discs are in the bag? **[2 marks]**

Direct proportion

Two quantities are in direct proportion if, when one quantity increases, the other quantity increases at the same rate and vice versa.

① Direct proportion

Direct proportion can be used in a lot of real-life situations, such as:

- exchange rates
- recipes
- shopping.

For example:

$\times 8$ ⌒ 1 kg of apples cost £1.05 ⌒ $\times 8$
8 kg of the same apples cost £8.40

Problem solving

There are two steps to this problem:

① Work out how many rupees Max got in 2012.

② Work out how many pounds he needs to change in 2017 to get the same number of rupees.

Use inverse operations to reverse the money change:

$\times 85.5$
2017: £1 = 85.50 rupees
$\div 85.5$

② Checklist

For direct proportion:

☑ As one quantity increases, the second quantity **increases** in the same ratio.

☑ As one quantity decreases, the second quantity **decreases** in the same ratio.

Remember to convert all the ingredients to grams so that the ratios are all described in the same unit.

Problem solving

Divide each ingredient by the amount needed in the recipe. Look for the lowest value and this will give the maximum number of batches. The number of batches of ginger biscuits is 30.

⑩ Worked example — Grade 4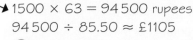

① 8 chopping boards cost £62.80. Work out the cost of 14 of these chopping boards.

Cost of 8 boards = £62.80
Cost of 1 board = £7.85
Cost of 14 boards = 14 × £7.85 = £109.90

② Max travels from the UK to India every year.
In 2012, the exchange rate was £1 = 63 rupees.
In 2017, the exchange rate was £1 = 85.50 rupees.
In 2012, Max changed £1500 into rupees.
How many pounds (£) did Max have to change to rupees in 2017 to get the same number of rupees as he did in 2012?

1500 × 63 = 94 500 rupees
94 500 ÷ 85.50 ≈ £1105

③ Asha made some ginger biscuits, which she sold at a charity event. She started with:

- 6 kg flour
- 3.75 kg butter
- 2.4 kg sugar
- 355 g ginger.

Here is the list of ingredients for making a batch of 18 ginger biscuits.

125 g flour, 100 g butter, 80 g sugar, 10 g ginger

(a) Asha made as many batches of ginger biscuits as she could, using the ingredients she had. Work out how many batches of ginger biscuits she made.

Flour	Butter	Sugar	Ginger
6000 ÷ 125	3750 ÷ 100	2400 ÷ 80	355 ÷ 10
= 48	= 37.5	= 30	= 35.5

Asha made 30 batches of biscuits.

(b) How many biscuits did Asha make in total?

Number of biscuits = 30 × 18 = 540

⑩ Exam-style practice — Grade 4

① Mohan has a plank of wood. The wood has a length of 12 metres. Mohan cuts the wood into two lengths, length X and length Y. The length X is 7 metres. The weight of length X is 10.5 kg. Work out the weight of length Y. **[3 marks]**

② In the UK, diesel costs £1.19 per litre. In the USA, diesel costs $2.95 per US gallon.
1 US gallon = 3.8 litres and £1 = $1.29.
Is diesel more expensive in the UK or in the USA? **[4 marks]**

☑ **Made a start** ☑ **Feeling confident** ☑ **Exam ready**

Inverse proportion

Two quantities are in inverse proportion when one quantity increases as the other quantity decreases, or vice versa, at the same rate.

 Inverse proportion

It takes 6 workers 15 days to complete a job. If the number of workers doubles, then the number of days needed will halve. This is an example of inverse proportion: when one quantity increases, the other decreases.

If it takes 6 workers 15 days to complete the job, then it will take 1 worker 6 times as long as that to do the same amount of work.

To work out how long it would take one worker to complete the job, set up the problem in a table.

$15 \times 6 = 90$ days. This is how long it takes one worker to complete the job. You can divide this number to work out how many days it will take any other number of workers.

Workers	Days
6	15
1	$15 \times 6 = 90$
2	$90 \div 2 = 45$

 Worked example | **Grade 5**

1 There is enough food to last 12 people for 10 days. How long would the food last if there were 15 people?

People	Days
12	10
1	$10 \times 12 = 120$
15	$120 \div 15 = 8$

2 A balloon contains a fixed amount of helium gas. The volume of the balloon is inversely proportional to the pressure.

When the pressure is 2 bars, the volume of the balloon is $3000\,\text{cm}^3$.
What is

(a) the volume of the balloon when the pressure is 5 bars?

Bars	Volume
2	3000
1	$3000 \times 2 = 6000$
5	$6000 \div 5 = 1200$

The volume is $1200\,\text{cm}^3$.

(b) the pressure when the volume is $8000\,\text{cm}^3$?

Volume	Bars
3000	2
1	$3000 \times 2 = 6000$
8000	$6000 \div 8000 = 0.75$

The pressure is 0.75 bars.

Work out how long the food will last for 1 person and then work out the number of days it would last for 15 people. Multiply 12 by 10 to find 120.

Problem solving

In this part, you are being asked to work out the pressure, not the volume. Use the values in the question to work out how many bars there will be when the balloon has a volume of $1\,\text{cm}^3$.

1 $3000\,\text{cm}^3$ of volume = 2 bars of pressure

2 You **divide** the volume by 3000, so you need to **multiply** the pressure by 3000: $3000 \times 2 = 6000$ bars

3 To get from $1\,\text{cm}^3$ to $8000\,\text{cm}^3$ you need to multiply by 8000. Therefore, you need to divide 6000 by 8000: $6000 \div 8000 = 0.75$ bars of pressure.

Don't forget to include the units in your answer.

 Exam-style practice | **Grade 5**

1 Four people can paint a fence in 6 hours.
How long will it take five people to paint it?
[2 marks]

2 An army base has provisions for 300 soldiers for 90 days. After 20 days, 50 soldiers leave the army base. How long will the food last if it is eaten at the same rate? **[4 marks]**

3 Emma draws some rectangles, which all have the same area. One of Emma's rectangles has length 10 cm and width 8 cm.

A second rectangle has length 4 cm.

(a) Work out its width. **[3 marks]**

A third rectangle has width 32 cm.

(b) Work out its length. **[2 marks]**

Percentages

Percentages are used to make comparisons in everyday life. 'Per cent' means 'out of 100' and a percentage is like a fraction but, instead of writing it over 100, you use the % sign.

(2) Percentages of a whole

100% means the whole of something. A number that is less than 100% represents part of a whole:

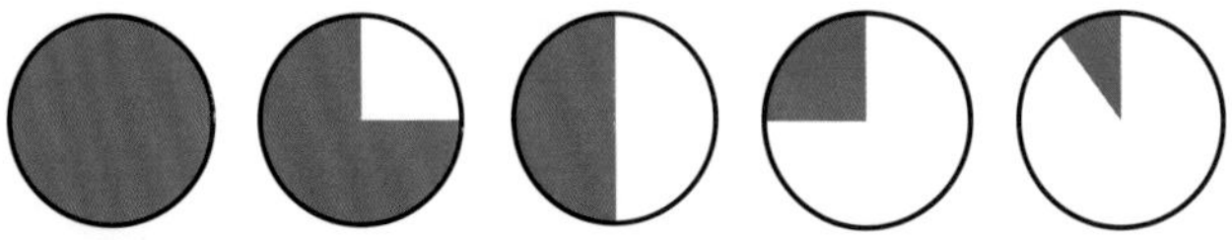

100% 75% 50% 25% 10%

(5) Converting into percentages

To express one quantity as a percentage of another:

1. Convert both quantities so that they are in the same units.
2. Write down the first quantity as a fraction of the second quantity.
3. Multiply this fraction by 100

For example: a student got 57 out of 80 possible marks on an exam. She needs 70% in this exam to pass.

To work out her percentage:

$$\frac{57}{80} \times 100 = 71.25\%$$

71.25% > 70% so she passes the exam.

(10) Worked example — Grades 2–3

1 Work out 35% of £360 without a calculator.

10% of £360 = £360 ÷ 10 = £36
30% of £360 = £36 × 3 = £108
5% of £360 = £36 ÷ 2 = £18
35% of £360 = £108 + £18 = £126

2 Work out 29.5% of 133 using a calculator.

$$29.5\% \text{ of } 133 = \frac{29.5}{100} \times 133$$
$$= 39.235 = 39.2 \text{ (3 s.f.)}$$

3 (a) Work out £480 as a percentage of £600

$$\frac{480}{600} \times 100 = 80\%$$

(b) Write 143 out of 800 as a percentage.

$$\frac{143}{800} \times 100 = 17.875 = 17.9\% \text{ (3 s.f.)}$$

29.5% means 29.5 out of 100.

If the required degree of accuracy is not stated, give your answer to 3 significant figures (3 s.f.).

(5) Calculating a percentage

Without a calculator

- Work out 10%: divide the quantity by 10
- Work out 1%: divide the quantity by 100
- Work out 2%: work out 1% of the quantity and then multiply by 2
- Work out 5%: work out 10% of the quantity and then divide by 2

Use different combinations of these to work out percentages of quantities without a calculator.

With a calculator

1. Divide the percentage by 100.
2. Multiply the answer by the quantity.

For example, to work out 45% of 320:

45 ÷ 100 = 0.45
0.45 × 320 = 144
45% of 320 is 144

Split the percentage into quantities that you know you can work out easily. 35% can be split into 30% and 5%.

Once you know 10% multiply by 3 to work out 30%.

(10) Exam-style practice — Grades 2–3

1 **(a)** Work out 28% of £85 000 **[2 marks]**
(b) Work out 40 out of 2000 as a percentage. **[2 marks]**

2 There are 200 counters in a bag.
80 of the counters are yellow.
(a) Work out 80 as a fraction of 200, giving your answer in its simplest form. **[2 marks]**
40 of the 200 counters in the bag are red.
(b) Work out 40 as a percentage of 200 **[2 marks]**

3 There are 350 people on the train at Wolverhampton.
22% of the 350 people are children.
(a) Work out 22% of 350 **[2 marks]**
103 of the 350 people are men.
(b) Work out 103 out of 350 as a percentage. **[2 marks]**
(c) How many women are there on the train? **[2 marks]**

Made a start | Feeling confident | Exam ready

Fractions, decimals and percentages

Fractions, decimals and percentages are simple ways of expressing a proportion of a quantity. You should be able to convert between them.

⑤ Rules of conversion

You can convert between fractions, decimals and percentages by using these rules.

Multiply by 100 and simplify, then write % at the end.

Divide by 100 to move the digits two places to the right. Insert zeros to fill any gaps.

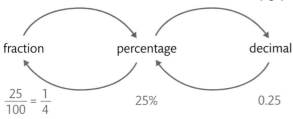

fraction percentage decimal

$\frac{25}{100} = \frac{1}{4}$ 25%   0.25

Write as a fraction of 100, remove the % sign and simplify the fraction.

Multiply by 100 to move the digits two places to the left. Insert zeros to fill any gaps and write % at the end.

⑤ Equivalent quantities

The table shows some equivalent fractions, decimals and percentages.

Fraction	Decimal	Percentage
$\frac{1}{4}$	0.25	25%
$\frac{1}{2}$	0.5	50%
$\frac{3}{4}$	0.75	75%
$\frac{1}{5}$	0.2	20%
$\frac{1}{10}$	0.1	10%
$\frac{1}{100}$	0.01	1%

⑤ Using your calculator

Fractions to decimals and percentages

For a fraction $\frac{a}{b}$, use the division button. $\boxed{a} \boxed{\div} \boxed{b} \boxed{=}$

Then multiply by 100 to get a percentage.

Decimals and percentages to fractions

Divide a percentage by 100 to convert it into a fraction.
Press the $\boxed{S \Leftrightarrow D}$ button to convert between fractions and decimals.

⑤ Worked example — Grade 2

① Write these in order of size. Start with the smallest number.

0.7 $\frac{2}{3}$ 65% $\frac{3}{5}$ 0.62

70%   66.67%   65%   60%   62%

So the order is:

$\frac{3}{5}$ 0.62   65% $\frac{2}{3}$ 0.7

② Tony spends 20% of his monthly salary on going out, $\frac{1}{4}$ of his salary on bills and $\frac{2}{5}$ on rent. The rest he saves. If his monthly rent is £450, how much will he save each month?

$20\% + \frac{1}{4} + \frac{2}{5} = 20\% + 25\% + 40\% = 85\%$

Savings $= 100\% - 85\% = 15\%$

40% = £450

1% = £11.25

15% = £11.25 × 15

= £168.75

Convert each of the numbers into a percentage and then write the original numbers in the correct order.

Remember, all the percentages must add up to 100%.

⑩ Exam-style practice — Grades 2–3

① Complete the table.

Fraction	Decimal	Percentage
$\frac{1}{8}$		
	0.15	
		40%

[3 marks]

② Circle the percentage closest in value to $\frac{2}{3}$.

[1 mark]

60%   67%   66.6%   66.7%

③ Andrew, Ben and Carina bought a present for their father. Andrew paid 32% of the total, Ben paid $\frac{2}{5}$ of the total and Carina paid the rest. Carina paid £252. How much was the present? **[4 marks]**

Percentage change

There are two methods you can use to increase or decrease an amount by a given percentage.

⑤ Finding-the-amount method

To increase or decrease a price by a percentage, first work out that percentage of the original amount, then add or subtract this to or from the original amount.

For example, a hotel adds an 18% service charge to the bill:

> **HOTEL HILLSIDE**
>
> £265 + 18% service charge
>
> *We hope you enjoyed your stay!*

To work out the total amount, first work out 18% of £265.

$$\frac{18}{100} \times £265 = £47.70$$

Add this to the original amount:

£265 + £47.70 = £312.70

⑤ Multiplier method

You can also increase or decrease an amount by a given percentage by finding the multiplier.

> **HOTEL HILLSIDE**
>
> £265 + 18% service charge
>
> *We hope you enjoyed your stay!*

To work out the total amount, first work out the multiplier.
The increased price is 100% + 18% = 118%.
Change this to a decimal: 118 ÷ 100 = 1.18
The multiplier is 1.18.
£265 × 1.18 = £312.70

⑤ Percentage increase or decrease

In one month, a plant grew from 80 cm to 92 cm.

What is the percentage increase?

Work out the amount of increase:

92 cm − 80 cm = 12 cm

Write this as a percentage of the original amount:

$$\frac{12}{80} \times 100 = 15\%$$

— 92 cm
— 80 cm

⑩ Worked example — Grade 3

1 A set of tyres normally costs £450. In a sale, there is a 35% discount. Work out the sale price of the set of tyres.

<u>Method 1</u>

Work out 35% of £450

> Find the amount of the change, then subtract this from the original amount.

$$\frac{35}{100} \times £450 = £157.50$$

£450 − £157.50 = £292.50

> To convert a percentage to a decimal, divide by 100.

<u>Method 2</u>

100% − 35% = 65%

65 ÷ 100 = 0.65 ← Or use a multiplier.

The multiplier is 0.65

£450 × 0.65 = £292.50

> Start by subtracting 35% from 100% and then converting the answer into a decimal.

2 David's weight decreases from 74.5 kg to 69 kg. Calculate the percentage decrease in David's weight. Give your answer correct to 3 significant figures.

Decrease = 74.5 kg − 69 kg = 5.5 kg

$$\text{Percentage decrease} = \frac{5.5}{74.5} \times 100 = 7.38\%$$

> Remember the increase or decrease is always written as a percentage of the original amount.

> The original weight is 74.5 kg.

⑩ Exam-style practice — Grades 3–4

1 Tom is buying a necklace. The necklace costs £195. He pays a deposit of 32%. Work out the amount he has to pay when he collects the necklace. **[3 marks]**

2 Alan needs to buy some oil for heating at his farm. The capacity of the oil tank is 2300 litres. The oil tank is already 20% full. Alan is going to fill the tank with oil. The price of oil is 73.4 pence per litre. Alan gets 8% off the price of oil. How much does Alan pay for the oil he needs to buy? **[5 marks]**

Reverse percentages

If you are given an amount after a percentage change, you need to be able to work out the original amount. There are two methods: the **unitary method** and the **multiplier method**.

 Calculating a reverse percentage

Amazing reduction! All prices reduced by 15% Sale price £204

You need to calculate a reverse percentage when you are given the final amount **after** a percentage change and you want to work out the original amount.

Using the unitary method

Taking the original price as 100%, after a reduction of 15%, the sale price is 100% − 15% = 85%.

The sale price is £204. So 85% is £204

You need to work out 1%.

1% = £204 ÷ 85 = £2.40

To work out the original price multiply this by 100

100% = £2.40 × 100 = £240

Using the multiplier method

To work out the multiplier: | Divide by 100 to convert the percentage to a decimal.

100% − 15% = 85%

85% ÷ 100 = 0.85

The multiplier is 0.85

So final price = original price × 0.85

To work out the original price, divide the final price by the multiplier.

£204 ÷ 0.85 = £240

 Worked example | **Grade 5**

The price of all plane tickets to Birmingham airport increased by 6%.

(a) The price of a plane ticket from New Delhi to Birmingham increased by £35.28. Work out the price before this increase.

$$6\% = £35.28$$
$$1\% = \frac{£35.28}{6}$$
$$100\% = \frac{£35.28}{6} \times 100 = £588$$

(b) After the increase, the price of a plane ticket from Shanghai to Birmingham was £466.93 Work out the price before this increase.

$$100\% + 6\% = 106\% = 1.06$$
$$£466.93 ÷ 1.06 = £440.50$$

> Part **(a)** is best answered by the unitary method.

> You can use either method to answer part **(b)**.

 Checklist

☑ To work out the multiplier for an increase, add the percentage increase to 100 and then divide by 100
$$\text{Multiplier} = \frac{100 + \% \text{ increase}}{100}$$

☑ To work out the multiplier for a decrease, subtract the percentage decrease from 100 and then divide by 100
$$\text{Multiplier} = \frac{100 - \% \text{ decrease}}{100}$$

 Exam-style practice | **Grade 5**

1 Kim is baking a cake. The icing makes up 12% of the cake's mass. Before the cake was iced it had a mass of 2.2 kg. Work out the mass of the iced cake. **[3 marks]**

2 Zak and Zoe are comparing this year's salaries with last year's. The table shows their salaries this year and the percentage increase since last year.

Find whose salary was greater last year.

	This year's salary	Percentage increase since last year
Jack	£33 450	4%
Zoe	£34 815	9%

[4 marks]

Growth and decay

You can use repeated percentages to model problems involving growth and decay. Typical examples of these are compound interest, population change and depreciation.

Compound interest

Most bank accounts pay **compound interest**. This means that the amount paid in interest is added to the balance of the account. The next time interest is calculated, the balance will be higher so the amount of interest will be higher. This is an example of **exponential growth**.

Suppose Anjali invests £1600 at 4.2% per annum compound interest. What is the value of Anjali's investment after 4 years?

Using the multiplier method in a table of values

To find the multiplier:

$100\% + 4.2\% = 104.2\%$

$104.2 \div 100 = 1.042$ so the multiplier is 1.042

End of year	Value (£)
1	$1600 \times 1.042 = 1667.20$
2	$1667.20 \times 1.042 = 1737.22$
3	$1737.22 \times 1.042 = 1810.19$
4	$1810.19 \times 1.042 = 1886.21$

With compound interest the value increases.

Using indices

Working with indices is a quicker method than using a multiplier.

$1600 \times 1.042 \times 1.042 \times 1.042 \times 1.042 = £1600 \times (1.042)^4$

$£1600 \times (1.042)^4 = £1886.21$

The golden rule

- ☑ Final amount = (starting amount) $\times$ (multiplier)^n
- ☑ n is the number of times the change happens.

The multiplier for a 3.5% increase is $\times 1.035$.

The car depreciates so it loses value. The multiplier will be less than 1.

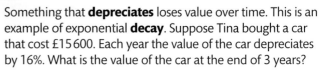 Depreciation

Something that **depreciates** loses value over time. This is an example of exponential **decay**. Suppose Tina bought a car that cost £15 600. Each year the value of the car depreciates by 16%. What is the value of the car at the end of 3 years?

Using indices

$100\% - 16\% = 84\%$

The multiplier is $84 \div 100 = 0.84$

The value after 3 years is $£15\,600 \times (0.84)^3 = £9246.18$

Depreciation is a decrease so the multiplier will be less than 1.

Worked example — Grade 5

1 Rita has £50 000 to invest. She is going to invest in either a savings account or a fixed bond.

Savings account
Invest £50 000 at 3.5% per annum compound interest for 3 years.

'Per annum' means 'per year'.

Fixed bond
Invest £50 000
Receive £5430 interest after 3 years.

Rita wants the maximum amount of money at the end of 3 years.

Savings account $£50\,000 \times (1.035)^3 = £55\,436$
Fixed bond $£50\,000 + £5430 = £55\,430$
She should invest in the savings account.

2 The value of a car depreciates at the rate of 20% per year. Hanna buys a new car for £36 500. Work out the value of the car after 3 years.

After 3 years: $£36\,500 \times (0.80)^3 = £18\,688$

Exam-style practice — Grade 5

1 Tom invests £1500 at 3.5% per annum compound interest.
Work out the value of Tom's investment after 3 years. **[3 marks]**

2 The value of a car depreciates by 15% each year. At the end of 2016 the value of the car was £6800
Work out the value of the car at the end of 2018 **[3 marks]**

3 Sandra invested £3250 for n years in a savings account. She was paid 3.2% per annum compound interest.
After n years, she will have more than £3650 in her savings account.
Work out the value of n. **[2 marks]**

 Made a start **Feeling confident** **Exam ready**

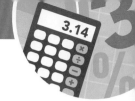

Compound measures

A **compound measure** is made up of two or more other measurements.

2 Compound measures

A **compound measure** is a mathematical or scientific measurement made up of two or more other measurements.

Speed and density are two common compound measures, covered on pages 58 and 59. You need to be able to use other compound measures, such as rates of change or pressure.

Problem solving

Make sure you convert 350 g/s into 0.35 kg/s because when you make comparisons, the units of any variable must be the same.

10 Worked example — Grade 5

1 Use the formula

$$\text{pressure} = \frac{\text{force}}{\text{area}}$$

to work out the pressure exerted by a force of 1200 newtons on a rectangular metal plate measuring 80 cm by 48 cm. Give your answer in newtons/m².

The answer needs to be in newtons per square metre, so you need to convert centimetres into metres.

Area = 0.8 m × 0.48 m = 0.384 m²

$$\text{Pressure} = \frac{\text{force}}{\text{area}} = \frac{1200}{0.384}$$

= 3125 newtons/m²

2 A full tank contains 540 litres of water. When a tap is opened, water flows out at the rate of 0.4 litres per second. How long will it take to empty the tank? Give your answer in minutes.

$$\text{Rate of flow} = \frac{\text{volume}}{\text{time}}$$

$$0.4 = \frac{540}{t} \Rightarrow t = \frac{540}{0.4}$$

t = 1350 seconds
= 22.5 minutes

You can work out the formula from the units. In this case, 'litres per second' means volume divided by time.

2 Checklist

- ✓ If you forget a formula you may be able to work it out from the given units. For example, if density is given in g/cm³, density must be $\frac{\text{mass}}{\text{volume}}$.
- ✓ Make sure you read the question carefully and convert any units correctly, if necessary.

5 Worked example — Grade 5

Sand was falling from lorry A at a rate of 0.3 kg/s and it took 15 minutes for all the sand to fall.

Sand was falling from lorry B at a rate of 350 g/s and it took 12 minutes for all the sand to fall.

Which lorry was carrying more sand?

350 g ÷ 1000 = 0.35 kg
15 minutes = 900 s
12 minutes = 720 s

$$\text{rate} = \frac{\text{mass}}{\text{time}}$$

Lorry A:

$$0.3 = \frac{\text{mass}}{900}$$

mass = 0.3 × 900
= 270 kg

Lorry B:

$$0.35 = \frac{\text{mass}}{720}$$

mass = 0.35 × 720
= 252 kg

Lorry A was carrying more sand, as 270 kg is more than 252 kg.

10 Exam-style practice — Grade 5

1 The combined force exerted by a boat and its crew on water is 1023 N. It exerts a pressure of 310 N/m² on the water.

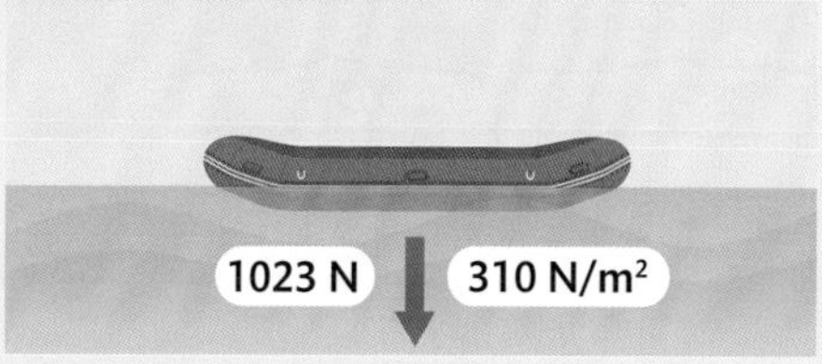

Work out the area of the raft in contact with the water. **[2 marks]**

2 An empty tank has a capacity of 720 litres. John wants to fill the tank, and has a choice of two hosepipes to fill the tank.

For hosepipe A, water flows out at a rate of 0.40 litres per second.

For hosepipe B, water flows out at a rate of 1728 litres per hour.

Work out the difference between the times taken to fill the tank using hosepipe A and hosepipe B.

Give your answer in minutes. You must show your working. **[4 marks]**

Speed

Speed describes how fast an object is moving. Speed is a compound measure (see page 57), with units such as miles per hour or metres per second.

Formula for speed

The formula for speed is:

$$\text{speed} = \frac{\text{distance}}{\text{time}}$$

This can be rearranged to:

$$\text{time} = \frac{\text{distance}}{\text{speed}} \text{ and distance} = \text{speed} \times \text{time}$$

You can remember the speed formula from this triangle. If you cover the variable you need to find, the other parts of the triangle show you how to calculate it.

Worked example — Grade 5

An athlete runs a distance of 660 metres in 1 minute and 15 seconds. Work out her average speed in metres per second.

Total time is
60 seconds + 15 seconds = 75 seconds

$$\text{speed} = \frac{\text{distance}}{\text{time}} = \frac{660}{75} = 8.8 \text{ m/s}$$

Worked example — Grade 5

On a journey from Paris to Lyon, René drove at an average speed of 50 mph for the first 2 hours and 30 minutes of his journey.

The remaining 210 miles of his journey were completed at an average speed of 70 mph.

René says that he completed the whole journey at an average speed of 55 mph.

Is René correct? You must show your working.

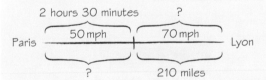

First part of the journey:
distance = speed × time = 50 × 2.5 = 125 miles
Total distance = 125 + 210 = 335 miles
Second part of the journey:

$$\text{time} = \frac{\text{distance}}{\text{speed}} = \frac{210}{70} = 3 \text{ hours}$$

Total time = 2.5 + 3 = 5.5 hours

$$\text{Average speed} = \frac{\text{total distance}}{\text{total time}}$$
$$= \frac{335}{5.5}$$
$$= 60.9 \text{ mph (1 d.p.)}$$

No, he is not correct.

Problem solving

You need to work out the total distance he travelled.

1 Divide the 30 minutes by 60, to convert to hours.

2 Rearrange the formula for distance to get time.

3 You need to work out the total time for which he travelled.

4 Now use the formula for speed.

Exam-style practice — Grades 4–5

1 Lorna drives 200 miles in 4 hours. Work out her average speed. **[2 marks]**

2 Dhillon goes for a walk. He walks for 5 hours at a speed of 2.5 miles per hour.
Work out the distance Dhillon walks. **[3 marks]**

3 Angela is driving along a motorway. Her satnav is showing that she will reach Vienna, which is 40 miles away, in 28 minutes. The speed limit on the motorway is 80 mph. She thinks she will exceed the speed limit. Is Angela correct? You must show how you get your answer. **[3 marks]**

4 Darren cycles 78 miles in 6 hours. His average speed for the first 30 miles is 15 miles per hour.
Work out Darren's average speed for the last 48 miles. **[3 marks]**

Density

Density is a compound measure (see page 57) that compares the mass of a given amount of a material to its volume. It is measured in units such as grams per cubic centimetre, g/cm^3.

5 Formula for density

The formula for density is:

$$density = \frac{mass}{volume}$$

This can be rearranged to:

$$volume = \frac{mass}{density} \text{ or mass} = density \times volume$$

You can remember the density formula from this triangle. If you cover the variable you need to find, the other side of the triangle shows you how to calculate it.

Use the total mass and the total volume to work out the density of the alloy.

Problem solving

When questions are given in context, you may need to identify which quantities you need to work out before you start. Here, you need to work out the volume of the cuboid.

Volume = length × width × height

The formulae for 3D shapes are given on page 71.

You need to change metres to centimetres because the density is given in g/cm^3.

Convert grams to kilograms by dividing by 1000, to compare with the maximum mass that can be supported on the pallet.

5 Worked example — Grade 5

210 g of zinc is mixed with 360 g of copper to make the alloy brass. The density of copper is $9\,g/cm^3$. The density of zinc is $7\,g/cm^3$.

(a) Work out the volume of zinc used in the alloy.

$$\text{Volume of zinc} = \frac{mass}{density} = \frac{210}{7} = 30\,cm^3$$

Use the version of the formula that will give the volume.

(b) What is the density of the alloy?

$$\text{Volume of copper} = \frac{mass}{density} = \frac{360}{9} = 40\,cm^3$$

Total volume of brass = 30 + 40 = 70 cm³

Total mass of brass = 210 + 360 = 570 g

$$\text{Density of brass} = \frac{mass}{volume} = \frac{570}{70} = 8.14\,g/cm^3$$

5 Worked example — Grade 5

A cuboid of rock measures 1 m by 0.7 m by 0.5 m. The density of the rock is $3.5\,g/cm^3$. The rock needs to be placed on a pallet. Can the rock be supported by a pallet that holds a maximum mass of 1200 kg? Justify your decision.

Volume of cuboid = 100 cm × 70 cm × 50 cm

= 350 000 cm³

Mass of rock = density × volume

= 3.5 × 350 000

= 1 225 000 g

= 1225 kg

The rock cannot be supported by the pallet as 1225 kg is more than 1200 kg.

10 Exam-style practice — Grade 5

1 The area of the cross-section of a prism is $85\,cm^2$. The length of the prism is 22 cm.

(a) Work out the volume of the prism. **[2 marks]**

The prism is made from wood and has a mass of 896 g.

(b) Work out the density, in g/cm^3, of the wood. Give your answer correct to 3 significant figures. **[2 marks]**

2 Nisha makes a lemon drink by mixing lemon cordial with water. She mixes $25\,cm^3$ of lemon cordial with $325\,cm^3$ of water. The density of lemon cordial is $1.40\,g/cm^3$. The density of water is $1.00\,g/cm^3$.

Work out the density of Nisha's lemon drink. Give your answer correct to 2 decimal places. **[4 marks]**

Proportion and graphs

Direct proportion and inverse proportion (see pages 50 and 51) can be shown graphically.

 Direct and inverse proportion

Direct proportion graphs look like this:

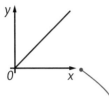

This is the graph of $y \propto x$ or $y = kx$. The graph is a straight line that passes through the origin.

Inverse proportion graphs look like this:

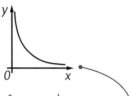

This is the graph of $y \propto \dfrac{1}{x}$ or $y = \dfrac{k}{x}$. The curve does not go through the origin or touch either axis.

 Worked example   **Grade 5**

1. This graph shows the conversion between gallons and litres.

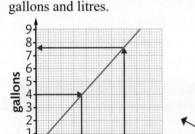

Draw lines on the graph to show the values you are working out. To convert 4 gallons to litres draw across from 4 on the vertical axis to the line, then down to the horizontal axis.

Use the graph to convert:
(a) 4 gallons to litres

18 litres ←

Make sure you use a sharp pencil and a ruler when drawing the lines on the graphs.

(b) 350 litres to gallons.

35 litres = 7.6 gallons
so 350 litres = 76 gallons

2. The acceleration, a, of a mass is directly proportional to the force, F, on the mass. Given that $F = 900$ when $a = 30$, work out the value of F when $a = 25$

$\dfrac{F}{25} = \dfrac{900}{30}$ ←   Use ratios to solve this type of question.

$F = 25 \times 30$

$= 750$

 The proportionality symbol

The quick way of writing that y is directly proportional to x is $y \propto x$.

This is the same as the equation $y = kx$.

The quick way of writing that y is inversely proportional to x is $y \propto \dfrac{1}{x}$

This is the same as $y = \dfrac{k}{x}$

If you see $y \propto x$ or $y \propto \dfrac{1}{x}$ in a question, you can convert it to the equivalent equation to help you answer the question.

 Checklist

☑ A graph of direct proportion goes through the origin.

☑ Direct proportion has equation $y = kx$.

☑ Inverse proportion has equation $y = \dfrac{k}{x}$

☑ Use ratios to work out proportion problems.

Exam-style practice   **Grade 5**

1. A and B are directly proportional. Which equation best describes the relationship between A and B?

$A = 3B + 2$

$A = \dfrac{4}{x}$

$A = 6B$

Give a reason for your answer.   **[2 marks]**

2. y is directly proportional to x.

$y = 42$ when $x = 5$

Work out the value of y when $x = 8$ **[2 marks]**

Ratio and proportion

Read the exam-style question and worked solution, then practise your exam skills with the two questions at the bottom of the page.

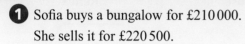

Worked example   Grade 5

1 Sofia buys a bungalow for £210 000.
She sells it for £220 500.

(a) Work out Sofia's percentage profit.

Profit = £220 500 − £210 000

    = £10 500

$\text{Percentage profit} = \dfrac{10\,500}{210\,000} \times 100\%$

    = 5%

> Work out the profit by taking away the original price from the selling price.

> To work out the percentage profit, work out the profit divided by the original price then multiply by 100.

Sofia invests £220 500 for 3 years at 4.5% per year compound interest.

(b) Work out the value of the investment at the end of 3 years.

100% + 4.5% = 104.5%

So multiplier = 104.5% ÷ 100 = 1.045

Value of the investment = £220 500 × (1.045)³

    = £251 627.13

    = £251 627 to the nearest pound

> Work out the multiplier by adding the percentage to 100% and then convert this into a decimal.

> Use the formula:
> value × (multiplier)^n
> where n is the number of years.

2 The diagram shows a solid wooden cuboid.

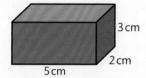

3 cm
2 cm
5 cm

The mass of the cuboid is 45 grams.

Wood will float on the Dead Sea only when the density of the wood is less than 1.24 g/cm³.

Will this wooden block float on the Dead Sea?

Density = mass ÷ volume

Volume of cuboid = 5 × 3 × 2 = 30 cm³

Density = 45 ÷ 30 = 1.5 g/cm³

It won't float because its density is higher than 1.24 g/cm³.

Checklist

- ☑ Work out the profit by taking away the original price from the selling price.
- ☑ Put the profit over the original price and then multiply by 100 to find the percentage profit.
- ☑ Work out the multiplier by adding the rate to 100% and then converting it into a decimal.

Exam-style practice   Grades 4–5

1 Amaya, Lexie and Yasmin did a Maths test.
The total for the test was 120 marks.
Amaya got 75 out of 120.
Lexie got 65% of the 120 marks.
Yasmin got $\dfrac{11}{15}$ of the 120 marks.
Who got the highest mark?
You must show all your working.   **[4 marks]**

2 Dmitri is going to make some concrete mix.
He needs to mix cement, sand and gravel in the ratio 2 : 3 : 5 by weight.
Dmitri wants to make 210 kg of concrete mix.
Dmitiri has:
18 kg of cement
95 kg of sand
110 kg of gravel.
Does Dmitri have enough cement, sand and gravel to make the concrete mix?   **[4 marks]**

Angle properties

Angles are measured in degrees. You need to be able to use a protractor to measure them. It is important that you learn the different types of angle and the properties of angles.

 Types of angle

Acute	Right angle	Obtuse	Reflex
		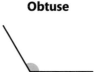	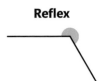
Less than 90°	90°	Between 90° and 180°	Between 180° and 360°

 Properties of angles

Alternate angles are equal.

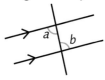

$a = b$

Corresponding angles are equal.

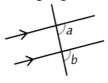

$a = b$

Allied or **co-interior** angles sum to 180°.

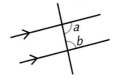

$a + b = 180°$

Angles on a straight line sum to 180°.

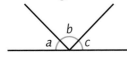

$a + b + c = 180°$

Vertically opposite angles are equal.

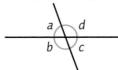

$a = c$ and $b = d$

Angles around a point add up to 360°.

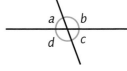

$a + b + c + d = 360°$

 Worked example Grade 2

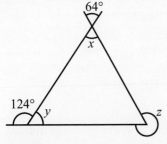

Use the properties of angles and then give clear reasons, even if it seems obvious.

(a) What type of angle is the angle labelled z?

Reflex

(b) Work out the value of x.

Give a reason for your answer.

$x = 64°$

(Vertically opposite angles are equal.)

(c) Work out the value of y.

Give a reason for your answer.

$y = 180° - 124° = 56°$

(Angles on a straight line add up to 180°.)

 Exam-style practice Grades 2–3

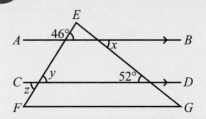

EFG is a triangle. *AB* is parallel to *CD*.

(a) What type of angle is the angle labelled x?

(b) Work out the value of x.

Give a reason for your answer. **[2 marks]**

(c) Work out the value of y.

Give a reason for your answer. **[2 marks]**

(d) Work out the value of z.

Give a reason for your answer. **[2 marks]**

Made a start Feeling confident Exam ready

Solving angle problems

When you solve angle problems, you must give a valid reason for each step of your working.

 Solving angle problems

When you are working out an angle in a given problem, you must give a reason for each step.

You should learn and be able to apply all the reasons in the checklist at the bottom of the page.

> Line segments with matching dashes are the same length.
> Line segments with matching arrows are parallel.

 Worked example Grade 4

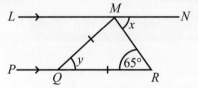

LMN is parallel to *PQR*. *QM* = *QR*.
Angle *RMN* = *x* and angle *MQR* = *y*.

(a) Work out the value of *x*.

Give a reason for your answer.

$x = 65°$

(Alternate angles are equal.)

(a) Work out the value of *y*.

Give a reason for your answer.

Angle $QMR = 65°$

(Base angles in an isosceles triangle are equal.)

$y = 180° - (65° + 65°) = 180° - 130° = 50°$

(Angles in a triangle add up to 180°.)

 Problem solving

You need to be confident applying the properties of angles (page 62) to problem-solving questions.

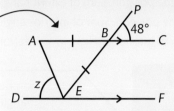

For example, in the diagram above:

ABC is parallel to *DEF*. *EBP* is a straight line.
AB = *EB*. Angle *PBC* = 48° and angle *AED* = *z*.

Work out the value of *z*.
Give a reason for each stage of your working.

You will need to work out the sizes of some of the other angles before you find *z*.

Start by annotating the angles that you know. Write a reason in each case. Angle *ABE* is a good starting point as vertically opposite angles are equal.

Angle ABE = angle $PBC = 48°$

(Vertically opposite angles are equal.)

Angle BEF = angle $ABE = 48°$

(Alternate angles are equal.)

Angle BAE + angle $BEA = 180° - 48° = 132°$

(Angles in a triangle add up to 180°.)

Angle $BEA = 132° ÷ 2 = 66°$

(Base angles in an isosceles triangle are equal.)

Angle $z = 180° - (66° + 48°) = 66°$

(Angles on a straight line add up to 180°.)

 Angles checklist

You need to learn these rules:

- ☑ Corresponding angles are equal.
- ☑ Alternate angles are equal.
- ☑ Angles in a triangle add up to 180°.
- ☑ Base angles in an isosceles triangle are equal.
- ☑ Vertically opposite angles are equal.
- ☑ Angles around a point add up to 360°.
- ☑ Angles on a straight line add up to 180°.

 Exam-style practice Grade 4

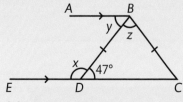

(a) Work out the value of *x*.

Give a reason for your answer. **[2 marks]**

(b) Work out the value of *y*.

Give a reason for your answer. **[2 marks]**

(c) Work out the value of *z*.

Give a reason for your answer. **[2 marks]**

 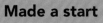

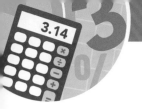

Angles in polygons

A polygon is a closed two-dimensional shape with three or more straight sides, such as a triangle, quadrilateral or hexagon. You can work out facts about the **interior angles** and **exterior angles** of a polygon.

5 Regular polygons

All the sides of a regular polygon are equal and all of its angles are equal. The number of sides in a polygon is represented by n.

Exterior angles are outside the polygon. Sum of exterior angles = 360°

Interior angles are inside the polygon. Sum of interior angles = $180° \times (n - 2)$

For a regular polygon: Sum of interior angles = $n \times$ interior angle

Angles on a straight line add up to 180°. Interior angle + exterior angle = 180°

For a regular polygon: Interior angle = $\dfrac{180° \times (n-2)}{n}$

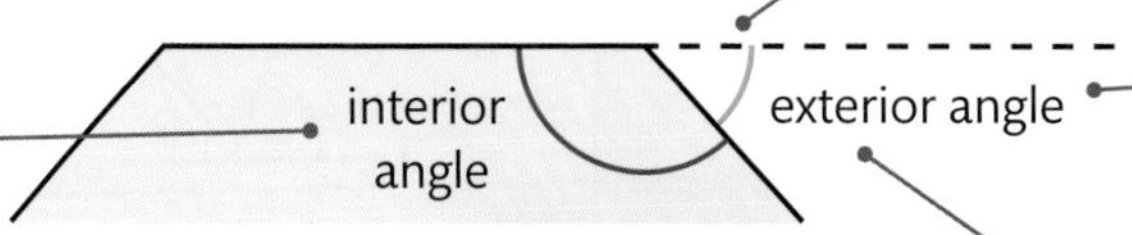

To measure an exterior angle, extend the side from the polygon.

For a regular polygon: Exterior angle = $\dfrac{360°}{\text{number of sides}}$

10 Worked example — Grade 5

1 The interior angle of a regular polygon is 160°.

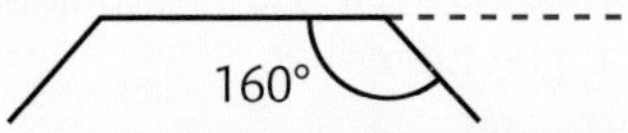

(a) (i) Write down the size of an exterior angle of the polygon.

Exterior angle = 180° − 160° = 20°

(ii) Work out the number of sides of the polygon.

Number of sides $= \dfrac{360°}{\text{exterior angle}} = \dfrac{360°}{20°}$

$= 18$

(b) What is the sum of the interior angles of the polygon?

Sum of interior angles = $180° \times (n - 2)$

$= 180° \times (18 - 2) = 2880°$

An alternative method (for a regular polygon) is:
Sum of interior angles = number of sides × interior angle
You will need to recall the formula to work out the number of sides.

2 The diagram shows two regular polygons. The exterior angle of the larger polygon is a and the exterior angle of the smaller polygon is b.

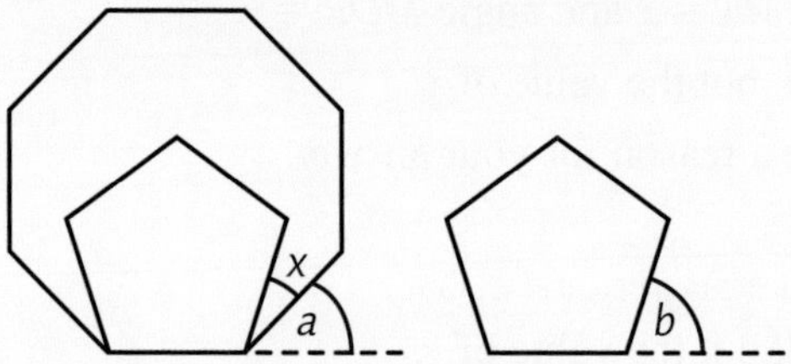

Work out the size of angle x.

Give reasons for your answer.

Work out the size of a, the exterior angle of the octagon.

$a = \dfrac{360°}{8} = 45°$

Work out b, the exterior angle of the pentagon.

$b = \dfrac{360°}{5} = 72°$

Then $x = 72° - 45° = 27°$

x is the difference between the two exterior angles.

2 Checklist

- ✓ Interior angles are inside the polygon.
- ✓ Exterior angles are outside the polygon.
- ✓ To measure an exterior angle, extend the side of the polygon.

10 Exam-style practice — Grade 5

ABCDE is a regular polygon.
EB is a straight line.
Angle *EBC* = 72°
Work out the size of the angle marked x. **[3 marks]**

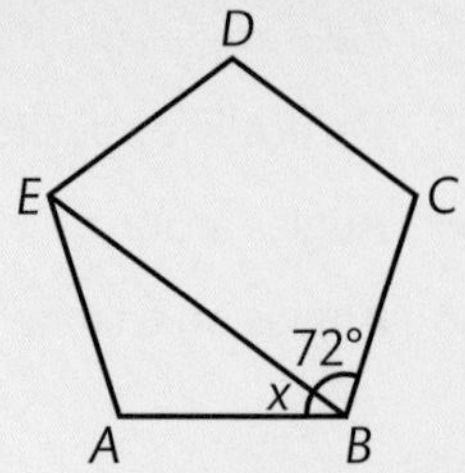

Constructing perpendiculars

You must be able to construct perpendicular lines using a pencil, a pair of compasses and a ruler.

5 Constructing perpendicular lines

You need to know three constructions involving perpendicular lines:

1 the midpoint and **perpendicular bisector** of a line segment

2 the perpendicular from a point to a line

3 the perpendicular from a point on a line.

To **bisect** means to cut something in half.

1. Place the compass point at *A* and then draw an arc.
2. Place the compass point at *B* and then draw an arc.
3. Join the two points where the arcs meet.

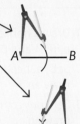

2 Checklist

☑ Make sure the joint of your pair of compasses is not loose and your pencil is clamped firmly in place.
☑ Use a transparent ruler and a sharp pencil.
☑ Always label your angles and sides.
☑ Never rub out your construction lines.

5 Worked example　Grade 5

Use a ruler and compasses to construct the perpendicular bisector of the line segment *AB*. You must show all your construction lines.

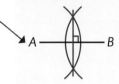

5 Worked example　Grade 5

Use a ruler and compasses to construct the perpendicular from point *A* to the line *XY*. You must show all your construction lines.

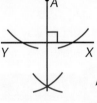

1. Draw two arcs from *A* to cut the line at *B* and *C*.
2. Place the compass point on *B* and draw an arc at *D*. Repeat this with the compass point placed on *C*.
3. Draw a line from *A* to *D*. This is the required perpendicular line.

5 Worked example　Grade 5

Use a ruler and compasses to construct the perpendicular at point *P* on the line *AB*. You must show all your construction lines.

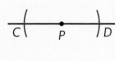

1. Place the compass point at *P* and draw arcs of equal radius from *P* to cross *AB* at *C* and *D*.
2. Extend the compasses and place the point on *C*. Draw an arc and repeat this from *D*. These arcs intersect at *E*.
3. Draw a perpendicular line from *E* to *P*.

5 Exam-style practice　Grade 5

Use a ruler and a compass to **construct** the perpendicular from point *C* to the line *AB*. You must show all your construction lines.　**[2 marks]**

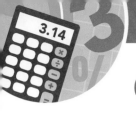

Constructions with angles

You can use compasses and a ruler to bisect angles, construct angles of 30° and 45° and construct triangles.

(10) Worked example — Grade 5

1 Construct an equilateral triangle with sides of length 6 cm. You must show all your construction lines.

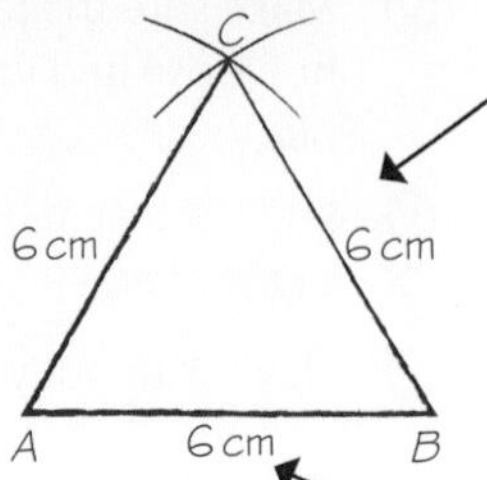

1. Draw a horizontal line of length 6 cm and label the ends *A* and *B*.
2. With compasses set to a radius of 6 cm, place the point on *A* and draw an arc.
3. With compasses still set to the same radius, place the point on *B* and draw another arc to intersect the first arc.
4. Label this point *C* then use a ruler to join *A* to *C* and *B* to *C*, to complete the equilateral triangle.

This method of construction is also used to construct a 60° angle as each angle in an equilateral triangle is 60°.

2 Construct a triangle ABC with $AB = 6$ cm, $BC = 5$ cm and $AC = 4$ cm. You must show all your construction lines.

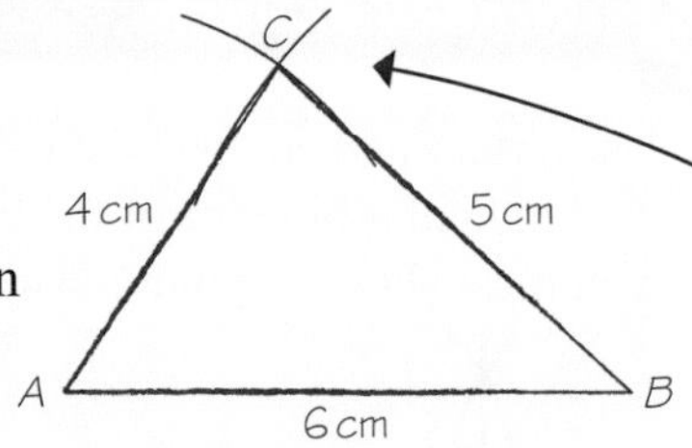

1. Draw a horizontal line of length 6 cm and label the ends *A* and *B*.
2. Set your compasses to 5 cm and, with the point on *B*, draw an arc.
3. Set your compasses to 4 cm and, with the point on *A*, draw an arc to intersect the first arc.
4. Label this point *C* and join *A* to *C* then *B* to *C* with a ruler to complete the triangle.

In this construction, you need to change the radius of your compasses to the lengths of the sides of the triangle.

(5) Bisecting an angle

To **bisect** an angle means to cut it in half. You can bisect an angle by following three simple steps.

1 With the compass point on *A*, sweep an arc and mark points *B* and *C*.

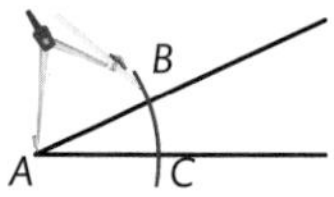

2 Using the same compass setting, draw arcs from the points *B* and *C* to intersect at *D*.

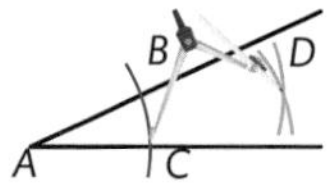

3 Draw a line from *A* to *D* to bisect the angle *CAB*.

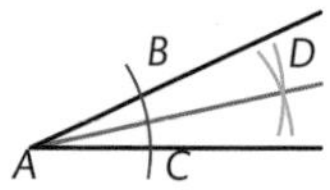

(2) Constructing 45° and 30° angles

A right angle can be bisected to construct a 45° angle and, in a similar way, a 60° angle can be bisected to construct a 30° angle.

(2) Checklist

- ✓ To construct a 45° angle, construct a 90° angle then bisect this angle.
- ✓ To construct a 30° angle, construct a 60° angle then bisect this angle.
- ✓ Construct a 60° angle in the same way as constructing an equilateral triangle.

(10) Exam-style practice — Grade 5

Use a ruler and compasses to construct the given angle at *P*. You must show all your construction lines.

(a) 30°

P

[3 marks]

(b) 45°

P

[3 marks]

Made a start | Feeling confident | Exam ready

Loci

A **locus** is a line or a path. The line or path is formed by a point that moves according to a particular rule. You will need to apply these rules with some of the techniques for constructing lines. The plural of locus is loci.

⑤ Common loci

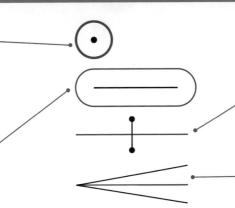

The locus of points that are a constant distance from one point is a circle.

The locus of points that are at a constant distance from a fixed line consists of two straight lines parallel to the original line, and two semicircles.

The locus of points that are equidistant from two fixed points is the perpendicular bisector of the line joining the points.

The locus of a point that is equidistant from two intersecting lines is the angle bisector of the lines.

You need to bisect the angle at *A* and construct part of a circle with radius 5 cm from *A*.

Problem solving

Construct each locus, then work out the region that satisfies **both** conditions at the same time.

⑤ Worked example — Grade 5

The diagram represents a triangular garden *ABC*. The scale of the diagram is 1 cm represents 1 m. A tree is to be planted in the garden so that it is nearer to *AB* than to *AC* and within 5 m of point *A*.

In the diagram, shade the region where the tree may be planted.

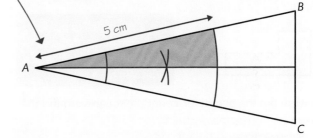

⑤ Worked example — Grade 5

(a) Draw the locus of all points that are equidistant from two points *P* and *Q*.

'Equidistant from two points' means you need to construct a perpendicular bisector.

(b) Draw the locus of all points that are exactly 1 cm from the line *PQ*.

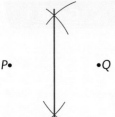

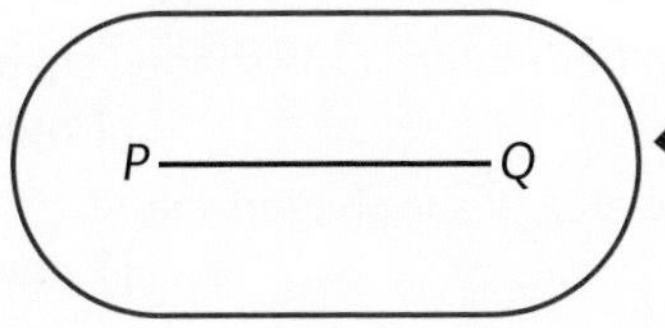

1. Draw two parallel lines above and below that are 1 cm from the line *PQ*.
2. Set your compasses to a radius of 1 cm.
3. Place your compass point at *P* and draw a semicircle so that it touches the two parallel lines.
4. Repeat this at *Q*.

⑩ Exam-style practice — Grade 5

This is a scale drawing of a rectangular garden *ABCD*. 1 cm represents 1 m.

Alan wants to plant a tree in the garden. It must be:

- at least 2 m from point *C*
- nearer to *AB* than to *AD*
- less than 1 m from *DC*.

Shade the region where Alan can plant the tree.

[4 marks]

Perimeter and area

You will need to know how to work out the distance around a shape and the amount of area a two-dimensional shape covers.

⑤ Perimeter

The perimeter is the distance around a shape.

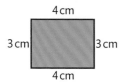

To work out the perimeter of a shape, add up the lengths of all the sides. Perimeter is measured in units of length, such as metres or centimetres.

Perimeter = 3 cm + 4 cm + 3 cm + 4 cm = 14 cm

Area

The area is the amount of space a shape takes up. It is measured in square units because it is a 2D measure, such as square metres or square centimetres.

Area = 3 cm × 4 cm = 12 cm²

⑤ Using squares

Sometimes shapes are drawn on centimetre-squared paper.

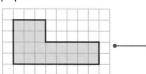

> It is a good idea to mark each side of the shape so you can keep track of which sides you have counted.

To work out the perimeter, count the squares around the shape.

In this case the perimeter is 24 cm.

To work out the area, count the squares inside the shape.

In this case the area is 22 cm².

⑤ Estimating area

The area of a shape on a centimetre grid can be estimated by using the following rules:

1 whole square is 1 cm² and 1 part square is $\frac{1}{2}$ cm².

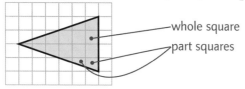
whole square
part squares

Whole squares = 6 so area is 6 cm²
Part squares = 12 so area is 6 cm²
Estimated area = 12 cm²

⑤ Worked example   Grade 1

1 The diagram shows the plan of the floor of Tanya's living room.

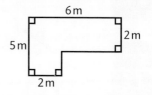

> Sometimes you need to work out missing lengths before you can work out the perimeter.

Work out the perimeter.

Missing length = 6 m − 2 m = 4 m
Missing height = 5 m − 2 m = 3 m
Perimeter = 6 m + 2 m + 3 m + 4 m + 2 m + 5 m
       = 22 m

2 This shaded shape is drawn on a centimetre grid.

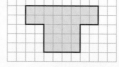

(a) Work out the perimeter of the shaded shape.
26 cm

(b) Work out the area of the shaded shape.
28 cm²

⑩ Exam-style practice   Grade 1

1 The shaded shape is drawn on a grid of centimetre squares.

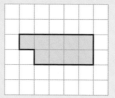

(a) Work out the perimeter of the shaded shape.
[1 mark]

(b) Work out the area of the shaded shape.
[1 mark]

2 The shaded shape is drawn on a grid of centimetre squares.

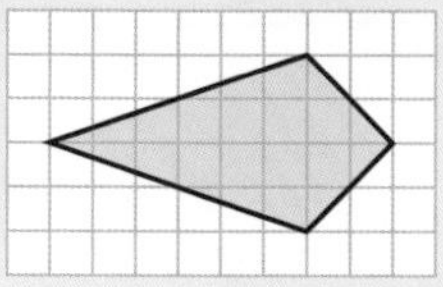

Estimate the area of the shaded shape.

[2 marks]

   ✓ **Made a start**   ✓ **Feeling confident**   ✓ **Exam ready**

Areas of 2D shapes

You can use formulae to work out the areas of simple shapes.

These formulae can be used to work out the areas of 2D shapes.

Rectangle	Parallelogram	Triangle	Trapezium
			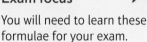
$A = l \times w$	$A = b \times h$	$A = \frac{1}{2} \times b \times h$	$A = \frac{1}{2}(a+b)h$

Exam focus 📌

You will need to learn these formulae for your exam.

Make sure that you have converted any lengths to the same units before you use any of these formulae.

---

1 Work out the area of this rectangle.

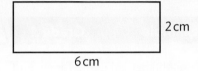
2 cm
6 cm

Area = length × width
= 6 × 2 = 12 cm²

2 Work out the area of this trapezium.

3 cm
7 cm
9 cm

Area = $\frac{1}{2}(a+b)h = \frac{1}{2} \times (9+3) \times 7$
= 42 cm²

You can work out the area of a **compound** shape by splitting the original shape into parts.

The red line splits the original shape into a triangle and a rectangle. Use the formulae to work out the area of the triangle and the area of the rectangle. Add these together to work out the area of the entire shape.

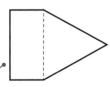

Split the shape up by drawing lines, or redraw the shapes separately.

Work out the area of this shape.

Area of rectangle
= 4 × 12 = 48 m²
Height of triangle
= 10 − 4 = 6 m

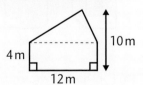
10 m
4 m
12 m

Area of triangle = $\frac{1}{2} \times 12 \times 6$ = 36 m²
Area of shape = 48 + 36 = 84 m²

---

1 The diagram shows a trapezium of height 3 m.

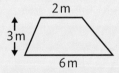
2 m
3 m
6 m

Work out the area of this trapezium. State the units with your answer. **[3 marks]**

2

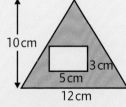
10 cm
3 cm
5 cm
12 cm

The diagram shows a rectangle inside a triangle.
The triangle has a base of 12 cm and a height of 10 cm. The rectangle is 5 cm by 3 cm.
Work out the area of the shaded region in the diagram. **[3 marks]**

3D shapes

You will need to know the mathematical names of 3D shapes.

⑤ Names of 3D shapes

You will need to recognise the mathematical names of these 3D shapes.

| Cube | Cuboid | Cylinder | Sphere |

| Cone | Square-based pyramid | Tetrahedron | Triangular prism |

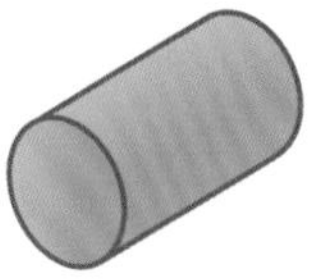

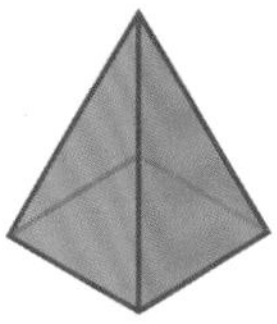

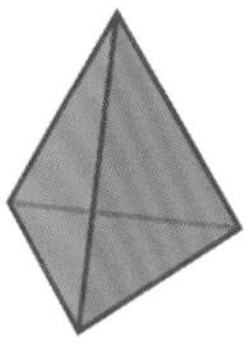

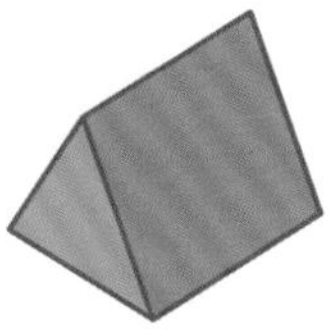

⑤ Faces, edges and vertices

You need to know the correct terms to describe a 3D shape.

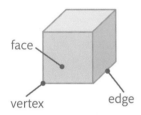

face
vertex   edge

Face: The flat surface on the side of the shape
Edge: The line where two faces meet
Vertex: A corner of the 3D shape

> The plural of vertex is 'vertices'.

⑤ Worked example   Grade 1

The diagram shows a solid triangular prism.

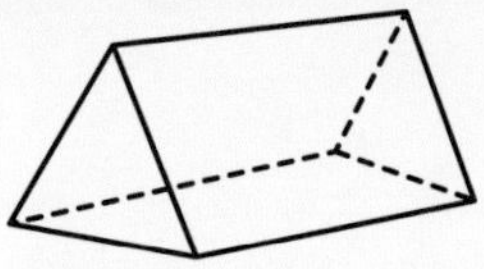

Write down
(a) the number of faces   5
(b) the number of edges   9
(c) the number of vertices.   6

Remember to include the part of the prism that you can't see.

⑤ Worked example   Grade 1

Write down the mathematical name for each of these three different 3D shapes.

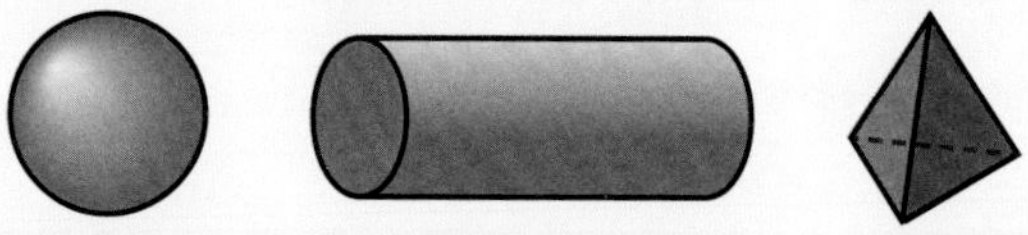

(a)   **(b)**   **(c)**

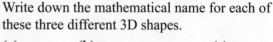

(a) sphere
(b) cylinder
(c) tetrahedron

> A prism is a 3D shape whose cross-section is the same shape along its full length.

⑤ Exam-style practice   Grade 1

(a) Write down the name of each of these 3D shapes.

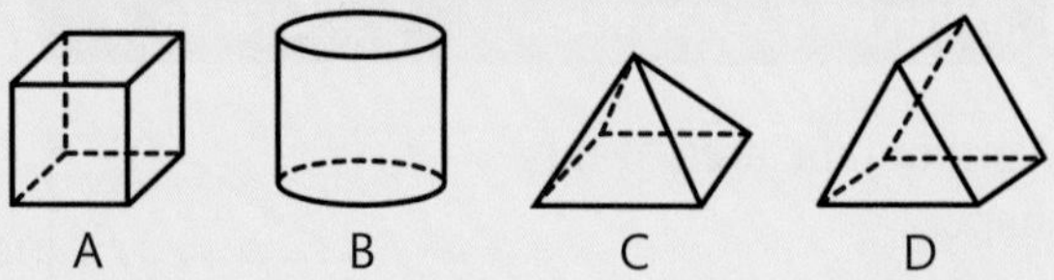

A   B   C   D

[4 marks]

(b) For shape C write down:
  (i) the number of faces
  (ii) the number of edges
  (iii) the number of vertices.   **[3 marks]**

✓ **Made a start**   ✓ **Feeling confident**   ✓ **Exam ready**

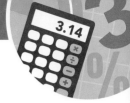

Volumes of 3D shapes

The volume of a 3D shape can be calculated from simple formulae and is measured in cubic units.

5 Formulae for 3D shapes

Cube

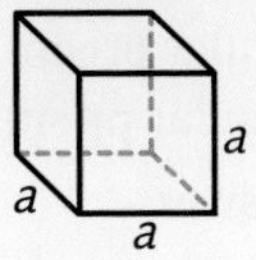

$V = a \times a \times a$

$V = a^3$

Cuboid

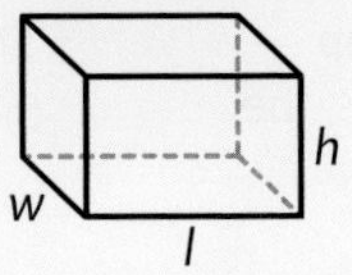

$V =$ length $\times$ width $\times$ height

$V = lwh$

Prism

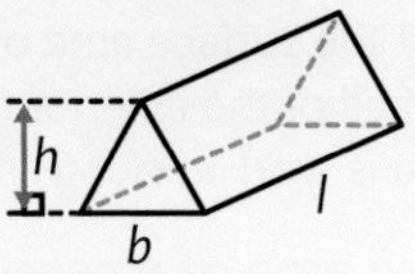

$V =$ cross-sectional area $\times$ length

Cone

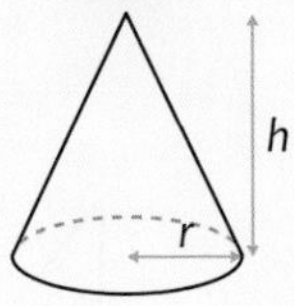

$V = \frac{1}{3} \times$ area of base $\times$ vertical height

Sphere

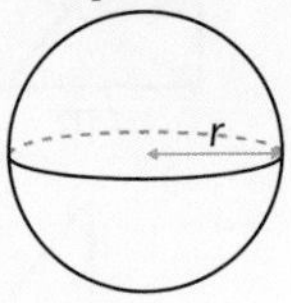

$V = \frac{4}{3} \times \pi \times r^3$

Square-based pyramid

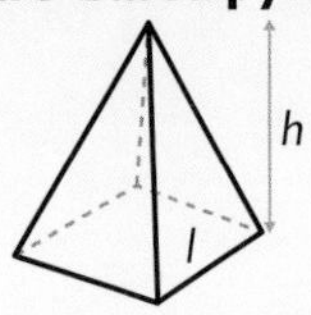

$V = \frac{1}{3} \times$ area of base $\times$ vertical height

Exam focus

If you need the formulae for a cone, sphere or square-based pyramid, they will be given in your exam.

10 Worked example — Grades 2–5

1

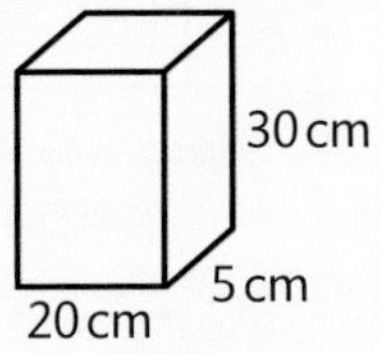

You will need to learn the formula for the volume of a cuboid: length × width × height

The diagram shows a cuboid.

Work out the volume of the cuboid.

Volume $= 20 \times 5 \times 30 = 3000\,\text{cm}^3$

2

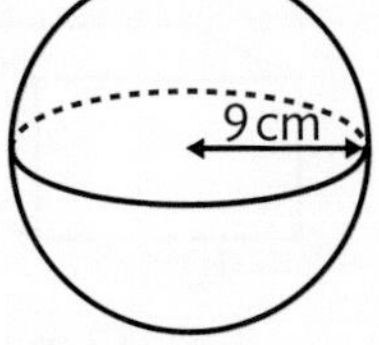

The diagram shows a sphere with radius 9 cm.

Work out the volume of the sphere.

Give your answer to the nearest whole number.

Volume $= \frac{4}{3} \times \pi \times r^3$

$= \frac{4}{3} \times \pi \times 9^3 = 3053.628\ldots$

$= 3054\,\text{cm}^3$

For this question, the formula for the volume of a sphere would be given in the exam.

2 Checklist

- Always write down the formulae first, then substitute the values into them.
- Rearrange equations carefully so that you do not make any errors.
- Learn the formulae for the volume of cubes, cuboids and prisms (you will **not** be given these in the exam).
- Make sure you know how to use the formulae for the volume of a pyramid, sphere and a cone (you do not need to remember these for the exam).

10 Exam-style practice — Grades 2–4

1 The diagram shows a cone.

Work out the volume of the cone. **[2 marks]**

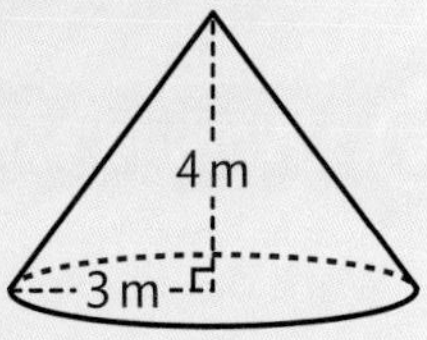

2 The diagram shows a triangular prism.

Work out the volume of the triangular prism.

[3 marks]

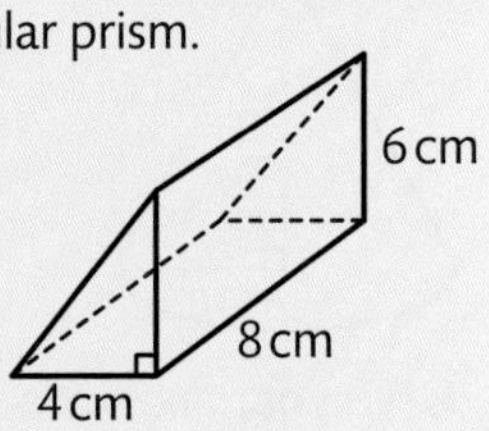

You need to learn the formula for the volume of a prism – it won't be given with the question.

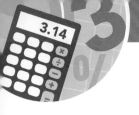

Surface area

The surface area is the area of all of the exterior surfaces of a 3D shape. It is measured in square units. You should be able to calculate the surface area and volume of different 3D shapes.

5 Surface area

To work out the surface area of shapes, simply add up the areas of all of the exterior faces. For some shapes, the surface area is worked out using a formula:

The surface area of a cone

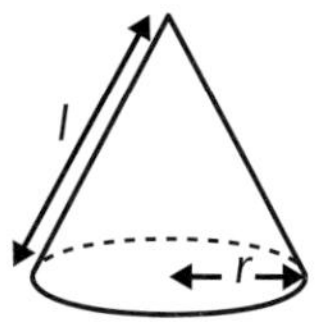

Total surface area $= \pi r^2 + \pi r l$

The surface area of a sphere

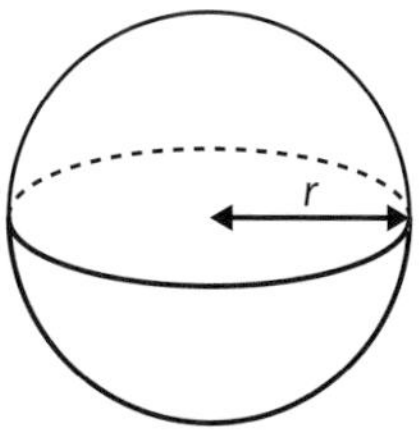

Total surface area $= 4\pi r^2$

A hemisphere is half of a sphere.

These formulae will be given in the exam if you need to use them in a question. Although you do not need to learn them off by heart, you do need to know how to use them.

Problem solving

For these types of question, always draw diagrams so that you can visualise each face and make sure you do not miss any.

5 Worked example — Grade 5

Work out the surface area of this cone.

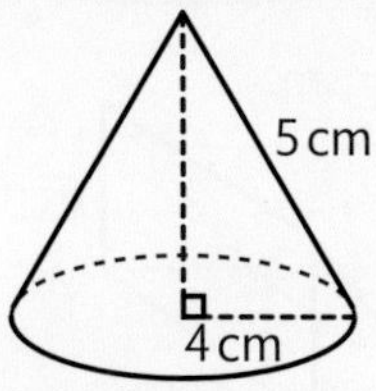

Give your answer correct to 1 decimal place.

Surface area $= \pi r^2 + \pi r l$

$= (\pi \times 4^2) + (\pi \times 4 \times 5)$

$= 16\pi + 20\pi$

$= 36\pi$

$= 113.1\text{ cm}^2$

You can leave your working in terms of π until the final step. Use the [S⇔D] button on your calculator to convert it to a decimal.

5 Worked example — Grade 5

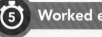

The diagram shows a triangular prism. Work out the surface area of the triangular prism.

State the units with your answer.

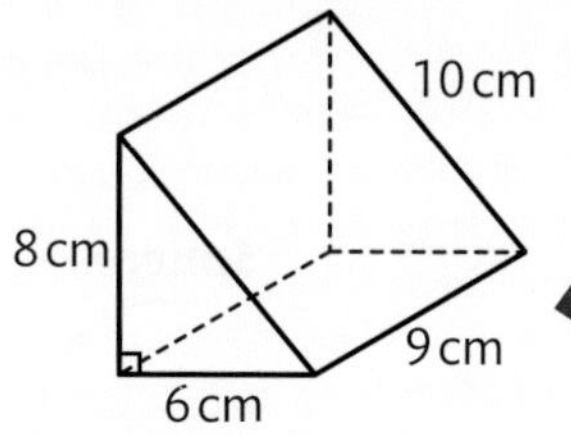

Always sketch each face and then work out the total surface area.

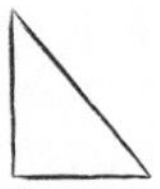

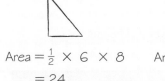

Area $= \frac{1}{2} \times 6 \times 8$
$= 24$

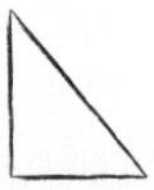

Area $= \frac{1}{2} \times 6 \times 8$
$= 24$

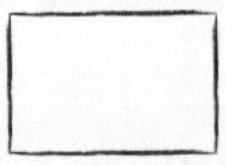

Area $= 10 \times 9$
$= 90$

Area $= 8 \times 9$
$= 72$

Area $= 6 \times 9$
$= 54$

Total surface area $= 24 + 24 + 90 + 72 + 54$
$= 264\text{ cm}^2$

15 Exam-style practice — Grade 4

1 The diagram shows a cuboid that measures 10 cm × 8 cm × 5 cm.

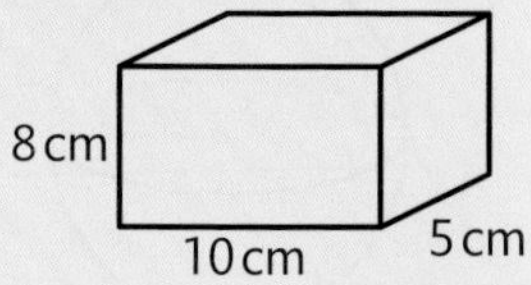

Work out

(a) the surface area **[2 marks]**

(b) the volume. **[2 marks]**

State your units in each case.

2 The diagram shows a right-angled triangular prism.

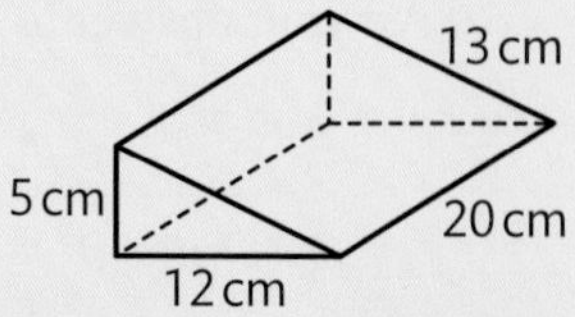

Work out

(a) the surface area **[3 marks]**

(b) the volume. **[2 marks]**

State your units in each case.

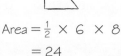

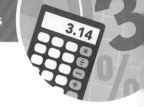

Circles and cylinders

A cylinder is a prism with a circular cross-section. The area of the cylinder's circular end is used to calculate the volume.

5 Circles and cylinders

xy²

Circle

Area of circle $= \pi r^2$

Circumference of circle $= \pi d = 2\pi r$

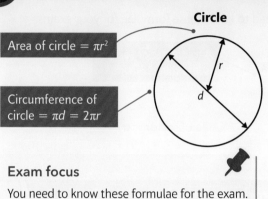

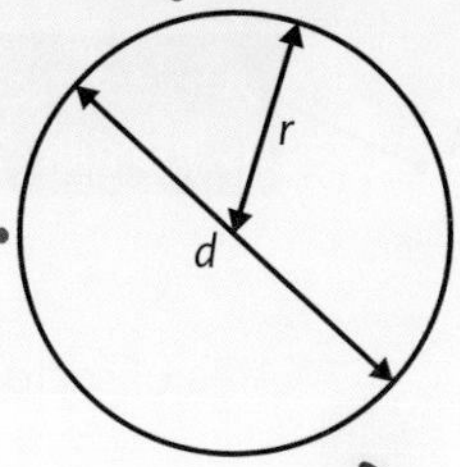
r
d

Cylinder

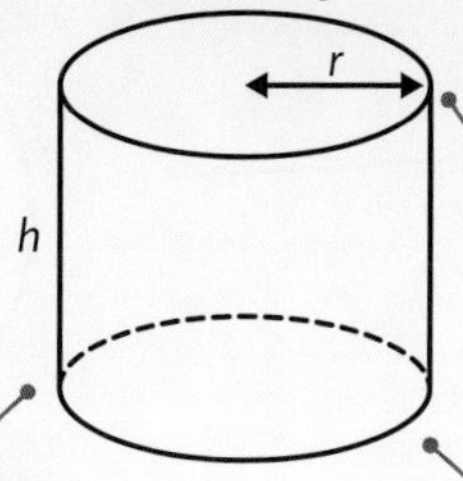
r
h

Area of top $= \pi r^2$

Area of curved surface $= 2\pi rh$

Volume of cylinder $= \pi r^2 h$

Surface area of cylinder $= 2\pi r^2 + 2\pi rh$

Exam focus

You need to know these formulae for the exam.

10 Worked example — Grade 5

1 The diagram shows a cylinder.

Work out

(a) the surface area. State the units. Give your answer correct to 3 significant figures.

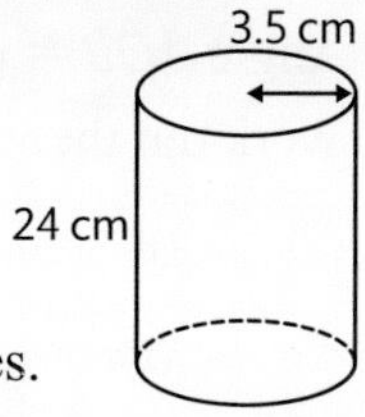
3.5 cm
24 cm

Surface area

$= 2\pi r^2 + 2\pi rh$

$= (2 \times \pi \times 3.5^2) + (2 \times \pi \times 3.5 \times 24)$

$= 605\text{ cm}^2$

(b) the volume. State the units. Give your answer correct to 3 significant figures.

Volume of cylinder $= \pi r^2 h$

$= \pi \times 3.5^2 \times 24$

$= 924\text{ cm}^3$

2 The diameter of Sandeep's bicycle wheel is 0.75 m.

He cycles 500 m.

Work out the number of complete turns the wheel makes.

Circumference $= \pi d = \pi \times 0.75 = 0.75\pi$

Number of turns $= 500 \div 0.75\pi$

$= 212.20659...$

Number of complete turns $= 212$

3 Work out the area of this compound shape.

Leave your answer in terms of π.

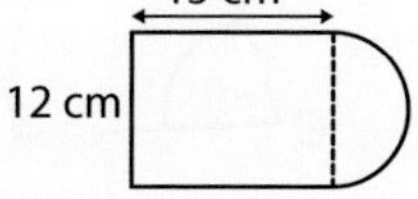
15 cm
12 cm

Area of rectangle $= 12 \times 15 = 180$

Area of semicircle $= \frac{1}{2} \times \pi \times 6^2 = 18\pi$

Area of compound shape $= 180 + 18\pi$

2 Checklist

- If the formula is in terms of the radius r, but the diameter is given, you can divide the diameter by 2 to find the radius.
- Always draw lines to break up a compound shape into simple shapes.

You might be asked to give an exact answer in terms of π.

Surface area $= \frac{385}{2}\pi$

Problem solving

1. Work out the circumference of the bicycle wheel.
2. Work out how many 'circumferences' go into 500 m.
3. Round down to work out the number of complete turns.

10 Exam-style practice — Grade 5

The diagram shows a roller in the shape of a cylinder.

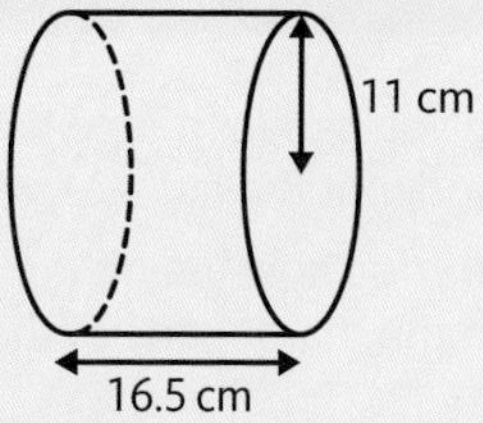
11 cm
16.5 cm

The roller has a radius of 11 cm and a length of 16.5 cm.
A company wants to make a new size of roller.
The new roller will have a radius of 12.4 cm.
It will have the same volume as the original roller.

Work out the length of the new roller. Give your answer correct to 1 decimal place. **[3 marks]**

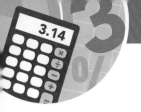

Circles, sectors and arcs

An arc length is a fraction of the circumference and the area of a sector is the area of a fraction of a circle.

[5] Minor and major xy^2 ☐

A circle can be divided into two parts called **minor** and **major**. You need to know these formulae for your exams.

A major arc or sector is greater than 180°.

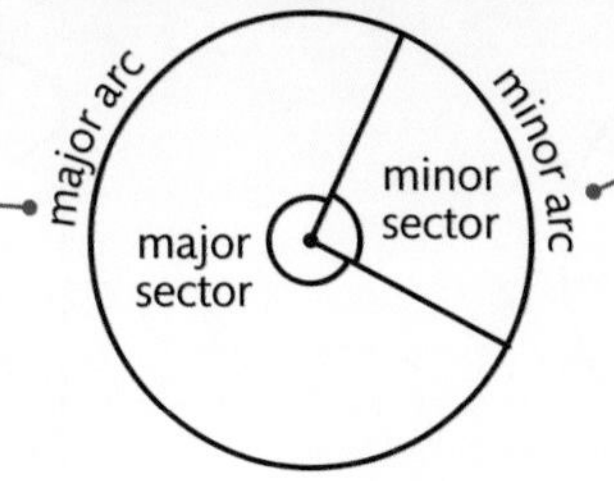

A minor arc or sector is less than 180°.

Arc length $= 2\pi r \times \dfrac{\theta}{360}$

Area of sector $= \pi r^2 \times \dfrac{\theta}{360}$

[5] Worked example — Grade 5 ☐

The diagram shows a sector of a circle, centre O.

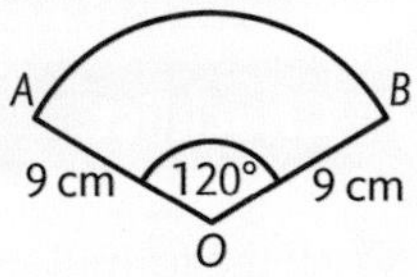

The radius of the circle is 9 cm.

Angle $AOB = 120°$.

Give your answers in terms of π.

Work out

(a) the arc length of the sector

$$\text{Arc length} = 2\pi r \times \frac{\theta}{360}$$
$$= 2 \times \pi \times 9 \times \frac{120}{360}$$
$$= 6\pi \text{ cm}$$

(b) the area of the sector.

$$\text{Area of sector} = \pi r^2 \times \frac{\theta}{360}$$
$$= \pi \times 9^2 \times \frac{120}{360}$$
$$= 27\pi \text{ cm}^2$$

[5] Worked example — Grade 5 ☐

The diagram shows a sector of a circle, centre O.

The arc length of the sector is 2π cm.

The radius of the sector is 12 cm.

Angle $AOB = x°$.

Work out the value of x.

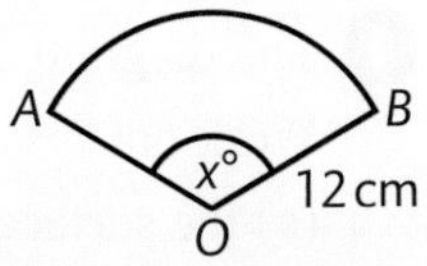

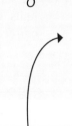

$$\text{Arc length} = 2\pi r \times \frac{\theta}{360}$$
$$2\pi = 2 \times \pi \times 12 \times \frac{x}{360}$$
$$\frac{360}{12} = x$$
$$x = 30$$

The left-hand side and right-hand side of the equation both contain π, which can be cancelled.

Write your final answer as a multiple of π. Your calculator might give answers in this form.

[2] Checklist ☐

- ✓ Make sure you can rearrange the formulae on this page to work out the radius, r, and the angle, θ.
- ✓ Make sure you know the difference between the minor and the major parts of the circle.

Exam focus

If the question asks you to give your answer correct to a number of significant figures, multiply out your answer and round it instead of leaving it in terms of π.

[10] Exam-style practice — Grade 5 ☐

The diagram shows a sector of a circle, centre O, radius 9.6 cm.

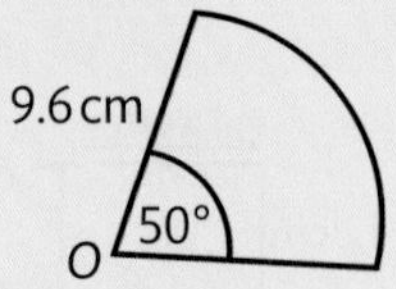

Work out

(a) the arc length **[2 marks]**

(b) the area of the sector. **[2 marks]**

Give your answers correct to 3 significant figures.

Circle facts

You will need to know the names of different parts of circles relating to chords, tangents, diameters and radii.

⑤ Properties of circles

Tangent and radius

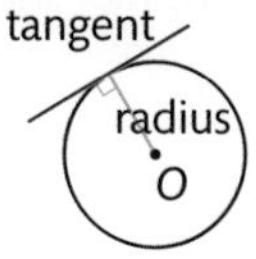

A tangent is a straight line that touches the circumference of the circle.

A tangent is **perpendicular** to the radius at that point.

Two tangents

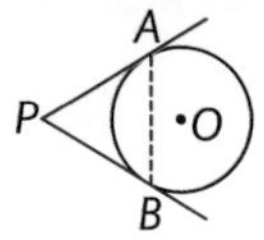

Two tangents intersecting at a point are **equal** in length.

They form two congruent triangles.

Triangle ABP is isosceles.

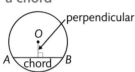

Perpendicular to a chord

A chord is a straight line joining two points on the circumference that does not pass through the centre of the circle. The perpendicular from the centre of the circle **bisects** the chord.

Segments

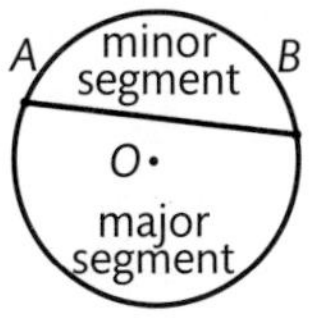

A chord of a circle divides the circle into two regions, which are called **segments** of the circle.

⑤ Worked example   Grade 1

Here are 5 diagrams and 5 labels. In each diagram the centre of the circle is marked with a cross (✖). Match each diagram to its label.

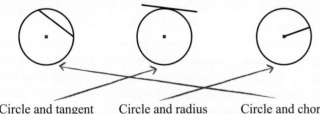

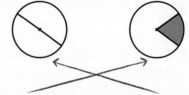

Circle and tangent   Circle and radius   Circle and chord   Circle and sector   Circle and diameter

⑤ Worked example   Grade 5

B and C are two points on a circle, centre O. Angle $OBC = 20°$. AB and AC are tangents to the circle.

Calculate the size of the angle marked x.

Give reasons for your answer.

> Make sure you learn the mathematical words linked to the different facts about circles.

> Start by looking for any angles you may know. An obvious starting place is a tangent touching the radius.
>
> You can write any angles that you work out on the diagram.

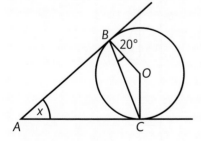

Angle $ABO = 90°$
(Angle between tangent and radius is 90°.)
Angle $ABC = 90° - 20° = 70°$
Angle $ACB = 70°$
(Base angles in an isosceles triangle are equal.)
So $x = 180° - 70° - 70° = 40°$
(Angles in a triangle add up to 180°.)

⑩ Exam-style practice   Grades 1–4

1 Draw a chord on the circle below. Shade your major segment. **[2 marks]**

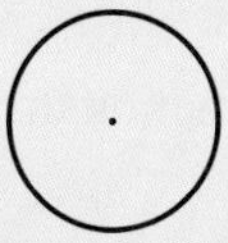

2 AP and BP are tangents to a circle, centre O. Angle $AOP = 80°$. Work out the size of angle APB. **[3 marks]**

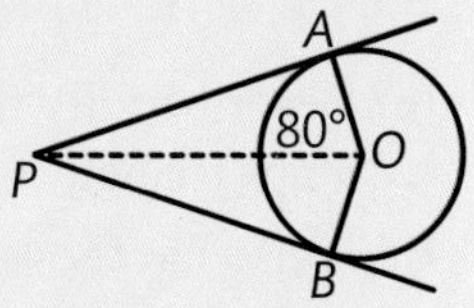

Transformations

A transformation changes the position, size or orientation of a shape.

 5 **Types of transformation**

Here are three out of the four transformations you need to know about. The original shape is the **object** and the final shape is its **image**. Rotation, reflection and translation always produce an image that is congruent to the original shape.

Reflection

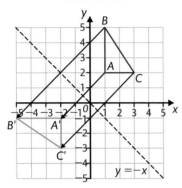

Rotation

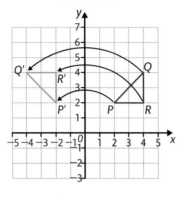

Translation

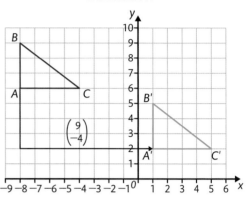

A **reflection** in a line makes another shape that is a mirror image of the original shape. The image is always the same distance from the mirror line as the object was. You can describe a reflection by giving the equation of its mirror line, for example $y = -x$, as above.

A **rotation** turns a shape through a clockwise or anticlockwise direction about a fixed point. The fixed point is the **centre of rotation**. Rotation changes the position and orientation of the shape.

A **translation** changes the position of the shape by moving all of its points the same distance in the same direction. A translation can be described by using vector notation, $\begin{pmatrix} a \\ b \end{pmatrix}$.

'a' moves to the right by 'a' units, '$-a$' moves to the left by 'a' units, 'b' moves upwards by 'b' units and '$-b$' moves downwards by 'b' units.

10 **Worked example** Grade 4

(a) Describe fully the single transformation that maps triangle A onto triangle B.

Rotation 90° clockwise about centre (1, 1)

(b) Describe fully the single transformation that maps triangle A onto triangle C.

Translation $\begin{pmatrix} 5 \\ -1 \end{pmatrix}$

(c) Describe fully the single transformation that maps triangle A onto triangle D.

Reflection in the line $x = 1$

15 **Exam-style practice** Grade 4

1 The vector $\begin{pmatrix} -5 \\ 4 \end{pmatrix}$ translates A to B. Circle the vector that translates B to A. **[1 mark]**

$\begin{pmatrix} -5 \\ 4 \end{pmatrix}$ $\begin{pmatrix} -4 \\ 5 \end{pmatrix}$ $\begin{pmatrix} 5 \\ -4 \end{pmatrix}$ $\begin{pmatrix} 4 \\ -5 \end{pmatrix}$

2

(a) Reflect shape P in the line $x = 3$ **[2 marks]**

(b) Rotate shape P 90° anticlockwise about (0, 2). **[2 marks]**

(c) Translate shape P by $\begin{pmatrix} -5 \\ -3 \end{pmatrix}$ **[2 marks]**

Made a start ✓ Feeling confident ✓ Exam ready

Enlargement

An enlargement changes the size of the shape.

 Enlargement

Enlargement makes a shape larger or smaller, depending on the scale factor. The scale factor is how much each length is multiplied by to get the enlarged shape.

$$\text{scale factor} = \frac{\text{enlarged length}}{\text{original length}}$$

All enlargements take place from a centre of enlargement. This is the point where lines drawn from both the original shape and the enlarged shape will meet.

 Worked example | **Grade 4** |

 ①

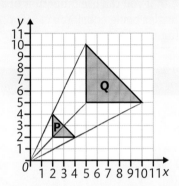

Describe fully the single transformation that maps shape **P** onto shape **Q**.

Enlargement of scale factor 2.5 about centre of enlargement (0, 0) ←

Draw lines on the grid that pass through the corners of the shapes. The centre of enlargement is the intersection of all the lines.

②

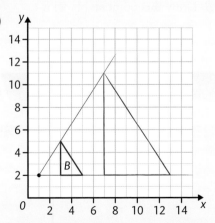

Enlarge triangle **B** by scale factor 3, centre (1, 2)

An enlargement with scale factor 3 means that all the sides are 3 times as long as in the original shape.

 Scale factors

For a scale factor greater than 1, the image is larger than the original shape.
Scale factor for image $A'B'C' = 2$

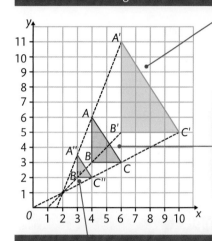

The original shape is *ABC*. The centre of enlargement is (2, 1), where the dotted lines intersect.

For a scale factor less than 1, the image is smaller than the original shape.
Scale factor for image $A''B''C'' = \frac{1}{2}$

 Checklist

When describing an enlargement, you need to remember to give two details:

① The scale factor

② The centre of enlargement

 Exam-style practice | **Grade 4**

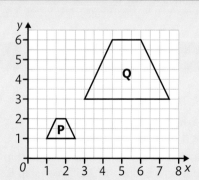

Describe fully the single transformation that maps shape **P** onto shape **Q**. **[3 marks]**

Bearings

A **bearing** is a measurement of the position of one point relative to another point.

② Language of bearings

Bearings are always measured from the **north** in a **clockwise** direction.

Bearings are measured in degrees and are always given as three digits.

Make sure you know the meaning of 'bearing of B from F'. This means you measure **from** F.

⑤ Worked example · Grade 5

(a) Write down the bearing of B from F.

Bearing of B from F = 075°

(b) Write down the bearing of F from B.

Bearing of F from B = 180° + 75° = 255°

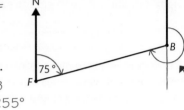

Draw extra lines so that you can use properties of angles, such as alternate angles being equal. You can work out the **reverse bearing** by adding or subtracting 180°.

⑩ Worked example · Grade 5

① The diagram shows the positions of two boats, A and B.

Boat C is on a bearing of 070° from boat A.

Boat C is on a bearing of 295° from boat B.

Draw an accurate diagram to locate the position of boat C.

Mark the position of boat C with a cross (✗).

Label it C.

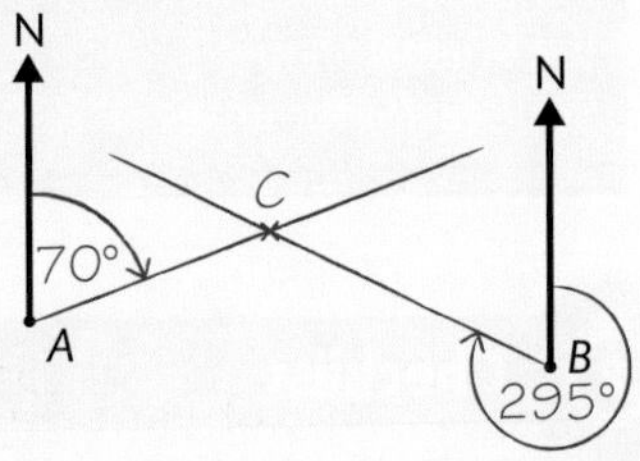

Use a protractor to measure the angles. C is where the two lines for the bearings cross.

② The diagram shows the positions of two points, A and B.

(a) Measure the angle marked x.

105°

(b) Write down the bearing of A from B.

Bearing of A from B = 180° + 105° = 285°

(c) Point C is 3 cm on a bearing of 060° from point B. Draw this point and label it C.

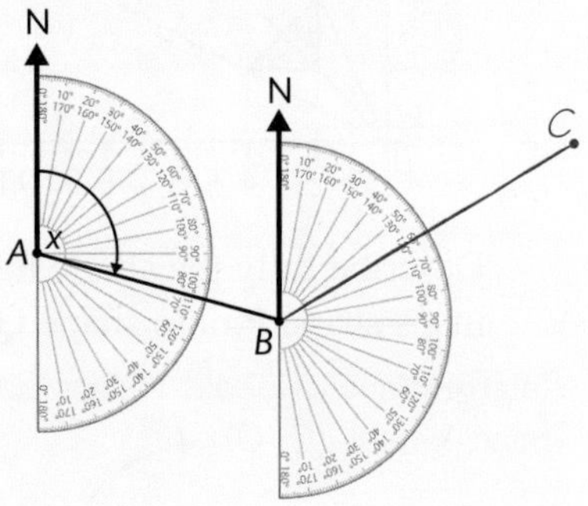

⑩ Exam-style practice · Grade 5

① The bearing of a ship from a lighthouse is 062°. Work out the bearing of the lighthouse from the ship. **[2 marks]**

② The diagram shows the positions of two ships, A and B.

Ship C is on a bearing of 062° from ship A, and is on a bearing of 285° from ship B. Draw an accurate diagram to show the position of ship C. **[3 marks]**

☑ **Made a start**   ☑ **Feeling confident**   ☑ **Exam ready**

Scale drawings and maps

You can use ratios to work out problems involving scale drawings and map scales.

 Scale drawings ✓

In a scale drawing, all the dimensions are changed by the same proportion.

You will need to know how to read a scale. It may be written in the form 1 cm = 2 m or as a ratio, in the form 1 : 200.

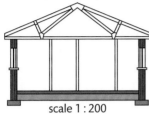

scale 1 : 200

What does a scale of 1 : 25 mean?

This scale can be applied to any units. Using this scale, 1 mm would represent 25 mm or 2.5 cm, 1 cm would represent 25 cm or 0.25 m, and so on.

> Use a ruler to measure the distance to the nearest mm.

 Maps ✓

Map scales may be written in the form 1 cm = 1 km or as ratios, such as 1 : 100 000. They tell you how real-life measurements are represented on a map. Here are four different ways in which a map scale can be shown.

1 scale 1 : 12 500 000

2
0   5   10   15
kilometres

3 1 centimetre = 1 kilometre (1 : 100 000)

4
0 1 2 3 4 5 6 7

What does a map scale of 1 : 25 000 mean?

If a distance is measured as 5 cm on the map, the real distance can be calculated:

5 cm represents 5 × 25 000 = 125 000 cm

It is not sensible to write a distance as 125 000 cm, so you can convert into km:

÷100   ÷1000

125 000 cm = 1250 m = 1.25 km

 Checklist ✓

- ✓ Make sure you can interpret scales such as 1 : n.
- ✓ Make sure you measure the map distance carefully.
- ✓ Make sure that the scale on the ruler begins at 0.
- ✓ Make sure you can recall conversion factors.
- ✓ Always give an answer in sensible units.

 Worked example | **Grade 5** ✓

The length of a van is 4.2 metres. Alice makes a scale model of the van. She uses a scale of 1 : 40.

Work out the length of the scale model of the van.

Give your answer in centimetres.

Length of van is 4.2 × 100 = 420 cm
Length of scale model is 420 ÷ 40 = 10.5 cm ◄

> Divide by 40, because every 40 cm on the van will be represented by 1 cm in the model.

 **Worked example** | **Grade 5** ✓

1 The diagram shows the positions of two hills, Penn and Hagley, on a map.

Penn ×

The scale of the map is 1 cm = 3.5 km. Work out the real distance between Penn and Hagley.

× Hagley

Map distance = 2.5 cm
Actual distance = 2.5 × 3.5 = 8.75 km

2 The scale of a map is 1 : 25 000. On the map, the distance between two villages is 21 cm. Work out the real distance between the two villages.

Give your answer in kilometres.

Actual distance = 21 × 25 000 = 525 000 cm
= 5250 m
= 5.25 km

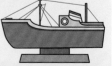 **Exam-style practice** | **Grade 5** ✓

1 A model ship has a length of 18 cm. The scale of the model is 1 : 250. Work out the length of the real ship.

Give your answer in metres. **[2 marks]**

2 On a map, 5 centimetres represents a real distance of 1 kilometre.

(a) On the map, the distance between two points is 16 cm. Work out the real distance between these two points. Give your answer in kilometres. **[2 marks]**

(b) Work out the scale of the map in the form 1 : n. **[2 marks]**

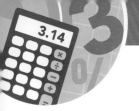

Pythagoras' theorem

If you know two sides of a right-angled triangle, you can use Pythagoras' theorem to work out the length of the third side.

5 Pythagoras' theorem xy^2

You can only apply Pythagoras' theorem to right-angled triangles.

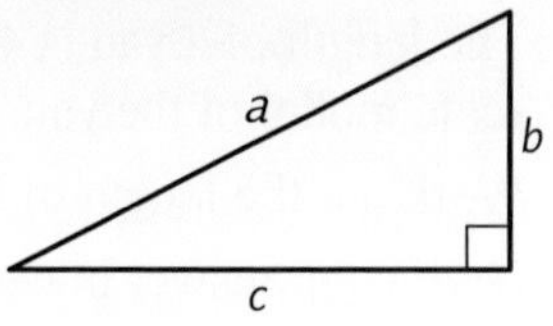

In any triangle, the longest side is opposite the largest angle. In this right-angled triangle, the side labelled *a* is the **hypotenuse,** and is opposite the right angle.

Pythagoras' theorem states that $a^2 = b^2 + c^2$

5 Worked example Grade 5

ABCD is a trapezium.
$AD = 18.4$ cm,
$AB = 15.5$ cm and
$DC = 6.2$ cm.
Angle ABC = angle $BCD = 90°$

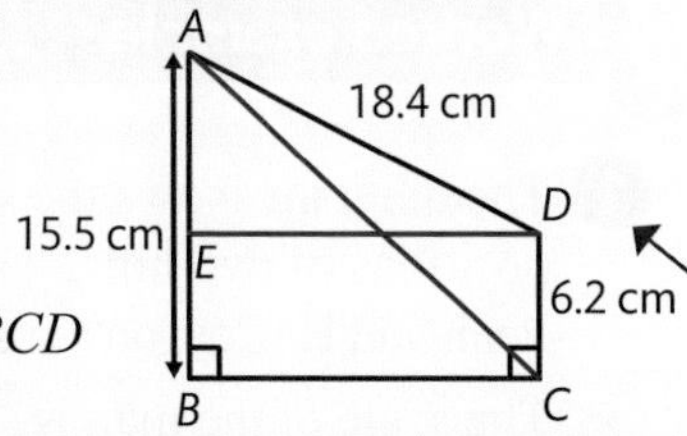

Join *AC* and draw a line from *D*, parallel to *BC*, to meet *AB* at *E*.

DE is equal to *BC* because it forms a rectangle.

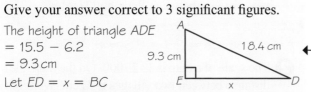

Work out the length of *AC*.

Give your answer correct to 3 significant figures.

The height of triangle *ADE*
$= 15.5 - 6.2$
$= 9.3$ cm

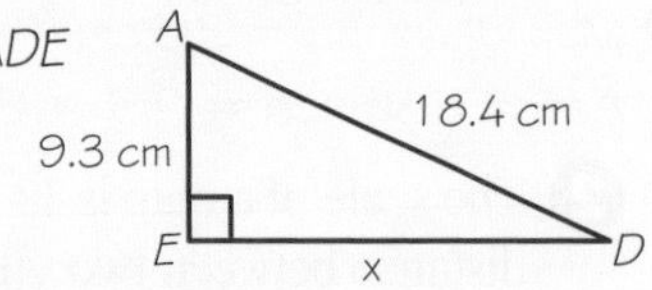

Sketch and label a diagram of triangle *ADE*, then apply Pythagoras' theorem.

Let $ED = x = BC$

$$18.4^2 = 9.3^2 + x^2$$
$$338.56 = 86.49 + x^2$$
$$338.56 - 86.49 = x^2$$
$$252.07 = x^2$$
$$x = \sqrt{252.07}$$

Apply Pythagoras' theorem again.

$$AC^2 = AB^2 + x^2$$
$$AC^2 = 15.5^2 + (\sqrt{252.07})^2$$
$$AC^2 = 240.25 + 252.07$$
$$AC^2 = 492.32$$
$$AC = \sqrt{492.32}$$
$$AC = 22.2 \text{ cm}$$

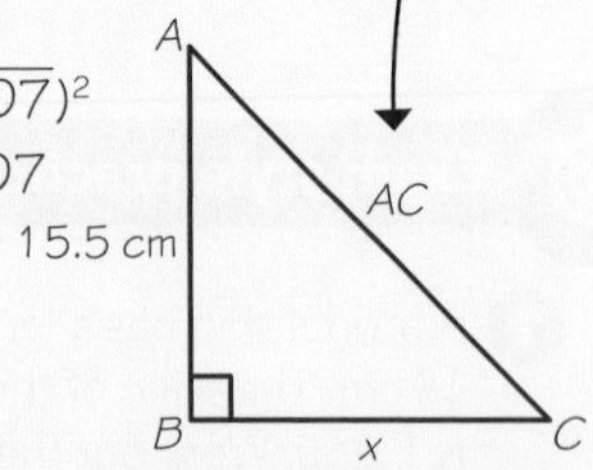

5 Worked example Grade 5

ABC is a right-angled triangle. $AC = 7$ cm and $AB = 16$ cm. Work out the length of *BC*.

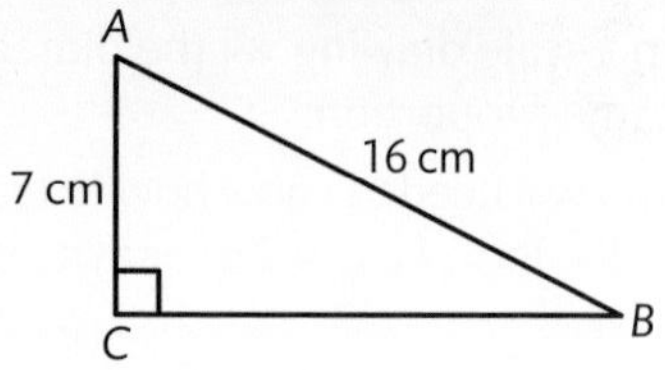

Give your answer correct to 3 significant figures.

$$a^2 = b^2 + c^2 \text{ where } a \text{ is the hypotenuse}$$
$$16^2 = 7^2 + BC^2$$
$$256 = 49 + BC^2$$
$$256 - 49 = BC^2$$
$$207 = BC^2$$
$$BC = \sqrt{207}$$
$$BC = 14.4 \text{ cm}$$

The square of the longest side is equal to the sum of the squares of the other two sides.

2 Checklist

- ✓ Pythagoras' theorem can only be applied to right-angled triangles.
- ✓ You must know the lengths of any two sides to work out the unknown length of the third side.
- ✓ Always round your answer to a sensible degree of accuracy such as 1 decimal place or 3 significant figures.

10 Exam-style practice Grade 5

1 The perimeter of triangle *ABC* is 24 cm. $AB = 11$ cm and $BC = 8$ cm.
By calculation, assess whether triangle *ABC* is a right-angled triangle. **[4 marks]**

2 A car park is in the shape of a trapezium, as shown in the diagram.
The council wants to put a fence all the way around the edge of the car park. The council has 60 m of fence. Do they have enough fence?
You must show all your working. **[3 marks]**

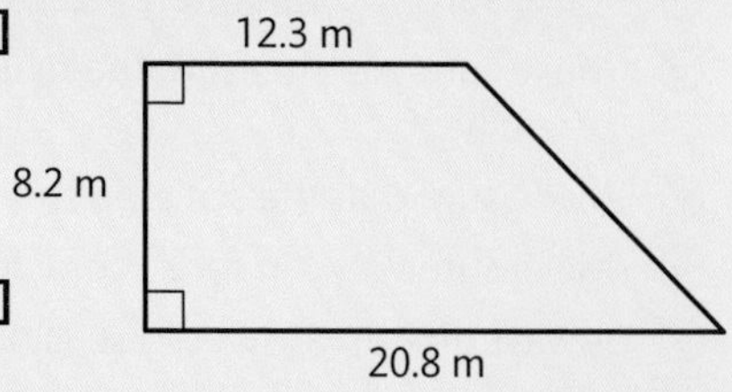

Units of length, area and volume

You should be able to convert between different units for lengths, areas and volumes.

 Conversions

Converting units of length

$1\,cm = 10\,mm$

Converting units of area

The area scale factor is the **square** of the length scale factor:

$1\,cm^2 = 10 \times 10 = 100\,mm^2$

Converting units of volume

The volume scale factor is the **cube** of the length scale factor:

$1\,cm^3 = 10 \times 10 \times 10 = 1000\,mm^3$

> This is area so the scale factor for cm² to mm² is 10 **squared**.
> cm² to mm² is $\times 10^2$

 Worked example | **Grade 5**

(a) Change $3.5\,cm^2$ to mm^2.

$3.5 \times 10^2 = 350\,mm^2$

(b) Change $635\,259.7\,cm^3$ to m^3.

$635\,259.7 \div 100^3 = 0.635\,259\,7\,m^3$

(c) Change 4.8 cubic metres to cubic centimetres.

4.8 cubic metres $= 4.8\,m^3$
$= 4.8 \times 100^3$
$= 4\,800\,000$ cubic centimetres

> This is volume so the scale factor for m³ to cm³ is 100³.
> m³ to cm³ is $\times 100^3$ so cm³ to m³ is $\div 100^3$

 Worked example | **Grade 5**

Ben and Nick went to London in their car. Ben said the speed of the car was 130 kilometres per hour. Nick told Ben that 130 kilometres per hour was about the same as 36 metres per second.

Was Nick correct? Show your working to justify your answer.

130 kilometres per hour
$= 130 \times 1000$ metres per hour
$= 130\,000 \div 60$ metres per minute
$= 130\,000 \div 60 \div 60$ metres per second
$= 36.1111$ metres per second
≈ 36 metres per second

Nick was correct.

> Change: kilometres to metres
> then: hours to minutes
> then: minutes to seconds
>
> Do the conversions one at a time, and write down the new units at each stage of your working.

Problem solving

This problem can also be approached by converting 36 metres per second to kilometres per hour.

Change: metres to kilometres

then: seconds to minutes

then: minutes to hours.

36 metres per second

$= 36 \div 1000$ kilometres per second

$= 0.036 \times 60$ kilometres per minute

$= 0.036 \times 60 \times 60$ kilometres per hour

$= 129.6$ kilometres per hour

≈ 130 kilometres per hour

 Exam-style practice | **Grade 5**

1 A rectangle has an area of $4\,m^2$. Write this area in cm^2. **[2 marks]**

2 The area of a tile is $9570\,mm^2$. Write $9570\,mm^2$ in cm^2. **[2 marks]**

3 Circle the longest length. **[1 mark]**

1800 cm   17 m   0.15 km   160 000 mm

4 Singh Systems is a company that makes computer processors. For shipping, processors are packed into boxes with 30 processors in each box. A machine can pack 2880 processors per hour. Work out how many seconds the machine takes to fill one box. **[3 marks]**

Trigonometry: lengths

Trigonometry can be used to work out the length of an unknown side of a right-angled triangle, using an angle and the length of another side.

 Working out unknown sides

You can use the trigonometrical ratios **sine** (sin), **cosine** (cos) and **tangent** (tan) to find missing lengths and angles in right-angled triangles.

Hypotenuse (hyp)

This is the longest side. It is always opposite the right angle.

Opposite (opp)

This is the side opposite the angle.

Adjacent (adj)

This is the side that is next to the angle.

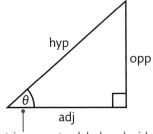

When using trigonometry, label each side in relation to the angle you know or are trying to find.

The ratios are:

$$\sin\theta = \frac{\text{opp}}{\text{hyp}} \qquad S = \frac{O}{H}$$

$$\cos\theta = \frac{\text{adj}}{\text{hyp}} \qquad C = \frac{A}{H}$$

$$\tan\theta = \frac{\text{opp}}{\text{adj}} \qquad T = \frac{O}{A}$$

SOH CAH TOA

 Problem solving

To calculate the value of x:

Step 1

Label the sides: **hyp** is the side opposite the right angle, **opp** is the side opposite the 60° angle and **adj** is the side next to the 60° angle.

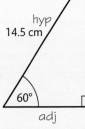

Step 2

Write down what you know and what you are looking for.

hyp = 14.5 and opp = x

Step 3

Write down SOH CAH TOA and then circle the ratio which has hyp and opp only.

SOH CAH TOA

Step 4

Write down the correct ratio, substitute the values from step 2 and work out x.

$$\sin\theta = \frac{\text{opp}}{\text{hyp}}$$

$$\sin 60° = \frac{x}{14.5}$$

To do this on a calculator, type in 1 4 . 5 × sin 6 0

$x = 14.5 \times \sin 60°$

$x = 12.6\,\text{cm}$

Give your answer correct to a suitable degree of accuracy. Here, 3 significant figures is suitable.

Check your answer makes sense. The hypotenuse is the longest side so your answer should be less than 14.5 cm.

 Worked example Grade 5

ABCD is a trapezium.
AD is parallel to *BC*.
Angle *C* = angle *D* = 90°
Angle *B* = 48°
AD = 6.3 cm
AB = 5.4 cm

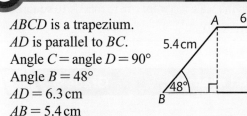

Work out the length of *BC*.
Give your answer in centimetres, correct to 1 decimal place.

hyp = 5.4 and adj = x
SOH CAH TOA

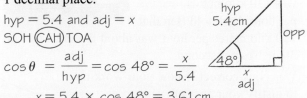

$$\cos\theta = \frac{\text{adj}}{\text{hyp}} = \cos 48° = \frac{x}{5.4}$$

$$x = 5.4 \times \cos 48° = 3.61\,\text{cm}$$

$$BC = 3.61\,\text{cm} + 6.3\,\text{cm} = 9.9\,\text{cm}$$

 Exam-style practice Grade 5

1 *ABCD* is a rectangle.
CDE is a straight line.

AB = 15 cm, angle *ACB* = 62°
and angle *EAC* = 90°.

Work out the length of *CE*.
You must show all of your working.

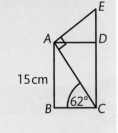

[4 marks]

2 Circle the correct calculation to work out the length x. **[1 mark]**

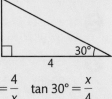

$$\sin 30° = \frac{x}{4} \qquad \tan 30° = \frac{4}{x} \qquad \cos 30° = \frac{4}{x} \qquad \tan 30° = \frac{x}{4}$$

Trigonometry: angles

You can use trigonometry to work out unknown angles in right-angled triangles.

 Inverse sin, cos and tan

You can use the formulae for sin, cos and tan to work out an unknown angle. You will need to use the **inverse trigonometric ratios** on your calculator:

$\sin^{-1}$ $\cos^{-1}$ $\tan^{-1}$

To access these ratios, you need to press SHIFT on your calculator and then one of the ratios sin , cos or tan .

> Make sure your calculator is in degree mode.

 Worked example Grades 4–5

Work out the value of x.
Give your answer correct to 1 decimal place.

hyp
opp
6.7 cm

x

8.3 cm adj

SOH CAH (TOA)

$\tan x = \dfrac{\text{opp}}{\text{adj}}$ $\tan x = \dfrac{6.7}{8.3}$

$x = \tan^{-1}\dfrac{6.7}{8.3} = 38.9°$ (1 d.p.)

 Worked example Grades 4–5

Angle $ABC = 90°$
Angle $BCD = 90°$
Work out the size of angle CDA.
Give your answer correct to 3 significant figures.

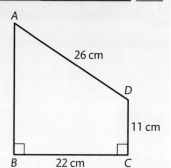

SOH (CAH) TOA

$\cos x = \dfrac{\text{adj}}{\text{hyp}}$

$\cos x = \dfrac{22}{26}$

$x = \cos^{-1}\dfrac{22}{26}$

$x = 32.2°$

Angle CDA
$= 32.2° + 90°$
$= 122.2°$
$= 122°$ (3 s.f.)

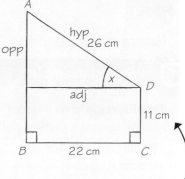

Split the trapezium into a right-angled triangle and a rectangle.

x is the angle in the right-angled triangle. You need to add 90° to find angle CDA.

On your calculator, remember to put brackets around $6.7 \div 8.3$ or use the fraction key.

---

⑮ **Exam-style practice** Grades 4–5

1 PQR is a right-angled triangle.
Angle $PQR = 90°$
$PR = 13\,\text{cm}$ and $QR = 5\,\text{cm}$.

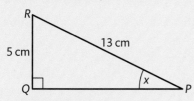

Work out the value of x.
Give your answer correct to 1 decimal place.

[3 marks]

2 The diagram shows triangle ADC.
ABC is a straight line.

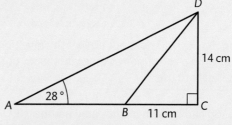

Angle $DAC = 28°$. $DC = 14\,\text{cm}$ and $BC = 11\,\text{cm}$.
Work out angle ADB.
Give your answer correct to 3 significant figures.

[4 marks]

 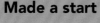

Trigonometry techniques

You need to able to use trigonometry to solve problems and to know the exact values of sin, cos, tan for certain angles without a calculator.

5 Without a calculator

You need to learn the exact values of sin, cos and tan for these angles:

θ	0°	30°	45°	60°	90°
sin θ	0	$\frac{1}{2}$	$\frac{1}{\sqrt{2}}$	$\frac{\sqrt{3}}{2}$	1
cos θ	1	$\frac{\sqrt{3}}{2}$	$\frac{1}{\sqrt{2}}$	$\frac{1}{2}$	0
tan θ	0	$\frac{1}{\sqrt{3}}$	1	$\sqrt{3}$	∞

5 Worked example Grade 5

The diagram shows a ladder leaning against a vertical wall.

The ladder stands on horizontal ground.

The length of the ladder is 8 m.

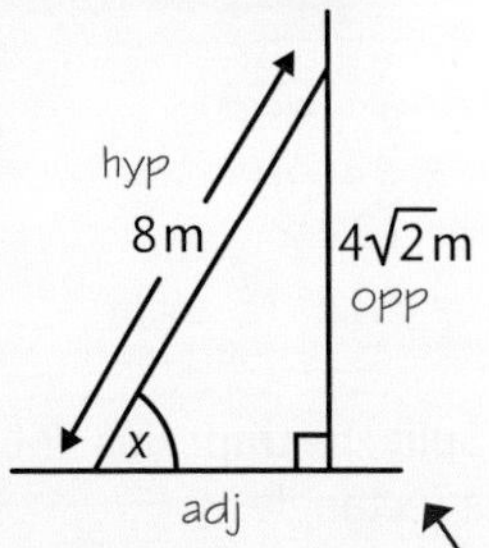

The top of the ladder is $4\sqrt{2}$ m high. It is safe to use the ladder when the angle marked x is between 60° and 80°. Is the ladder safe to use?

You must show all of your working.

opp $= 4\sqrt{2}$ and hyp $= 8$

[SOH] CAH TOA

$$\sin x = \frac{4\sqrt{2}}{8} = \frac{\sqrt{2}}{2} = \frac{1}{\sqrt{2}}$$

$x = 45°$

This is not between 60° and 80° so the ladder is not safe to use.

Just writing that $x = 45°$ does not answer the question. You need to write a conclusion stating whether or not the ladder is safe to use.

Divide the top and bottom by the same number to write the fraction in its simplest form. Compare it to the trigonometry values you know to work out x.

5 Worked example Grade 5

Work out the value of x.

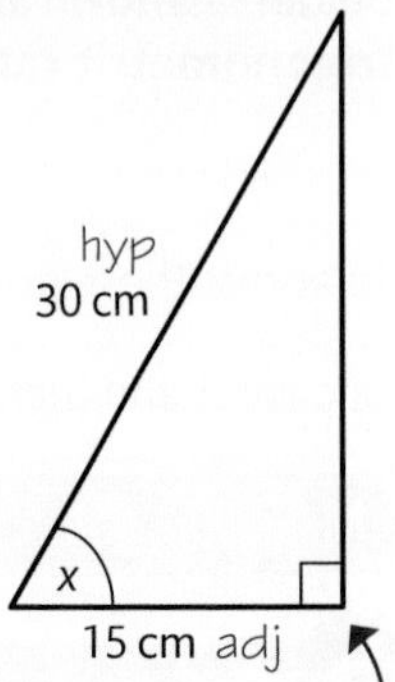

adj = 15 and hyp = 30

SOH [CAH] TOA

$$\cos x = \frac{15}{30}$$

$$\cos x = \frac{1}{2}$$

$x = 60°$

Always label the diagram clearly.

To answer this question you need to know that the cosine of 60° is $\frac{1}{2}$.

2 Checklist

- It is important that you learn the values for sin, cos and tan of 0°, 30°, 45°, 60° and 90°
- You must be able to apply trigonometry to simple problems.

Exam focus

When answering trigonometry questions, always label the sides of your triangle hyp, opp and adj. Remember to check that your final answer makes sense by making sure that it is a realistic value for the triangle given.

10 Exam-style practice Grade 5

1 Work out the value of x. **[3 marks]**

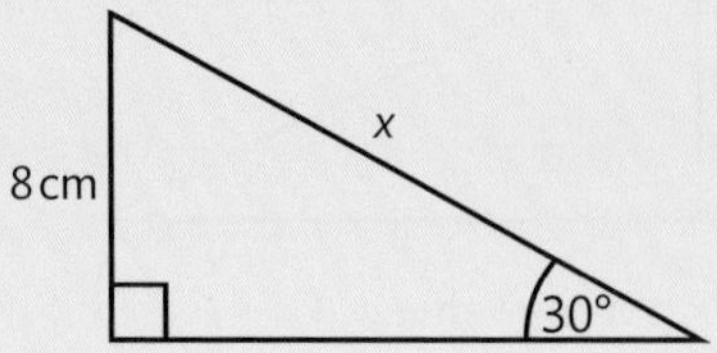

2 Work out the value of y. **[2 marks]**

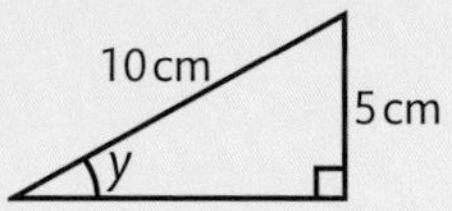

Time and timetables

Time can be displayed in two formats: 12-hour and 24-hour. It is important to be able to read timetables.

5 Time format

Time can be given in a 12-hour format or in a 24-hour format.

12-hour	24-hour
8:25 a.m.	08:25
8:25 p.m.	20:25

Rules for changing 12-hour clock times to 24-hour clock times:

Up to 12 noon, the times are the same	Between 1 p.m. and midnight, add 12 to the hour number	Times between midnight and 1 a.m. start 00

10 Worked example — Grade 1

1 Sandeep looks at his clock and realises that it's his bed time.

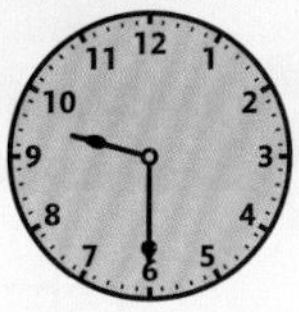

Write his bed time in

(a) the 12-hour clock.

9.30 p.m.

(b) the 24-hour clock.

9.30 + 12:00
= 21:30

9.30 p.m. is between 1 p.m. and midnight, so add 12 to the hour number.

When using the 12-hour format you must write a.m. for times before 12 noon and p.m. for times after 12 noon.

2 Kiran lives in Birmingham. He is planning to travel from Birmingham to Manchester.

The timetable shows information about the times of the trains Kiran can catch from Birmingham.

Birmingham	08:00	09:15	10:30
Wolverhampton	08:20	09:30	10:57
Stafford	08:45	09:55	11:25
Manchester	09:30	10:40	11:52

Kiran is going to meet Mai in Manchester at 11 a.m.

(a) What is the time of the latest train he can catch?

09:15

You need to identify the latest train Kiran can catch to get to Manchester by 11 a.m. The next train will reach Manchester too late.

(b) Work out which train takes the least amount of time to travel from Birmingham to Manchester.

08:00 → 09:30 = 90 minutes
09:15 → 10:40 = 85 minutes
10:30 → 11:52 = 82 minutes
The 10:30 train takes the least amount of time.

2 Timetables

Bus and train timetables use the 24-hour clock. A train timetable looks like this.

Birmingham New Street	10:14	10:30	10:33
Marston Green	10:26	↓	10:42
Birmingham International	10:30	10:40	10:45
Hampton-in-Arden	10:33	↓	10:48
Tile Hill	10:41	↓	10:55
Coventry	10:47	10:50	11:00

For example, a train leaves Birmingham New Street at 10:14 and arrives in Coventry at 10:47.

10 Exam-style practice — Grades 1–2

1 **(a)** Write 14:18 in the 12-hour clock. **[1 mark]**

(b) Write 4.29 p.m. in the 24-hour clock. **[1 mark]**

2 Emil lives in Liverpool. He goes to a meeting in London.
Emil leaves his home in Liverpool at 08:10.
He catches a train in Liverpool at 08:35.
The train takes 2 hours 35 minutes to get to London.
It then takes Emil 25 minutes to get to his meeting.

At what time does Emil get to his meeting? **[3 marks]**

3 Here is part of a train timetable from Stamford to Stansted Airport.

Stamford	08:59	09:59	10:59	11:59
Peterborough	09:18	10:18	11:18	12:18
Ely	09:53	10:53	11:53	12:53
Cambridge	10:08	11:08	12:08	13:08
Stansted Airport	10:45	11:45	12:45	13:45

A train leaves Stamford at 09:59.

(a) At what time should this train get to Ely? **[1 mark]**

Jess gets to Cambridge station at 10:45.
She wants to catch a train to Stansted Airport.

(b) How many minutes should Jess have to wait? **[1 mark]**

Reading scales

You will need to be able to read scales from instruments including rulers, weighing scales, measuring jugs and odometers.

(5) Reading scales ✓

When reading a scale, work out what each mark represents.

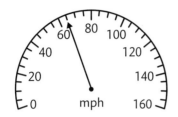

- The pointer is between 60 and 80
- There are 4 spaces between 60 and 80, so each mark shows 5 units.
- As the pointer is on the first mark, it must be 5 more than 60
- The reading is 65 mph.

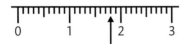

- The pointer is between 1 and 2
- There are 10 spaces between 1 and 2 so each mark shows 0.1 unit.
- As the pointer is on the eighth mark it must be 0.8 more than 1
- The reading is 1.8

- The pointer is between 8.3 and 8.4
- There are 10 spaces between 8.3 and 8.4 so each mark shows 0.01 unit.
- As the pointer is on the second mark it must be 0.02 more than 8.3
- The reading is 8.32

(5) Marking scales ✓

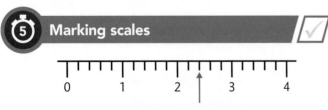

To find the number 2.4 on the scale:

- Work out what each mark represents: there are 5 spaces between 2 and 3 so each mark is 0.2 units.
- Work out how many spaces you need to get to the right number.
- Place the pointer on the second mark after 2

(5) Worked example | Grade 1 ✓

1 Write down the number shown by the arrow.

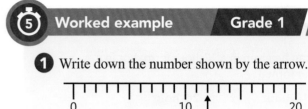

12 | There are 10 spaces and each mark is 1 unit.

2 Write down the number shown by the arrow.

2.24 | There are 10 spaces and each mark is 0.01 unit.

(5) Worked example | Grade 1 ✓

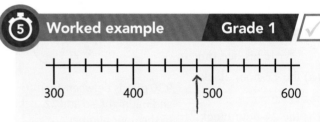

On the scale show a reading of 480

There are 5 spaces and each mark is 20 units, so place the pointer on the fourth mark.

(10) Exam-style practice | Grade 1 ✓

1 (a) Write down the number marked by the arrow. **[1 mark]**

(b) On the scale show a reading of 4.6 **[1 mark]**

2 Each box has the same weight. The scale measures in grams.

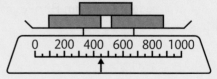

Work out the weight of one box. **[2 marks]**

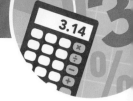

Symmetry

Some shapes have symmetry. There are two types of symmetry: reflective symmetry and rotational symmetry.

5 Reflective symmetry

The picture below is a two-dimensional picture of a butterfly.

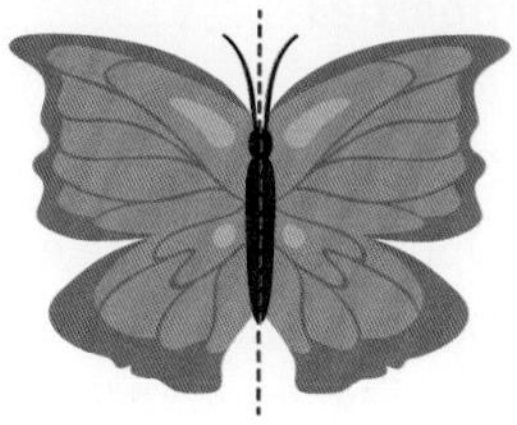

If the picture is folded along the dotted line then one half is an exact image of the other half.

The dotted line is called a **line of symmetry**.

One half of the shape is a mirror image of the other half.

In this case the butterfly has **one** line of symmetry.

A line of symmetry is sometimes called a mirror line.

5 Rotational symmetry

The diagram shows a rectangle being rotated.

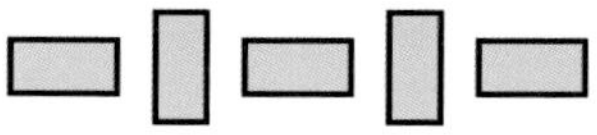

- When the rectangle is rotated through 90°, it does not look like its original shape.
- When the rectangle is rotated through 180°, it does look like its original shape.
- When the rectangle is rotated through 270°, it does not look like its original shape.
- When the rectangle is rotated through 360°, it does look like its original shape.

In one full turn, there are two positions in which it looks like its original shape.

The rectangle is said to have a rotational symmetry of order 2.

The order of rotational symmetry is the number of times the original shape is repeated in a 360° turn. All shapes have an order of rotational symmetry of at least 1.

5 Worked example — Grade 1

1 Here is a shape.

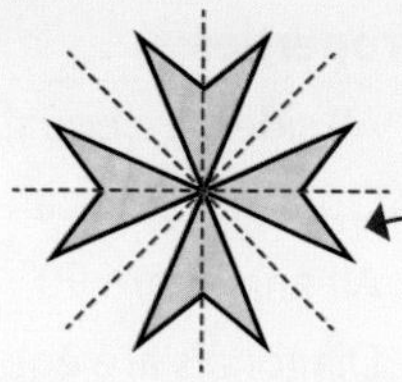

Write down the number of lines of symmetry of this shape.

4

A line of symmetry is drawn in such a way that one half of the shape is a mirror image of the other half.

2 Here is a shape.

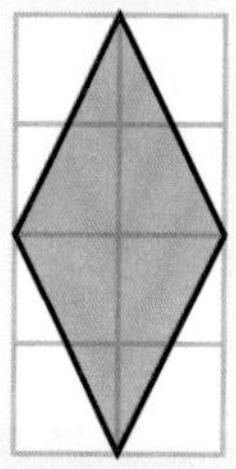

Write down the order of rotational symmetry of this shape.

2

Turn the shape and count how many times it looks like the original shape. This shape looks the same as the original shape at 180° and 360°.

10 Exam-style practice — Grade 1

1 Here are five shapes.

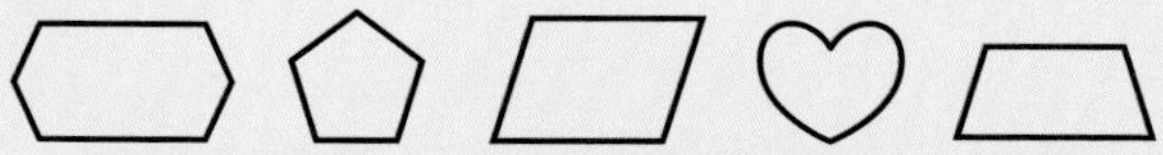

A B C D E

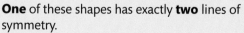

One of these shapes has exactly **two** lines of symmetry.

(a) Write down the letter of this shape. **[1 mark]**

(b) Write down the order of rotational symmetry of shape B. **[1 mark]**

2 The diagrams show patterns made from grey tiles and white tiles.

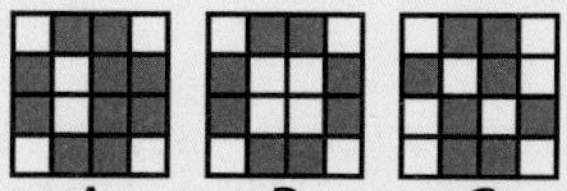

A B C

One of the patterns has exactly 1 line of symmetry.

(a) Write down the letter of this pattern. **[1 mark]**

(b) Write down the order of rotational symmetry of pattern C. **[1 mark]**

Quadrilaterals

A quadrilateral is a four-sided two-dimensional shape. The interior angles of a quadrilateral always add up to 360°.

 Types of quadrilateral

The table shows the different types of quadrilateral, with their properties.

Square	Properties	Rhombus	Properties
	• All sides are equal. • Opposite sides are parallel. • All angles are 90°. • Diagonals are equal and bisect at 90°.		• All sides are equal. • Opposite sides are parallel. • Opposite angles are equal. • Diagonals bisect each other at 90°.
Rectangle		**Trapezium**	
	• Opposite sides are equal. • Opposite sides are parallel. • All angles are 90°. • Diagonals bisect each other.		• Sides might not be equal. • One pair of sides is parallel. • Angles might not be equal.
Parallelogram		**Kite**	
	• Opposite sides are equal. • Opposite sides are parallel. • Opposite angles are equal. • Diagonals bisect each other.		• Two pairs of equal adjacent sides. • One pair of opposite equal angles. • Diagonals cross at 90° and one bisects the other.

 Worked example **Grade 1**

1 Here is a quadrilateral.

What type of quadrilateral is it? Give a reason for your answer.

The quadrilateral has four equal sides and four right angles, so it is a square.

2 On the grid below, draw a trapezium.

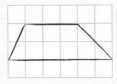

Include all the details. If you only say that the four sides are equal but don't mention the angles, the shape could be a square or a rhombus.

Exam focus 📌

You need to learn the names and the properties of the different quadrilaterals for your exam.

 **Exam-style practice** **Grade 1**

1 Write down the mathematical name of each of these quadrilaterals.

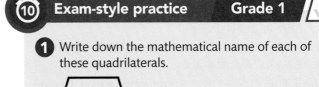

(a) [1 mark]

(b) [1 mark]

2 On the grid below, draw a kite. [1 mark]

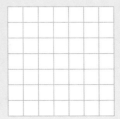

✓ **Made a start** ✓ **Feeling confident** ✓ **Exam ready**

3.14

Plans and elevations

Plans and elevations are 2D drawings representing 3D shapes.

 Plans and elevations

The diagram below shows the different sides of a 3D shape. Each view has a special name.

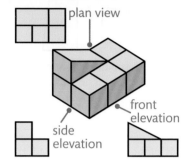

plan view

front elevation

side elevation

Plan view

The plan view is the view looking down onto the shape from above.

Front elevation

The front elevation is the view looking at the shape from the front.

Side elevation

The side elevation is the view looking at the shape from the side.

Exam focus

You will need to learn the different types of plan and elevation.

 Worked example | Grade 2

The front elevation and the side elevation of a cuboid are drawn on the grid.

On the grid, draw the plan of the cuboid.

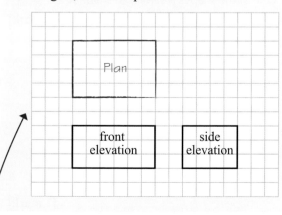

Plan

front elevation

side elevation

Use the same scale as the elevations given.

 Worked example | Grade 2

Here is a 3D object.

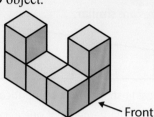

Front

Draw

(a) the plan view of the object

(b) the side elevation of the object

(c) the front elevation of the object.

Make sure your drawings are clear. Use a ruler and a sharp pencil.

From above, you will not be able to see the two cubes sticking out on the top.

 Exam-style practice | Grade 2

1 Here is a 3D object.

On the grid below, draw the view of the solid shape from the direction shown by the arrow.

[2 marks]

2 Here are the plan, front elevation and side elevation of a 3D shape.

plan

front elevation

side elevation

Draw a sketch of the 3D shape. **[2 marks]**

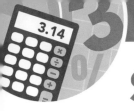

Similarity and congruence

Shapes that are exactly the same shape and size are congruent. Shapes that have the same shape but are different sizes are similar.

5 Similarity

These two shapes are **similar**.

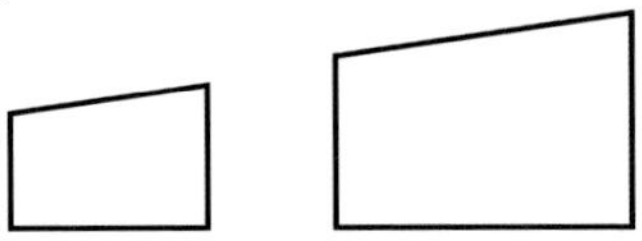

They are identical in shape **but not** identical in size.

Similar shapes are enlargements of one another. Even if one shape is flipped or rotated, they would still be similar.

5 Congruence

These two shapes are **congruent**.

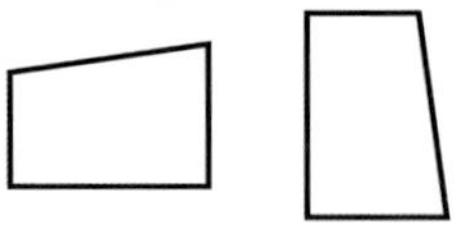

They are identical in shape **and** identical in size.

Congruent shapes have exactly the same size and shape as each other. Even if one shape is flipped or rotated, they would still be congruent.

5 Worked example — Grades 1–2

1 **(a)** Write down the letters of the two triangles that are congruent.

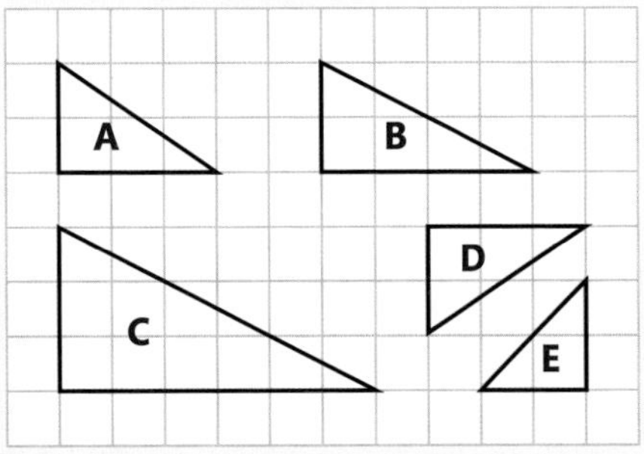

A and D

Notice that **D** is flipped over, but it is still the same shape and size as **A**.

One of the triangles is similar to triangle **B**.

(b) Write down the letter of this triangle.

C

Remember that similar shapes are enlargements of one another. Count the squares to work out which shape has the same ratio of width to height.

2 **(a)** On the grid below, draw a triangle that is congruent to the shaded triangle.

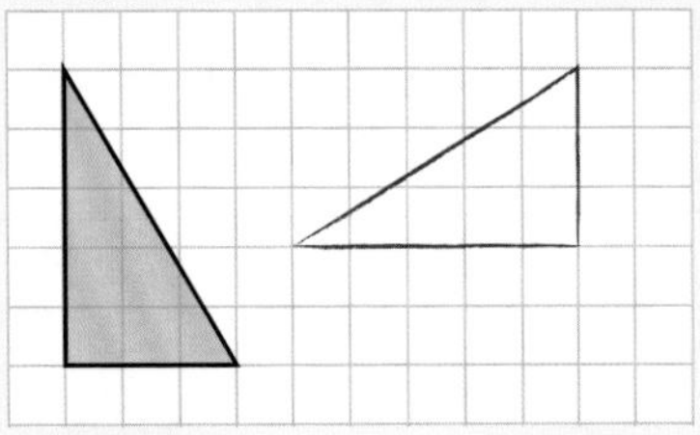

Congruent shapes have exactly the same size and shape. However, they can be rotated or reflected.

(b) On the grid below, draw a triangle that is similar to the shaded triangle, but not congruent.

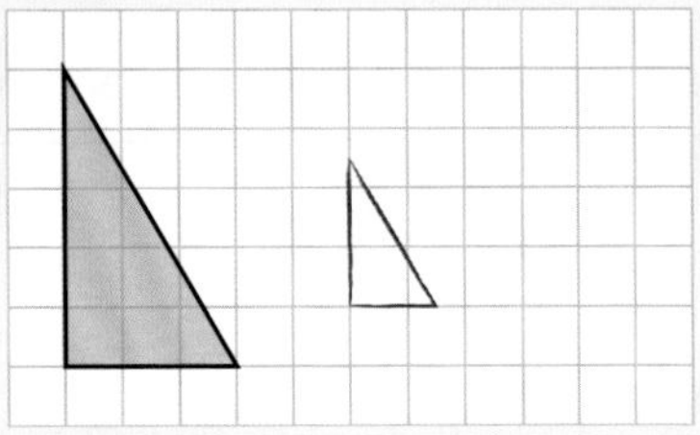

Similar shapes are the same shape, but can be a different size. You need to draw a triangle that is either bigger or smaller than the original.

10 Exam-style practice — Grades 1–2

1 Two of the seven shapes on the grid are congruent.

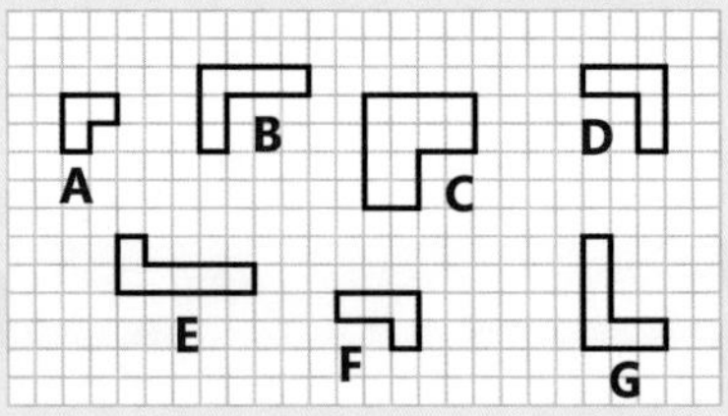

(a) Write down the letters of these two shapes. **[1 mark]**

One of the shapes is similar to shape **A**.

(b) Write down the letter of this shape. **[1 mark]**

2 Two of the six shapes on the grid are congruent.

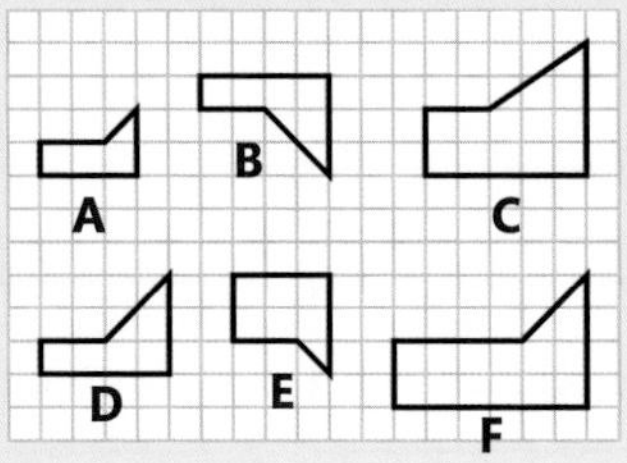

(a) Write down the letters of these two shapes. **[1 mark]**

One of the shapes is similar to shape **A**.

(b) Write down the letter of this shape. **[1 mark]**

Similar shapes

Using the idea of similar shapes, you can use scale factors to calculate corresponding unknown lengths.

⑤ Understanding scale factors ✓

When a shape is an enlargement of another shape then the two shapes are similar.

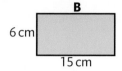

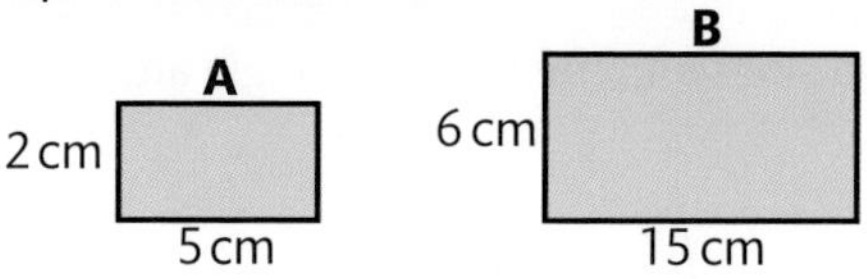

You can work out the scale factor of enlargement by considering corresponding lengths in both shapes.

Comparing corresponding sides:

- the scale factor from shape **A** to shape **B** is $\frac{6}{2} = 3$
- the scale factor from shape **B** to shape **A** is $\frac{2}{6} = \frac{1}{3}$

⑤ Working out lengths ✓

Once you have worked out the scale factor, you can work out missing lengths of sides of similar shapes.

Trapezium **A** is similar to trapezium **B**.

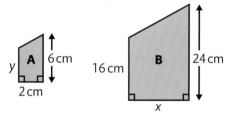

To work out the scale factor, choose a side that you know the length of on both shapes.

The height on the right-hand side of trapezium **A** is 6 cm, and on trapezium **B** is 24 cm.

$24 \div 6 = 4$, so **B** is an enlargement of **A** by a scale factor of 4.

To work out length x:

$x = 2$ cm $\times 4$

$x = 8$ cm

To work out length y:

$y = 16$ cm $\div 4$

$y = 4$ cm

The corresponding angles in similar shapes are the same.

⑤ Worked example — Grade 2–4 ✓

① Here are two similar shapes.

Parallelogram **B** is similar to parallelogram **A**.

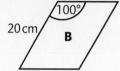

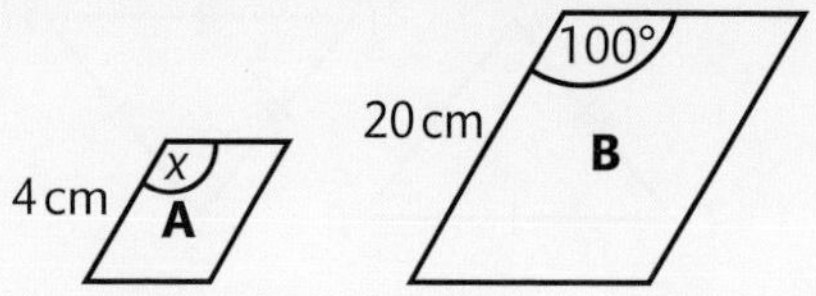

(a) Write down the size of the angle marked x.

$x = 100°$

(b) Write down the scale factor from parallelogram **A** to parallelogram **B**.

Scale factor $= 20 \div 4 = 5$

② Quadrilaterals $ABCD$ and $LMNP$ are mathematically similar.

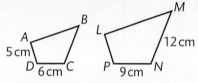

(a) Work out the length of LP.

$DC = 6$ cm and $PN = 9$ cm

$\frac{9}{6} = \frac{3}{2}$

$5 \times \frac{3}{2} = \frac{15}{2}$

$LP = 7.5$ cm

To find a scale factor, divide one side by the corresponding side.

(b) Work out the length of BC.

$12 \div \frac{3}{2} = 12 \times \frac{2}{3} = 8$

$BC = 8$ cm

To divide by a fraction, turn the fraction upside down and multiply. Go to page 10 to revise dividing fractions.

⑮ Exam-style practice — Grade 4 ✓

① Triangle ABC is similar to triangle PQR.

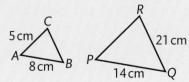

Diagram not accurately drawn

(a) Work out the length of PR. **[2 marks]**

(b) Work out the length of BC. **[2 marks]**

② The diagram shows triangle ACD.

B is a point on AC and E is a point on AD so that BE is parallel to CD. Triangle ABE is similar to triangle ACD.

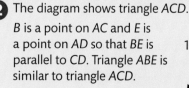
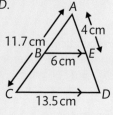

(a) Work out the length of AB. **[2 marks]**

(b) Work out the length of ED. **[2 marks]**

Congruent triangles

Congruent triangles are identical in size and shape, although their position relative to each other may be different.

(10) Conditions for congruency

Two triangles are congruent if they satisfy any one of these conditions.

SSS	**SAS**
All three sides are equal.	Two sides and the included angle are equal.
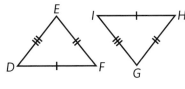	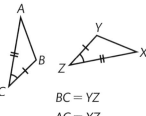
$DF = HI$	$BC = YZ$
$EF = GH$	$AC = XZ$
$DE = GI$	angle C = angle Z
RHS	**AAS**
Right angle, hypotenuse and another side are equal.	Two angles and one side are equal.
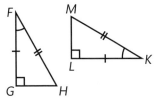	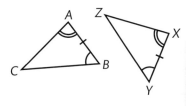
$FG = KL$	$AB = XY$
$FH = KM$	Angle B = angle Y
Angle G = angle L = 90°	Angle A = angle X

You will need to remember the four different conditions for congruent triangles.

(5) Worked example — Grade 5

CDE is an equilateral triangle.

F lies on DE. CF is perpendicular to DE.

Show that that triangle CFD is congruent to triangle CFE.

CDE is equilateral
CD = CE
CD is the hypotenuse of triangle CDF
CE is the hypotenuse of triangle CEF
CF is common to triangle CDF and triangle CEF
Angle CFD = angle CFE = 90°
Triangle CDF is congruent to triangle CEF by the RHS rule

Perpendicular means that one line is at right angles to another. If CF is perpendicular to DE, then the angles CFD and CFE must both be right angles.

Exam focus

You will need to show each step clearly, and state which condition you are using to show congruence.

(2) Checklist

To show that triangles are congruent you must prove that one of these conditions is met.

☑ SSS ☑ SAS ☑ RHS ☑ AAS

Start with the rules you know about triangles, and then see what you can work out. In equilateral triangles, all sides are the same length.

(10) Exam-style practice — Grade 5

In the diagram, $AB = BC = CD = DA$.

Show that triangle ADB is congruent to triangle CDB.

[3 marks]

Line segments

You need to be able to work out the length of a straight line on a coordinate grid. You can use Pythagoras' theorem (page 80) to do this.

 Working out the length

You can use Pythagoras' theorem to work out the length of a line segment on a coordinate grid.

Use the grid lines to draw a right-angled triangle.

Then apply Pythagoras' theorem.

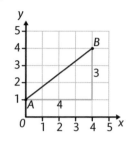

$AB^2 = 4^2 + 3^2$

$AB^2 = 16 + 9$

$AB^2 = 25$

$AB = \sqrt{25}$

$AB = 5$

You can use a formula to work out the length of any line segment, if you know the coordinates of the end points. Taking the points $A(x_1, y_1)$ and $B(x_2, y_2)$, then the length of AB is:

$$AB = \sqrt{(x_2 - x_1)^2 + (y_2 - y_1)^2}$$

Learn this formula, or draw a triangle and use Pythagoras' theorem.

 The mid-point

You calculate the coordinates of the mid-point of a line segment between $A(x_1, y_1)$ and $B(x_2, y_2)$, as the mean (average) of the x values and the mean of the y values:

Mid-point of $AB = \left(\dfrac{x_2 + x_1}{2}, \dfrac{y_2 + y_1}{2}\right)$

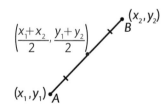

 Worked example **Grade 5**

A is the point with coordinates (3, 6).

B is the point with coordinates (9, 14).

Work out the length AB.

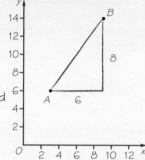

$x_2 - x_1 = 9 - 3 = 6$ and

$y_2 - y_1 = 14 - 6 = 8$

$AB^2 = 6^2 + 8^2$

$AB^2 = 100$

$AB = \sqrt{100}$

$AB = 10$

You can work out this example by drawing a right-angled triangle or by using the formula.

 Worked example **Grade 5**

1 P is the point with coordinates (1, 4).

Q is the point with coordinates (4, 8).

Work out the length PQ.

$PQ = \sqrt{(x_2 - x_1)^2 + (y_2 - y_1)^2}$

$PQ = \sqrt{(4 - 1)^2 + (8 - 4)^2} = \sqrt{(3)^2 + (4)^2}$

$PQ = \sqrt{9 + 16} = \sqrt{25}$

$PQ = 5$

2 Work out the coordinates of the mid-point of the line segment between $A(3, 7)$ and $B(13, 11)$.

Mid-point $= \left(\dfrac{3 + 13}{2}, \dfrac{7 + 11}{2}\right) = \left(\dfrac{16}{2}, \dfrac{18}{2}\right)$

Mid-point $= (8, 9)$

 Exam-style practice **Grade 5**

P has coordinates (2, 1) and Q has coordinates (10, 7).

(a) Give the coordinates of the mid-point of the line segment PQ. **[2 marks]**

(b) Work out the length PQ. **[3 marks]**

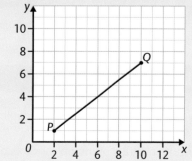

Vectors

Vectors are quantities, such as force or velocity, that have both **magnitude** (size) and **direction**.

5 About vectors

A vector quantity acts in a specific direction, like the force on a snooker ball hit by a cue. In the diagram, *A* and *B* are two points. The length of the line *AB* represents the magnitude of the vector from *A* to *B* and the arrow shows the direction.

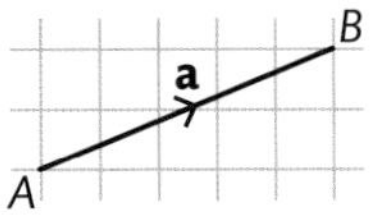

The vector from *A* to *B* can be described in three ways:

$\overrightarrow{AB} = \mathbf{a} = \begin{pmatrix} 5 \\ 2 \end{pmatrix}$

$\begin{pmatrix} 5 \\ 2 \end{pmatrix}$ is a **column vector** that represents a move of 5 to the right and 2 upwards.

Column vectors are generally written as $\begin{pmatrix} x \\ y \end{pmatrix}$.

5 Parallel vectors

If two vectors are parallel, one is a scalar multiple of the other.

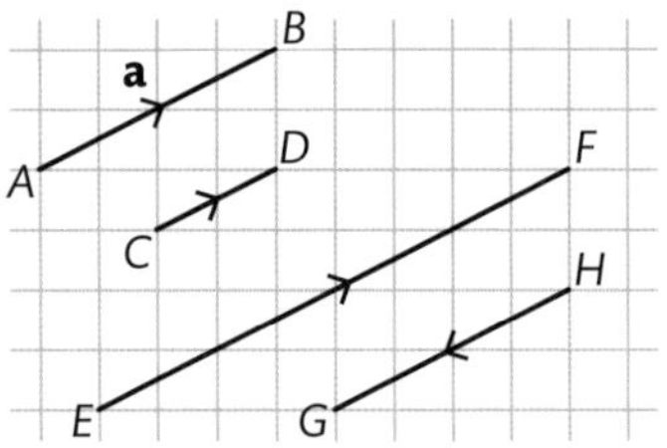

In the diagram, all the vectors are parallel and $\overrightarrow{AB} = \mathbf{a}$

$\overrightarrow{CD}$ and $\overrightarrow{EF}$ are positive multiples of $\overrightarrow{AB}$ because they act in the same direction.

$\overrightarrow{CD} = \begin{pmatrix} 2 \\ 1 \end{pmatrix} = \frac{1}{2}\begin{pmatrix} 4 \\ 2 \end{pmatrix} = \frac{1}{2}\mathbf{a}$ $\quad$ $\overrightarrow{EF} = \begin{pmatrix} 8 \\ 4 \end{pmatrix} = 2\begin{pmatrix} 4 \\ 2 \end{pmatrix} = 2\mathbf{a}$

$\overrightarrow{HG} = \begin{pmatrix} -4 \\ -2 \end{pmatrix} = -\mathbf{a}$

Vector $-\mathbf{a}$ is parallel to $\mathbf{a}$ but in the opposite direction.

10 Worked example — Grade 5

$\mathbf{a} = \begin{pmatrix} -7 \\ 3 \end{pmatrix}$ and $\mathbf{b} = \begin{pmatrix} 6 \\ -1 \end{pmatrix}$

Work out

(a) $3\mathbf{a}$

$3\mathbf{a} = 3\begin{pmatrix} -7 \\ 3 \end{pmatrix} = \begin{pmatrix} -21 \\ 9 \end{pmatrix}$

(b) $\mathbf{a} + \mathbf{b}$

$\mathbf{a} + \mathbf{b} = \begin{pmatrix} -7 \\ 3 \end{pmatrix} + \begin{pmatrix} 6 \\ -1 \end{pmatrix} = \begin{pmatrix} -1 \\ 2 \end{pmatrix}$

(c) $\mathbf{a} - \mathbf{b}$

$\mathbf{a} - \mathbf{b} = \begin{pmatrix} -7 \\ 3 \end{pmatrix} - \begin{pmatrix} 6 \\ -1 \end{pmatrix} = \begin{pmatrix} -13 \\ 4 \end{pmatrix}$

You add or subtract column vectors by combining *x*-values and combining *y*-values.

2 Checklist

- ✓ If two vectors are parallel, one is a multiple of the other.
- ✓ You can add, subtract or multiply vectors or multiply them by scalars.

10 Worked example — Grade 5

OAB is a triangle.

$\overrightarrow{OA} = \mathbf{a}$ and $\overrightarrow{OB} = \mathbf{b}$

Write, in terms of **a** and **b**

(a) $\overrightarrow{AB}$

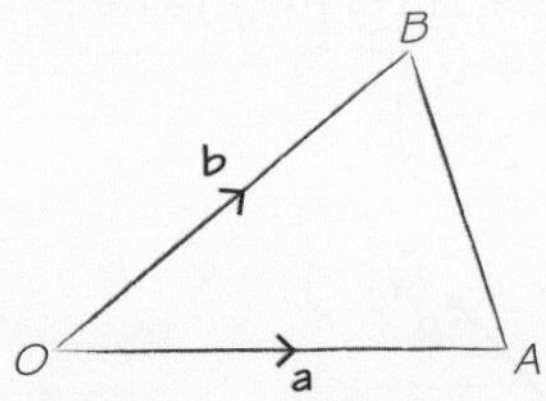

Find a path from *A* to *B* using the vectors **a** and **b**. If you go backwards along a vector, subtract it.

$\overrightarrow{AB} = -\mathbf{a} + \mathbf{b}$ or $\mathbf{b} - \mathbf{a}$

(b) $\overrightarrow{BA}$

$\overrightarrow{BA} = -\mathbf{b} + \mathbf{a}$ or $\mathbf{a} - \mathbf{b}$

15 Exam-style practice — Grade 5

ABCDEF is a regular hexagon with centre *O*.

$\overrightarrow{OA} = \mathbf{a}$ and $\overrightarrow{OB} = \mathbf{b}$

Write these vectors in term of **a** and **b**

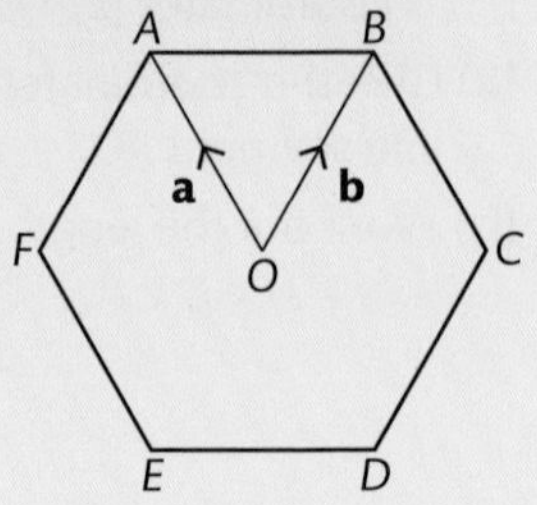

(a) $\overrightarrow{EF}$ **[2 marks]**

(b) $\overrightarrow{AD}$ **[2 marks]**

(c) $\overrightarrow{AB}$ **[2 marks]**

(d) $\overrightarrow{CF}$ **[2 marks]**

Pages 62–94 LINKS

Geometry and measures

Read the exam-style question and worked solution, then practise your exam skills with the two questions at the bottom of the page.

Worked example — Grade 5

The diagram represents a wooden frame.

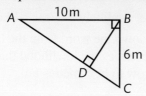

The frame is made from four wooden bars, AB, AC, BC and BD.

Angle ABC = angle ADB = 90°.

$AB = 10$ m and $BC = 6$ m

Work out the total length of the four wooden bars of the frame. Give your answer correct to 3 significant figures.

$AC^2 = 6^2 + 10^2$

$AC^2 = 36 + 100$

$AC^2 = 136$

$AC = \sqrt{136}$

$\tan BAC = \dfrac{opposite}{adjacent}$

$\tan BAC = \dfrac{6}{10}$

$BAC = \tan^{-1}\left(\dfrac{6}{10}\right)$

$BAC = 30.96°$

$\sin x = \dfrac{opposite}{hypotenuse}$

$\sin 30.96° = \dfrac{BD}{10}$

$BD = 10 \times \sin 30.96° = 5.1445$

Total length of bars

$= \sqrt{136} + 5.1445 + 10 + 6 = 32.8$ m

You need to know how to apply Pythagoras' theorem and trigonometry to 2D diagrams.

Trigonometry is only applied to right-angled triangles, using sin, cos and tan.

Sketch a right-angled triangle and label it with any angles and lengths that you know.

Do not round any answers until the final answer is obtained. It is sometimes better to leave intermediate answers in terms of square roots and then convert to decimals at the end.

The trigonometrical ratios for right-angled triangles are

$\sin \theta = \dfrac{opposite}{hypotenuse}$ $\cos \theta = \dfrac{adjacent}{hypotenuse}$

$\tan \theta = \dfrac{opposite}{adjacent}$

Checklist

- ☑ Draw a right-angled triangle and label the sides correctly.
- ☑ Apply Pythagoras' theorem if two sides are given and you want to work out the third side.
- ☑ Use SOH CAH TOA to work out the unknown angle.
- ☑ Round your final answer to a suitable degree of accuracy.

Exam-style practice — Grade 5

1 $ABCD$ is a parallelogram.

$DC = 6$ cm

Angle $ADB = 35°$

Work out the length of AD. Give your answer correct to 3 significant figures.

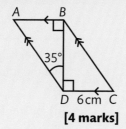

[4 marks]

2 OAB is a sector of a circle, centre O.

OCD is a sector of a circle, centre O.

OCA and ODB are straight lines.

Angle $AOB = 75°$, $OD = 7$ cm and $DB = 5$ cm

Work out the perimeter of the shaded region. Give your answer correct to 3 significant figures.

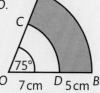

[4 marks]

 Made a start   **Feeling confident**   **Exam ready**   95

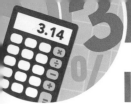

Introduction to probability

Probability is a measure of the likelihood of an event happening. Probability is a branch of mathematics that is used to predict future events.

(5) The language of probability

All probabilities must have a value that is greater than or equal to 0 and less than or equal to 1.

This is a probability scale.

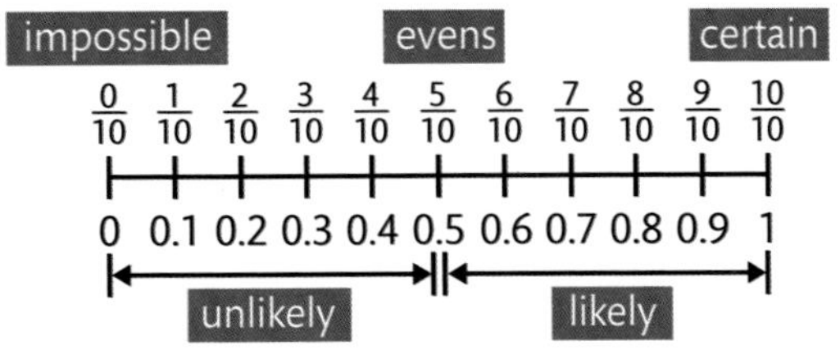

All probabilities can be written as fractions, percentages or decimals.

If there are n independent outcomes that are **equally likely**, then the probability of one outcome is $\frac{1}{n}$

(5) Equally likely outcomes

Probabilities can be calculated by using the formula

$$\text{probability} = \frac{\text{number of successful outcomes}}{\text{total number of outcomes}}$$

The outcomes have to be equally likely for the rule to work.

For example, when drawing counters out of a bag you are equally likely to pick any counter.

A bag contains 3 yellow counters, 2 blue counters and 4 red counters.

$$\text{P(blue counter)} = \frac{2}{3 + 2 + 4} = \frac{2}{9}$$

So the probability of picking a blue counter is $\frac{2}{9}$

As Saskia has selected a cat **at random**, it is equally likely that she has picked any of the cats. You need to use the formula for equally likely outcomes.

(5) Sample space diagrams

A sample space diagram shows all the possible outcomes of an event.

For example, this sample space diagram shows all 12 possible outcomes for a fair coin and a fair dice being thrown together.

		Dice					
		1	**2**	**3**	**4**	**5**	**6**
Coin	**H**	H1	H2	H3	H4	H5	H6
	T	T1	T2	T3	T4	T5	T6

(10) Worked example — Grades 1–3

1 This is a list of words used in probability.

impossible unlikely evens likely certain

(a) Write down the word from the list which best describes the likelihood that a man will grow to be 5 metres tall.

impossible

(b) On the probability scale, mark with a cross (×) the probability that when a fair coin is thrown it will land on heads.

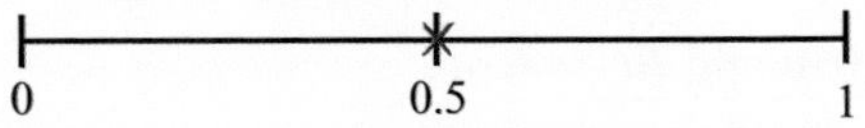

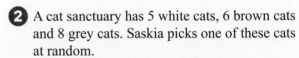

Remember that a coin has a side with a head and a side with a tail, so the probability of scoring a head on a fair coin is $\frac{1}{2}$

2 A cat sanctuary has 5 white cats, 6 brown cats and 8 grey cats. Saskia picks one of these cats at random.

Work out the probability that she picks a grey cat.

$$\text{P(grey cat)} = \frac{8}{5 + 6 + 8} = \frac{8}{19}$$

(15) Exam-style practice — Grades 2–3

1 Mina has a fair six-sided spinner. The sides of the spinner are numbered 1, 1, 2, 3, 3 and 5.

Mina spins the spinner once.

Write down the probability that the spinner will land on

(a) 2 **[1 mark]**

(b) 3 **[2 marks]**

2 Matt throws two fair six-sided dice. He adds the scores on the dice together.

(a) Draw a sample space diagram to show all the possible total scores. **[2 marks]**

(b) Use the diagram to work out the probability that the total score is

(i) 4 **[2 marks]**

(ii) greater than 8 **[2 marks]**

(iii) even. **[2 marks]**

More about probability

Probability is the likelihood of an event occurring.

(2) All possible outcomes

The sum of the probabilities of all the possible outcomes is **1**.

P(outcome occurs) = 1 − P(outcome does not occur)

For example, Neela's football team have a 1 in 3 chance of winning their next match.

P(winning) = $\frac{1}{3}$

P(not winning) = $1 - \frac{1}{3} = \frac{2}{3}$

(10) Worked example   Grade 5

1 A box contains only red, green, blue and orange pencils. Burt takes a pencil from the box at random. The table shows the probability of selecting each colour.

Colour	red	green	blue	orange
Probability	0.24	0.18		

The probability that Burt selects a green pencil is twice the probability that he selects a blue pencil. Work out the probability that he will:

(a) take a blue pencil

$\boxed{P(\text{not B}) = 1 - P(B)}$

P(blue) = 0.18 ÷ 2 = 0.09

(b) not take a blue pencil

P(not blue) = 1 − 0.09 = 0.91

(c) take a red pencil or a green pencil

P(red or green) = P(red) + P(green)
P(red or green) = 0.24 + 0.18 = 0.42

(d) take an orange pencil.

P(orange) = 1 − (0.24 + 0.18 + 0.09)
= 1 − 0.51 = 0.49

2 There are 35 boys and 48 girls in a club. The ratio of boys who play pool to boys who do **not** play pool is 2 : 5. The ratio of girls who play pool to girls who do **not** play pool is 1 : 3. The club leader picks one child at random from all of those who play pool.

Work out the probability that this child is a girl.

The number of boys who play pool is $\frac{2}{7} \times 35 = 10$

The number of girls who play pool is $\frac{1}{4} \times 48 = 12$

Total number who play pool is 10 + 12 = 22

The probability that this child is a girl = $\frac{12}{22} = \frac{6}{11}$

(2) Types of event

Independent events can happen at the same time, but the outcome of one does not affect the outcome of the other. For independent events A and B:

P(A and B) = P(A) × P(B)

Mutually exclusive events cannot happen at the same time. For mutually exclusive events A and B:

P(A or B) = P(A) + P(B)

Problem solving

Burt cannot take a red pencil and a green pencil at the same time so these events are mutually exclusive.

Problem solving

To work out the probability that the child is a girl, you first need to work out the total number of children who play pool:

1 Work out the number of boys who play pool, then the number of girls who play pool.

2 Whether the child is a boy or a girl is a mutually exclusive event, so add the outcomes to get the total number of children who play pool.

(1) Checklist

☑ **Or** means add the probabilities.
☑ **And** means multiply the probabilities.

(10) Exam-style practice   Grade 5

1 A bag contains only red counters, yellow counters, blue counters and green counters. Ken takes a counter from the bag at random. The table shows each of the probabilities.

Colour	red	yellow	blue	green
Probability	0.19	0.42	x	$2x$

Work out the value of x.   **[3 marks]**

2 Sandeep has a biased coin. The probability that the coin will land tails up is 0.7

Sandeep is going to throw the coin 3 times. He says the probability that the coin will land heads up 3 times is less than 0.1

Is Sandeep correct? Show all your working.
    [3 marks]

Relative frequency

Relative frequency is the number of times an outcome occurs in a series of trials. You need to be able to estimate the probability of an outcome using the relative frequency.

2 Relative frequency

The more times a trial is carried out, the closer a relative frequency gets to the theoretical frequency.
Relative frequency can be used as an estimate for the probability of the outcome.

$$\text{Relative frequency} = \frac{\text{frequency of outcome}}{\text{total frequency}}$$

2 Estimating probabilities

You can use relative frequency as an estimate for probability. As the total frequency gets larger, the estimate will get more accurate.

10 Worked example Grade 5

Rebecca surveyed the number of times customers go to a supermarket. She asked 80 customers at random how many times they went to the supermarket last month.
The table shows her results.

Visits	0	1	2	3	4	5 or more
Frequency	6	24	17	16	10	7

A customer is picked at random.
Estimate the probability that the customer went to the supermarket

(a) exactly 2 times

$$\text{P(exactly 2 times)} = \frac{17}{80}$$

From the table, total frequency is $6 + 24 + 17 + 16 + 10 + 7 = 80$

(b) 3 or more times.

$$\text{P(3 or more times)} = \frac{16 + 10 + 7}{80} = \frac{33}{80}$$

Customers who visited 3 or more times are those who visited 3, 4 or 5 or more times.

5 Worked example Grade 5

In an experiment a drawing pin is thrown. The number of times it lands point up is recorded.

The drawing pin is thrown 12 times and lands point up 8 times.

(a) From this data, estimate the probability that it lands point up.

$$\frac{8}{12} = \frac{2}{3} = 0.6\dot{6}$$

The drawing pin is thrown 100 times and lands point up 61 times.

(b) From this data, estimate the probability that it lands point up.

$$\frac{61}{100} = 0.61$$

10 Exam-style practice Grade 5

1 A bag contains only red, green, yellow and blue counters. The table gives information about the counters.

Colour	red	green	yellow	blue
Frequency	28	21	24	17

A counter is to be taken from the bag at random.
Work out the probability that the counter will be

(a) yellow **[1 mark]**
(b) red or green or blue **[2 marks]**
(c) not green. **[2 marks]**

2 The table shows some information about the time, in seconds, people spent in a queue at a supermarket.

Time spent x (seconds)	Frequency
$0 < x \leqslant 50$	3
$50 < x \leqslant 100$	4
$100 < x \leqslant 150$	6
$150 < x \leqslant 200$	2

(a) Estimate the probability that a new customer visiting the supermarket spends

(i) more than 150 seconds in a queue **[1 mark]**
(ii) 100 seconds or less in a queue. **[2 marks]**

(b) Comment on the accuracy of your estimates. **[1 mark]**

Venn diagrams

A Venn diagram represents connections between different sets of data. For a diagram showing two sets, the overlapping region of the circles represents the elements that are in both sets. Any values outside of the circles are not in either set.

 What is a Venn diagram?

A **Venn diagram** shows information about sets or groups of data. Consider two events A and B.

The probability of event A is written as P(A). The probability that A does not happen is $P(A') = 1 - P(A)$, and is displayed outside of the circle.

The intersection between the circles shows the elements that are in both sets, $A \cap B$.

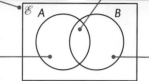

The square contains all possible outcomes. This is called the **universal set** and is shown by $\mathscr{E}$

This area contains outcomes that are in both A **and** B.

This area contains outcomes that are in A but **not** in B.

This area contains outcomes that are in B but **not** in A.

 Worked example **Grade 5**

1 $\mathscr{E} = \{$square numbers less than 100$\}$

$A = \{$multiples of 3$\}$

$B = \{$multiples of 4$\}$

(a) Draw a Venn diagram to represent this information.

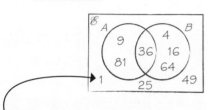

Square numbers less than 100 that are not multiples of 3 or 4 should go outside the two circles, but inside the rectangle.
The universal set is square numbers **less than** 100. This means that 100 should not be included, even though it is a multiple of 4

A number is selected from the universal set, $\mathscr{E}$, at random.

(b) Work out the probability that the number is a multiple of 3 only.

P(A but not B) $= \dfrac{2}{9}$

(c) Work out the probability that the number is in the set $A \cap B$.

P(A $\cap$ B) $= \dfrac{1}{9}$

(d) Work out the probability that the number is not a multiple of 3 or a multiple of 4.

P(neither A nor B) $= \dfrac{3}{9} = \dfrac{1}{3}$

This is the elements outside both circles. There are three numbers in the Venn diagram not in either circle (1, 25 and 49) so the probability is 3 out of 9

 Exam-style practice **Grade 5**

1 Simon gathered some information about the pet dogs and pet cats around the estate he lives in.

There are 90 families in this estate. 65 families have a dog, 34 have a cat and 12 have a dog and a cat. No family had more than 1 cat or more than 1 dog.

(a) Draw a Venn diagram to represent this information. **[3 marks]**

(b) What is the probability that a family, chosen at random, has neither a dog nor a cat? **[2 marks]**

2 A running club has 60 members. 44 of the members take part in a cross-country run, 27 of the members take part in a marathon and 6 of the members do not run in the cross country or the marathon.

Work out the probability that a member only takes part in the cross country run or in the marathon but not both. **[4 marks]**

 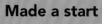 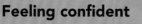

Tree diagrams

A tree diagram is a simple diagram that represents a sequence of two or more events.

Tree diagrams ✓

Tree diagrams are particularly useful in answering probability questions as they record all possible outcomes in a clear and logical manner.

For example, Liz makes a spinner. The spinner can land on green or on blue. The probability that the spinner will land on green is 0.65. Liz spins the spinner twice.

> As a general rule: **multiply along the branches and add between the branches.**

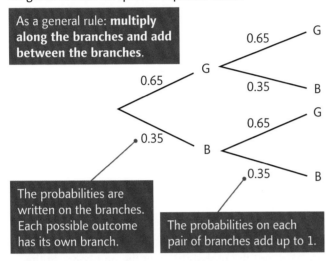

> The probabilities are written on the branches. Each possible outcome has its own branch.

> The probabilities on each pair of branches add up to 1.

To work out the probability that the spinner lands on two different colours:

P(two different colours) = GB or BG
$$= (0.65 \times 0.35) + (0.35 \times 0.65)$$
$$= 0.2275 + 0.2275 = 0.455$$

Checklist ✓

- ☑ One branch for each possible outcome.
- ☑ Along the branches you multiply the probabilities.
- ☑ Between the branches you add the probabilities.
- ☑ The sum of all the probabilities at the ends of the branches is 1

Worked example   Grade 5 ✓

There are 12 pens in a box.

5 of the pens are yellow.

7 of the pens are red.

Andy takes a pen from the box at random. He records the colour and puts the pen back into the box. He then takes another pen from the box at random and records the colour.

(a) Show this information on a tree diagram.

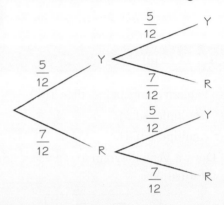

(b) Work out the probability that Andy takes two pens of the same colour.

P(one of each colour) = YY or RR
$$= \left(\frac{5}{12} \times \frac{5}{12}\right) + \left(\frac{7}{12} \times \frac{7}{12}\right)$$
$$= \frac{25}{144} + \frac{49}{144}$$
$$= \frac{74}{144}$$

> You can leave probability answers as fractions, and you don't need to simplify them unless you are told to.

Exam-style practice   Grade 5 ✓

1 The probability that it will rain on Saturday is 0.7. When it rains on Saturday, the probability that it will rain on Sunday is 0.75
When it does not rain on Saturday, the probability that it will rain on Sunday is 0.4

    (a) Show this information on a tree diagram.   **[3 marks]**

    (b) Work out the probability that it will rain on both Saturday and Sunday.   **[2 marks]**

    (c) Work out the probability that it will rain on at least one of the two days.   **[2 marks]**

2 Rajesh has 20 medals in a box. He has 11 gold medals, 6 silver medals and 3 bronze medals.

Rajesh takes a medal from the box at random and records the colour. He puts the medal back into the box. He then takes another medal at random and records the colour.

Work out the probability that the two medals were the same type.   **[5 marks]**

Pages 96–100 LINKS

Probability

Read the exam-style question and worked solution, then practise your exam skills with the questions at the bottom of the page.

(10) Worked example — Grade 5

There are 12 counters in a bag.

5 of the counters are red. 7 of the counters are green.

Rishi takes a counter from the bag at random. He puts the counter back in the bag. He then takes another counter from the bag at random.

(a) Complete the tree diagram.

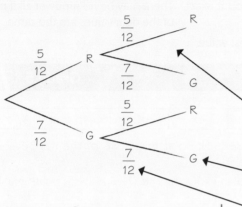

The counter has been put back into the bag, so there are always 12 counters in the bag for Rishi to choose from.

(b) Work out the probability that Rishi takes one counter of each colour. You must show your working.

$$P(\text{one of each colour}) = P(R \text{ and } G) + P(G \text{ and } R)$$
$$= \left(\frac{5}{12} \times \frac{7}{12}\right) + \left(\frac{7}{12} \times \frac{5}{12}\right)$$
$$= \frac{35}{144} + \frac{35}{144}$$
$$= \frac{70}{144} = \frac{35}{72}$$

You need to know that a red counter followed by a green counter OR a green counter followed by a red counter can be chosen. There are two possible outcomes.

Write down the probabilities on each branch.

The probabilities for each pair of branches add up to 1.

The probabilities are multiplied along the branches and added between the branches.

(2) Checklist

- ✓ If the object is replaced, the probabilities remain the same.
- ✓ **AND** means multiplication of probabilities.
- ✓ **OR** means addition of probabilities.

(10) Exam-style practice — Grade 5

1 There are 14 white beads and 11 black beads in a bag.

There are no other beads in the bag.

Sam takes a bead from the bag at random.

(a) Write down the probability that the bead will be white. **[2 marks]**

There are 7 red beads and 13 yellow beads in a box.

Sam adds 10 more beads to this box.

Sam is going to take a bead at random from the 30 beads in the box. The probability that he will take a red bead is $\frac{1}{3}$

(b) Work out how many red beads Sam adds to the box. **[3 marks]**

2 Andrea and Nisha take a test.

The probability that Andrea will pass the test is 0.65

The probability that Nisha will pass the test is 0.75

(a) Work out the probability that both of these girls fail the test. **[3 marks]**

(b) Work out the probability that both of these girls pass the test or that both of these girls fail the test. **[3 marks]**

3 The table shows the probabilities that a spinner will land on 2 or on 4

Number	1	2	3	4
Probability		0.25		0.15

The probability that the spinner will land on 1 is the same as the probability that the spinner will land on 3

(a) Work out the probability that the spinner will land on 3 **[3 marks]**

Lisa is going to spin the spinner 400 times.

(b) Work out an estimate for the number of times the spinner will land on 4 **[2 marks]**

Averages and range

There are three different types of average that you need to know how to use to analyse and compare data. The spread of data is given by the range.

5 The three averages and the range

Type of average	Mean	Median	Mode
How to find it	Add up all the values and divide by how many values there are.	Put the values in order, then find the middle value (or the mean of the middle two values.)	The value or observation that occurs most frequently.
Advantage	Uses all the data	Not affected by extreme values	Good for data that is in words
Disadvantage	Affected by extreme values	Does not take into account exact values of all the data	There may be no mode at all if none of the data values are the same.

Range = highest value − lowest value

5 Worked example — Grade 5

Nisha has five cards. She wants to write down a number on each card so that

- the mode of the five numbers is 9
- the median of the five numbers is 10
- the mean of the five numbers is 12
- the range of the five numbers is 8

Work out the five numbers on the cards.

| 9 | 9 | 10 | 15 | 17 |

The mode is 9, so at least two of the numbers must be 9.
The median is 10, so the third highest value must be 10.
The range is 8 so the largest number must be 9 + 8 = 17
The mean is 12, so the total of all 5 numbers must be 12 × 5 = 60
60 − (9 + 9 + 10 + 17) = 15

Problem solving

The mean is equal to the sum of the values divided by the number of values. To work out the sum of the values, multiply the mean by the number of values. Here, the mean is 12, so the total of the 5 numbers must be 60.

5 Worked example — Grade 1

Here are nine numbers:

4 8 6 9 10 4 8 3 4

(a) Write down the mode.
Mode = 4

(b) Work out the median.
3 4 4 4 ⑥ 8 8 9 10
Median = 6

(c) Work out the mean.
Mean = (4 + 8 + 6 + 9 + 10 + 4 + 8 + 3 + 4) ÷ 9
= 6.22

(d) Work out the range.
Range = 10 − 3 = 7

You need to remember the definitions of mean, median, mode and range.

15 Exam-style practice — Grades 1–5

1 These are the numbers of goals a hockey team scored in each of 10 matches:

4 5 4 3 6 4 6 7 3 5

Work out the
(a) mode **[1 mark]** **(b)** median **[2 marks]**
(c) mean **[2 marks]** **(d)** range. **[2 marks]**

2 There are 30 students in a class.
18 are boys and 12 are girls.
The mean height of the boys is 152 cm.
The mean height of the girls is 147 cm.
Work out the mean height of all the students in the class. **[2 marks]**

3 Here is a list of numbers written in order of size:

4 7 x y

The numbers have
- a median of 9
- a mean of 12.

Work out the value of x and the value of y. **[3 marks]**

Pictograms

A pictogram is a simple diagram used to display data.

5 Drawing and interpreting pictograms

The pictogram shows the numbers of tins of cat food sold in a shop on Monday, Tuesday and Wednesday last week.

Monday	O O O O
Tuesday	O O ◖
Wednesday	O O O ◿
Thursday	O O ◔
Friday	O O

Key O represents 8 tins

On Thursday, 22 tins of cat food were sold in the shop.

On Friday, 16 tins of cat food were sold in the shop.

This data can be represented on the pictogram.

One circle represents 8 tins.

22 tins are represented by 2 whole circles and another $\frac{3}{4}$ of a circle.

16 tins are represented by 2 whole circles.

You can work out the number of tins sold on Monday as $4 \times 8 = 32$ tins

Always refer to the key as it will tell you what each symbol represents.

Half a circle represents 4 tins, a quarter of a circle represents 2 tins and three-quarters of a circle represents 6 tins.

5 Worked example — Grade 1

The pictogram gives information about the numbers of points scored by two boys in a computer game.

Sandeep	O O O O
Avi	O O ◖
Jonny	O O O ◿

Key O represents 20 points

Jonny scored 65 points.

(a) Use this information to complete the pictogram.

(b) Write down the number of points that Avi scored.

20 + 20 + 10 = 50 points

(c) Work out the total number of points that all three boys scored.

(20 × 4) + 50 + 65 = 80 + 50 + 65
= 195 points

10 Exam-style practice — Grade 1

This pictogram shows the numbers of radios sold in a shop on Thursday, on Friday and on Saturday.

On Sunday the shop sold 11 radios.

(a) Use this information to complete the pictogram. **[1 mark]**

(b) Work out the total number of radios sold on these four days. **[2 marks]**

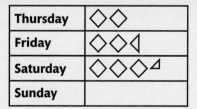

Thursday	◇ ◇
Friday	◇ ◇ ◖
Saturday	◇ ◇ ◇ ◿
Sunday	

Key ◇ represents 4 radios

Line graphs

You can use different types of line graph to represent different types of information.

 Vertical line graph

This is similar to a bar graph, showing discrete data, except that lines are drawn instead of bars. The height of each line represents a particular frequency.

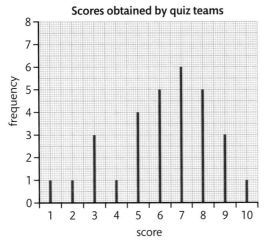

From this line graph you can work out the different averages and the spread.

 Time series graph

A time series graph displays continuous data. You plot values of a given variable against time. Time is always on the horizontal axis.

From this time series graph you can work out the trend of the data.

 Worked example **Grade 5**

The vertical line graph shows the numbers of children absent each day over 20 school days.

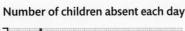
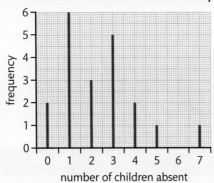

Work out the mean number of children absent per day.

Mean =
$$\frac{[(0 \times 2) + (1 \times 6) + (2 \times 3) + (3 \times 5) + (4 \times 2) + (5 \times 1) + (6 \times 0) + (7 \times 1)]}{20}$$

Mean = $\frac{47}{20}$

= 2.35

To work out the mean from a frequency diagram, multiply the value for each line by the frequency and add all your answers together. This gives you the total number of children absent over the 20 day period.

Divide this number by 20 to find the mean number of children absent each day.

When describing a trend, always use the words 'downwards' or 'upwards'. You just need to look at the shape of the graph and the slope of the line.

 Exam-style practice **Grade 5**

The table gives information about the profits made by a company, in the summer (S) and in the winter (W), over three years.

	Year 1		Year 2		Year 3	
	S	**W**	**S**	**W**	**S**	**W**
Profit (£)	12 000	24 000	18 000	33 000	23 000	39 000

(a) Draw a time series graph for this information.

[3 marks]

(b) Describe the trend in the profits made over these three years.

[1 mark]

 Made a start **Feeling confident** ✓ **Exam ready**

Pie charts

A pie chart is a visual representation of data. It shows frequencies as proportions of a circle.

 Drawing a pie chart

A pie chart is a circle divided into different sectors. Each sector is a slice of the pie chart.

You need to work out the angle for each sector of the pie chart before you can draw it.

The angles at the centre of the pie chart add up to 360°.

Mike asked 60 students to name their favourite fruit.
Here are his results.

Fruit	Frequency	Angle
Apple	18	$\frac{18}{60} \times 360° = 108°$
Banana	24	$\frac{24}{60} \times 360° = 144°$
Orange	5	$\frac{5}{60} \times 360° = 30°$
Pear	13	$\frac{13}{60} \times 360° = 78°$

Draw a circle, using your compasses and a pencil.
Draw a vertical line from the centre of the circle to the top.
Use a protractor to measure and draw the first angle of 108°.

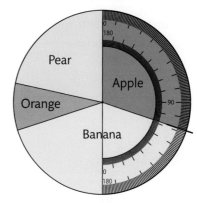

Then draw the remaining angles carefully, in order.

Add a column to the table to work out the angles:
$$\frac{\text{frequency for this sector}}{\text{total frequency}} \times 360°$$

 Worked example   **Grade 2**

Imran recorded the musical instrument played by each of 30 students in the school orchestra.

The table shows his results.

Draw an accurate pie chart to show this information.

Instrument	Frequency	Angle
Drums	8	$\frac{8}{30} \times 360° = 96°$
Guitar	5	$\frac{5}{30} \times 360° = 60°$
Recorder	10	$\frac{10}{30} \times 360° = 120°$
Piano	7	$\frac{7}{30} \times 360° = 84°$

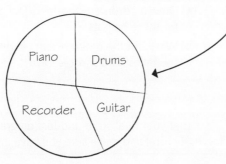

Work out the angles and label each sector clearly.

 Exam-style practice   **Grade 2**

The pie chart shows information about the numbers of votes cast for each of four candidates in an election.

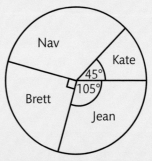

(a) What fraction of the votes did Nav get?   **[2 marks]**

Brett got 600 votes.

(b) Work out the total number of votes the four candidates got.   **[2 marks]**

Stem-and-leaf diagrams

A **stem-and-leaf diagram** is a special table in which each data value is split into a 'stem' (the first digit or digits) and a 'leaf' (usually the last digit).

 Drawing a stem-and-leaf diagram

You need to order the data in a stem-and-leaf diagram to make it useful. The first part of each data value is the stem and the last digit is the leaf.

For example, Bob catches 15 fish. These are the weights, in grams, of the fish:

40   51   47   37   43   65   52   54   63   41   56   56   38   45   40

To draw an ordered stem-and-leaf diagram for these weights:

Step 1 Draw an **unordered** stem-and-leaf diagram.

The first digits are in the first column, the second digits are listed on the right of the line.

```
3 | 7 8
4 | 0 7 3 1 5 0
5 | 1 2 4 6 6
6 | 5 3
```

> It is always helpful to draw an unordered stem-and-leaf diagram and then order the leaves in a second stem-and-leaf diagram.

Step 2 Draw the **ordered** stem-and-leaf diagram.

Now all the digits on the right of the line are put into ascending order.

```
3 | 7 8
4 | 0 0 1 3 5 7
5 | 1 2 4 6 6
6 | 3 5
```

Key: 3 | 7 represents 37 g

> Remember to add a key to a stem-and-leaf diagram.

 Worked example | Grade 3 |

Here are the heights, in centimetres, of 15 children.

113   137   125   140   137   119   138   139
123   128   123   120   141   115   127

Show this information in an ordered stem-and-leaf diagram.

Unordered:

```
11 | 3 9 5
12 | 5 3 8 3 0 7
13 | 7 7 8 9
14 | 0 1
```

Ordered:

```
11 | 3 5 9
12 | 0 3 3 5 7 8
13 | 7 7 8 9
14 | 0 1
```

Key: 11 | 3 represents 113 cm

 Exam-style practice | Grade 3 |

1 Alexi plays 15 games of ten-pin bowling. Here are his scores.

72   58   75   66   79
75   66   63   89   76
65   78   77   71   83

Draw an ordered stem-and-leaf diagram to show Alexi's scores. **[3 marks]**

2 Here are the heights, in cm, of 19 plants.

72   83   77   95   97   83   102   94   72
105   82   93   96   102   100   97   88   92   87

(a) Draw an ordered stem-and-leaf diagram for these heights. **[3 marks]**

(b) Work out the difference in height between the tallest and shortest plants. **[2 marks]**

> Check that your final stem-and-leaf diagram contains 15 'leaves' in total and make sure you have included a key.

Scatter graphs

A scatter graph is a visual representation of two variables. It can show a trend or a **correlation**. **Strong correlation** is shown by the points being clustered along a line. **Weak correlation** is shown by the points being more openly dispersed along a line.

 Types of correlation

Positive correlation	Negative correlation	No correlation
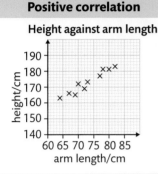	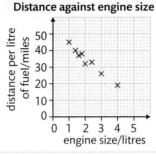	
As one variable increases, the other variable increases. **In context**, as the arm length increases the height increases.	As one variable increases, the other variable decreases. **In context**, as the engine size increases, the distance travelled per litre of fuel decreases.	There is no linear relationship between the two variables. **In context**, there is no linear relationship between money and happiness.

You can only draw a **line of best fit** if the scatter graph shows negative or positive correlation.

Outliers are values that lie outside the 'trend' shown by the rest of the data.

Making predictions
- **Interpolation** is when you make a prediction when the value is within the given data range.
- The predicted value is reliable.

- **Extrapolation** is when you make a prediction when the value is outside the given data range.
- The predicted value is not reliable.

Worked example   Grade 5

A garage sells motorcycles. The scatter graph shows information about the price and age of the motorcycles.

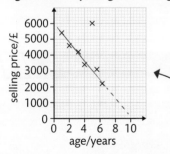

The line of best fit should go approximately through the middle of all the points, ignoring any outliers.

(a) Write down the coordinates of the outlier.

(5, 6000)

(b) (i) Draw the line of best fit.

(ii) Describe the correlation.

There is a negative correlation between the selling price of a motorcycle and its age.

A motorcycle is 9 years old.

(c) Estimate the price of this motorbike. Is this estimate reliable? Give a reason for your answer.

£700

9 years is outside the range of the data, so this is not reliable (extrapolation).

 Exam-style practice   Grade 5

10 students each took a French test and a German test. The table shows their marks.

French marks	44	30	40	50	14	20	32	34	20	45
German marks	48	35	45	54	18	22	36	38	25	50

(a) Show this information on a scatter graph.   **[2 marks]**

(b) Describe the relationship, if any, between French marks and German marks.   **[1 mark]**

(c) Use a line of best fit to estimate:

   (i) the German mark for a student with a French mark of 27   **[1 mark]**

   (ii) the French mark for a student with a German mark of 42   **[1 mark]**

 Made a start   Feeling confident   Exam ready

Frequency tables

You can use data presented in frequency tables and grouped frequency tables to work out averages.

5 Working out averages

This table records the numbers of matches in 80 match boxes.

Number of matches, *x*	Frequency *f*	$x \times f$
49	23	1127
50	22	1100
51	20	1020
52	15	780
	80	4027

Draw an extra column in the table to show your working out.

To work out the **mean**:

Work out the total number of matches, by multiplying each number by the frequency.

Identify the total of the frequencies.

$$\text{Mean} = \frac{\text{total of all values}}{\text{number of values}} = \frac{\sum fx}{\sum f} = \frac{4027}{80} = 50.3$$

This symbol means 'sum of', and shows you have to add up all the values in that column of the table.

The mean number of matches in a box is **50**

To work out the **median**:

The total number of boxes is 80

The median is the $\frac{80 + 1}{2}$ value, when they are written in order.

This is the 40.5th value. The first 23 values are 49, then the next 22 values are 50 so the 40.5th value must be **50**

To work out the **mode**:

The mode is the value that occurs the most.

The highest frequency is **23**, so the mode is **49**

5 Worked example — Grade 5

The table shows information about the numbers of hours spent on the internet last week.

Number of hours, *h*	Frequency *f*	Mid-point *x*	$x \times f$
$0 \leqslant h < 2$	5	1	5
$2 \leqslant h < 4$	6	3	18
$4 \leqslant h < 6$	4	5	20
$6 \leqslant h < 8$	10	7	70
$8 \leqslant h < 10$	12	9	108
	37		221

(a) Write down the modal class.

$8 \leqslant h < 10$

(b) Write down the class interval that contains the median.

Median is the $\frac{37 + 1}{2}$ = 19th value, which is in the class $6 \leqslant h < 8$

(c) Work out an estimate for the mean number of hours.

$$\text{Mean} = \frac{\sum fx}{\sum f} = \frac{221}{37} = 5.97 \text{ hours}$$

(d) Explain why your answer to part **(c)** is an estimate.

The data is grouped. We don't know exact values.

For grouped data you need to find the mid-point of each class interval.

15 Exam-style practice — Grade 5

1 Adam watched 40 cars go onto a ferry. He counted the number of people in each car. The table shows his results.

Number of people in a car	Frequency
1	6
2	14
3	10
4	6
5	4

(a) Write down the mode. **[1 mark]**

(b) Work out the median. **[1 mark]**

(c) Work out the mean number of people in a car. **[1 mark]**

2 The table gives information about the temperature, *T* °C, at noon in a town for 50 days.

Temperature (*T* °C)	Frequency
$4 \leqslant T < 8$	6
$8 \leqslant T < 12$	8
$12 \leqslant T < 16$	13
$16 \leqslant T < 20$	21
$20 \leqslant T < 24$	2

(a) Write down the modal class. **[1 mark]**

(b) Write down the class interval which contains the median. **[1 mark]**

(c) Estimate the mean temperature. **[3 marks]**

(d) Explain why your answer to part **(c)** is an estimate. **[1 mark]**

Two-way tables

Two-way tables show frequencies for two different categories. One category is given in the row headings, and one category is given in the column headings.

A two-way table shows two variables. For example, 60 children went on school trips to Paris or to Rome. 19 boys and 12 girls went to Paris. 14 boys went to Rome.

One variable is the gender of the children, girl or boy. The second variable is the location of their trip, Paris or Rome. To show this in a two-way table:

1. Draw a table and add headings for the rows and columns to fit the given data.
2. Fill in the information you have been given, and calculate any missing numbers.
3. Add up the numbers in each row to get the row total.

There were 33 boys in total.

	Paris	Rome	Total
Boys	19	14	33
Girls	12	15	27
Total	31	29	60

15 girls went to Rome.

You could also represent this in a **frequency tree**.

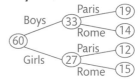

On an activity day, students each play one sport.
They play football, rugby or tennis.
120 students are on the activity day.
72 of the students are boys.
19 of the boys and 10 of the girls play rugby.
42 of the students play football.
11 of the 42 students who play football are girls.
Work out the number of girls who play tennis.

	Football	Rugby	Tennis	Total
Boys		19		72
Girls	11	10		
Total	42			120

	Football	Rugby	Tennis	Total
Boys	31	19	22	72
Girls	11	10	27	48
Total	42	29	49	120

Number of girls who play tennis = 27

$48 - (10 + 11) = 27$, the number of girls who played tennis.

$120 - (42 + 29) = 49$, the total number of students who play tennis.

19 boys and 10 girls play rugby, so there are 29 students playing rugby in total.

Start by filling in all the numbers you know.

$120 - 72 = 48$, so there were 48 girls in total.

1 The two-way table shows some information about the numbers of cakes sold in a shop.

	Monday	Tuesday	Wednesday	Total
Morning	14		13	53
Afternoon		9	17	
Total	35			100

(a) Complete the two-way table. **[3 marks]**

One of these cakes is picked at random.

(b) Write down the probability that this cake is sold on a Wednesday morning. **[1 mark]**

One of the cakes sold on a Tuesday is picked at random.

(c) Write down the probability that this cake is sold in the afternoon. **[2 marks]**

2 There are 130 adults at a language school.

Each adult studies one of Latin or Russian or Mandarin.

96 of the adults are women.
12 of the women study Latin.
73 of the adults study Russian.
55 of the women study Russian.
9 of the men study Mandarin.

How many of the adults study Latin? **[4 marks]**

 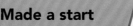 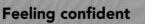

Sampling

The way in which data is collected can have a big impact on the validity of any conclusions.

⑤ About sampling

A **population** is every single person or item you might be interested in.

A **sample** is a selection of people or items taken from the whole population.

To represent the population accurately, the sample should be **random** and free from **bias**.

Bias can occur in many ways. For example:

- The sample may not be representative of the population, for example, a weighted dice that is designed to give one result more often the others.
- The population may not be appropriate for the survey being carried out, for example, it may leave out a group who ought to be included.

How do you avoid bias?

- Use a larger sample.
- Use a random sample.

Advantages and disadvantages of samples

👍 Cheaper than using the entire population

👍 Less time-consuming

👍 Less data to handle (easier)

👎 Not completely representative

👎 May be biased

⑤ Worked example | Grade 5

Ellen asks 10 of her friends at her running club to take part in a survey. Give **one** reason why this may not be a suitable sample.

The sample could be biased as it only includes her friends who go to the running club.

You could also suggest that the sample size is too small or may not be representative of all the members of the club.

⑤ A random sample

A random sample is a sample drawn randomly from a population so that every individual has an **equal chance** of being chosen. It is assumed to be representative of the whole population.

To carry out a random sample, you can number each person or item and then use a random number generator.

Another way to generate a random sample would be to write everyone's name on a piece of paper, and then randomly pick pieces of paper out of a hat or bag without looking.

⑩ Worked example | Grade 5

1 Sam wants to take a random sample of students from her year group.

(a) Explain what a random sample means here.

Each member of the year group has an equal chance of selection.

(b) Describe a method Sam could use to take her random sample.

Number each student and then use a random number generator.

2 Ray wants to work out how much time people spend watching football on television. He is going to use a questionnaire to carry out a survey. Ray asks the boys in his class to complete his questionnaire. Give **two** reasons why his sample is biased.

He only asks boys, and they are all in the same class/year/school.

Try to give answers in the context of the question not just quote standard answers.

⑩ Exam-style practice | Grade 5

1 The manager of a shop is carrying out a survey on the ages of his customers. He records the ages of the first 10 customers in his shop after 8.30 a.m. one morning. Give **two** reasons why this may **not** be a suitable sample.

[2 marks]

2 Tania carries out a survey to work out how much money people spend buying trainers. She asks 100 people in a sports shop to do her questionnaire. Explain why her sample is biased.

[1 mark]

✓ Made a start | ✓ Feeling confident | ✓ Exam ready

Analysing data

You need to be able to use averages and measures of spread to analyse and compare data.

 Comparing data

To compare two sets of data you should compare an average and a measure of spread: use the mean or the median, and the range.

Averages	Measure of spread
Mean	Range
Median	

 Checklist

- ☑ Always calculate the average you are asked for in the question, for the data given. If the question asks for the mean, don't give the median.
- ☑ Calculate the range to see how the data is spread out.
- ☑ Use the correct vocabulary when comparing data.

 Worked example | Grade 3

Harry and Suki recorded the times, in minutes, they exercised each morning for five days. Harry's times are shown below:

12 16 12 13 19

Suki exercised for a mean of 16.2 minutes each day.

Who exercised for longer on average each day? You must justify your answer.

Mean for Harry
$$= \frac{12 + 16 + 12 + 13 + 19}{5} = 14.4 \text{ minutes}$$

16.2 > 14.4 so Suki exercised for longer on average as her mean is greater.

 Worked example | Grade 3

The stem-and-leaf diagrams below give information about the times taken by some boys and some girls to complete a puzzle.

Boys

1	7 8 8 8 8 9
2	0 3 4 4 5 6 6 7 9
3	2 5

Key: 1 | 7 represents 17 minutes

Girls

1	8 8 9 9
2	0 3 4 4 7 7 8
3	0 1 1 2

Key: 1 | 8 represents 18 minutes

> Make sure you interpret your answer in context.

(a) Work out and compare the ranges of the times taken by the boys and by the girls.

Boys' range = 35 − 17 = 18   Girls' range = 32 − 18 = 14

The boys' range is greater than the girls' range, so the times taken by the boys were more spread out than the times taken by the girls.

(b) Work out and compare the medians of the times taken by the boys and the girls.

Boys: Total of 17

$$\frac{17 + 1}{2} = 9 \text{ so the median is the 9th time}$$

Median of boys' time is 24 minutes.

Girls: Total of 15

$$\frac{15 + 1}{2} = 8 \text{ so the median is the 8th time}$$

Median of girls' time is 24 minutes.

The boys and girls have the same median times, so on average they took the same amount of time to complete the puzzle.

 **Exam-style practice** | Grade 3

Joanne is recording the times, in minutes, that some people spent at a motorway café during the day and during the night. The two boxes give this information.

Compare the distribution of the times spent in the café during the day to the distribution of the times spent in the café during the night.

[4 marks]

Day time
6 10 12 15 16
21 23 26 28 28
29 31 33 36 45

Night time
Median = 15
Range = 35

Statistics

Read the exam-style question and worked solution, then practise your exam skills with the question at the bottom of the page.

 Worked example   **Grade 3**

Simran recorded the shoe size of each of the boys in her class.

Here are the shoe sizes of the boys:

5   6   7   5   6   7   5   10   8   9

(a) Work out the mean shoe size.

Mean = (5 + 6 + 7 + 5 + 6 + 7 + 5 + 10
        + 8 + 9) ÷ 10

     = 68 ÷ 10

     = 6.8

(b) Work out the range.

Range = 10 − 5

      = 5

She then recorded the shoe sizes of the girls in her class. For the shoe sizes of the girls in her class:

- the mean is 5.9
- the range is 4

(c) Compare the shoe sizes of the boys and the shoe sizes of the girls.

The mean shoe size of the boys is greater than the mean shoe size of the girls, so on average the boys' shoe sizes are greater than the girls' shoe sizes.

The range of the shoe sizes of the boys is greater than the range of the shoe sizes of the girls, so the boys' shoe sizes were more spread out than the girls' shoe sizes.

> To work out the mean, add up all the values and then divide by the total number of values.

> To work out the range, subtract the lowest value from the highest value.

> Write the average comparison in context.

> In this scenario, compare the means using the correct words, such as 'greater than' or 'less than'.

> In this scenario, compare the ranges using the correct terms, such as 'greater than' or 'less than'.

 Checklist

- ☑ Compare the mean and the range.
- ☑ One of your statements must be in context.

 Exam-style practice   **Grade 5**

Mr Smith's students did a maths test and a science test. The scatter graph shows the marks of 12 of these students.

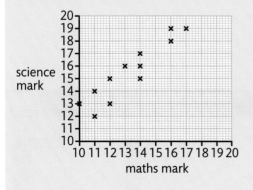

The table shows the marks of two more students.

Name	Maths	Science
Katy	13	15
Ava	16	17

(a) Show this information on the scatter graph. **[1 mark]**

(b) What type of correlation does this scatter graph show? **[1 mark]**

Jake did the maths test, but he was absent for the science test.

Jake's mark in the maths test was 15

(c) Use the graph to estimate what mark Jake might have got in the science test. **[2 marks]**

Problem-solving strategies

In your exam, questions might require you to make connections between different parts of mathematics, interpret results and evaluate methods within a certain context or think about problems as a series of mathematical processes.

5 How to answer problem-solving questions

Ask yourself these **five** sets of questions.

1 Do I understand the problem?

Have I identified the type of problem?
Have I read through the problem carefully?
Have I thought about the problem in my own words?
Have I reviewed my thoughts and ideas?

2 What information do I need?

Have I looked at the key words used in the question?
Have I understood the mathematical language used?
What is the style of the question – describe, show, solve, prove or state?
How do I respond to these key mathematical words?

3 What maths do I know?

What topic(s) do I need to recall?
What formulae do I need?
What steps are required to reach the answer?
What would a sensible answer look like?

4 Is my solution correct?

Have I carried out my plan logically?
Have my methods worked?
Are my answers sensible?

5 Have I completed everything?

Have I answered every part of the question?
Have I given the information that was being asked for?
Have I shown all my working?
Have I given units with my answer?

5 Worked example — Grade 5

This is a diagram of Harry's patio.

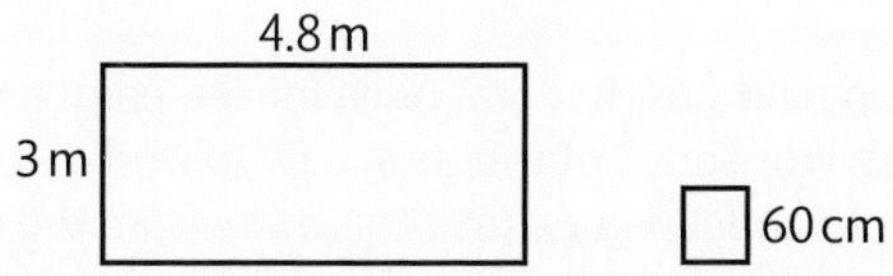

Harry wants to cover all of the patio with slabs.
The slabs are squares with sides of length 60 cm.
The slabs are sold in packs of 10
Each pack of slabs costs £175. Harry only has £650
Can he buy enough packs of slabs to cover the patio? **[5 marks]**

What is my plan to solve the problem?

I need to convert 3 m and 4.8 m into cm.
$3 \times 100 = 300$ cm and $4.8 \times 100 = 480$ cm
I need to work out the area of the patio and slab.
Patio: $300 \times 480 = 144\,000$
Slab: $60 \times 60 = 3600$
I need to work out the number of slabs for the patio.
$144\,000 \div 3600 = 40$
I need to work out the number of packs.
$40 \div 10$
I need to work out the cost.
$4 \times £175$
I need to compare the cost with £650

5 Worked example — Grade 5

Anjali makes a spinner.
The spinner can stop on either green or red.
The probability that the spinner will stop on green is 0.7
Anjali spins the spinner twice.
Work out the probability that the spinner stops on two different colours. **[4 marks]**

What is my plan to solve the problem?

I need to draw a tree diagram.
I need to label the first green branch as 0.7
I need to label the second green branch as 0.7
I need to label the first red branch as 0.3
I need to label the second red branch as 0.3
I need to multiply along the branches for green and red.
0.7×0.3
I need to multiply along the branches for red and green.
0.3×0.7
I need to add the probabilities to work out the probability that the spinner lands on two different colours.
$(0.7 \times 0.3) + (0.3 \times 0.7)$

10 Exam-style practice — Grade 5

Using the five point plan to problem solving, complete the two problems set on this page. **[4 marks]**

Solving number problems

Number skills are often tested in particular contexts, such as problems with money.

 Worked example | Grade 5

Sandeep is decorating his bedroom.

£18.90   £10.65 each   £7.35

He buys four tins of paint.

One of the tins costs £18.90

The other three tins each cost £10.65

Sandeep also buys a pack of paint brushes.

The pack costs £7.35

Sandeep gets $\frac{1}{4}$ off the total cost.

He pays with three £20 notes.

How much change should Sandeep get?

Cost of 3 tins = 3 × £10.65 = £31.95
Total cost = £31.95 + £18.90 + £7.35
           = £58.20
$\frac{1}{4}$ of £58.20 = £14.55
Cost = £58.20 − £14.55
      = £43.65
Total money given = 3 × £20 = £60
Change = £60 − £43.65
       = £16.35

> When working with money, be careful with place value.
> Money written in pounds should always have 2 decimal places.

> Start by working out the cost of the three tins.

> Work out the total cost of the paint tins and the paint brushes.

> Sandeep paid $\frac{3}{4}$ of the total price for the paint and brushes. Work out $\frac{1}{4}$ of the total cost to work out the discount Sandeep gets. Take this away from the total cost to work out out how much he paid.

Problem solving

When you are answering a problem-solving question, make sure that you lay your answer out neatly, starting a new line for each equation.

You may need to use information you worked out earlier, so it is a good idea to write down what you are working out at the start of each line to help you find it again quickly.

 Problem solving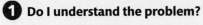

1 **Do I understand the problem?**

The question is asking you to work out the total cost of the four tins of paint and the paint brushes, and then to work out the change.

2 **What information do I need?**

You need all the underlined information.

3 **What maths do I know?**

- how to add and multiply decimals
- how to work out a fraction of an amount

4 **Is my solution correct?**

The answer is sensible considering the total amount of money that has been spent.

5 **Have I completed everything?**

Reread the question. You need to make sure you subtract $\frac{1}{4}$ of the total cost and work out the change.

 Exam-style practice | Grade 4

Ravina buys 80 rings.

She pays £3.50 for each ring.

Ravina sells $\frac{1}{2}$ of the rings for £6 each.

She sells $\frac{1}{5}$ of the rings for £5 each.

Ravina wants to make a total profit of £100

How much should she sell each of the remaining rings for? **[4 marks]**

Solving graphical problems

Graphical skills are often tested in particular contexts, such as problems with plotting and using conversion graphs.

 Worked example | **Grade 5** | ☑

The table shows some lengths in inches changed into lengths in centimetres.

Length (inches)	0	2	6	10
Length (centimetres)	0	5	15	25

(a) Use the information in the table to draw a line graph that can be used to convert between inches and centimetres. Use the grid provided below.

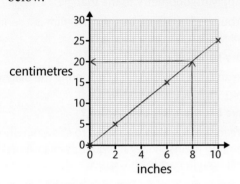

Anna's height is 56 inches and Ben's height is 125 centimetres.

(b) Who is taller?

8 inches = 20 centimetres
56 ÷ 8 = 7
Anna's height = 7 × 20 = 140 centimetres
140 cm is more than 125 cm so Anna is taller.

 Problem solving ⚙ ☑

1 **Do I understand the problem?**
The question is asking you to draw a line on the graph paper to show the conversion between inches and centimetres.

2 **What information do I need?**
You need to know how to plot points on the graph paper and draw a straight line. You then need to use the conversion graph to convert between inches and centimetres.

3 **What maths do I know?**
- how to plot points clearly at the correct coordinates and then draw a straight line
- how to use the conversion graph to convert between inches and centimetres

4 **Is my solution correct?**
125 cm and 140 cm are both realistic heights, so the answer is sensible.

5 **Have I completed everything?**
Reread the question. You need to interpret the conversion graph and write your answer in context.

Plot these points on the grid and then draw a straight line through all of them.

Convert both heights into the same units. Your graph does not go up to 56 inches. You can convert 8 inches to centimetres then multiply by 7.

Alternatively, you could convert Ben's height into inches and then compare it with Anna's height in inches.

 Exam-style practice | **Grade 5** | ☑

One apple and four pears cost 95 pence.
Six apples and two pears cost £1.30
Let *a* represent the cost of one apple in pence.
Let *p* represent the cost of one pear in pence.
Use a graphical method to work out the cost of four apples and seven pears. **[4 marks]**

Problem solving

Write the information given in the question using algebra:
$a + 4p = 95$
$6a + 2p = 130$
Draw these lines on the grid then find the point of intersection to solve the simultaneous equations. This will give the price of **one** apple and **one** pear.

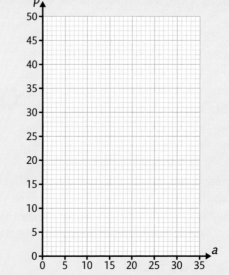

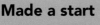

Solving geometric problems

Geometric skills are often tested in particular contexts, such as using similar triangles to work out lengths of sides.

 Worked example | **Grade 5** ✓

The diagram shows a metal frame *ABCDEFGHJ*.

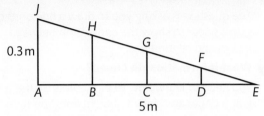

The line *AE* is horizontal and the line *AJ* is vertical.
$AE = 5$ m and $AJ = 0.3$ m.

The legal requirement is that the angle *AEJ* of the ramp is a maximum of 3.8°.

(a) Does this ramp meet the legal requirement?

Opposite = 0.3
Adjacent = 5

SOH CAH (TOA)

$\tan x = \dfrac{\text{opposite}}{\text{adjacent}} = \dfrac{0.3}{5}$

$x = \tan^{-1}\left(\dfrac{0.3}{5}\right)$

$x = 3.43°$

The angle meets the legal requirement.

(b) The length of *BE* is 3.75 m. Show that *BH* is 22.5 cm.

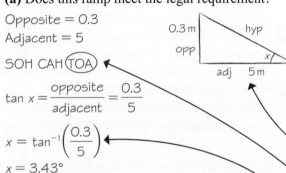

$\dfrac{y}{0.3} = \dfrac{3.75}{5}$

$y = \dfrac{3.75}{5} \times 0.3$

$y = 0.225$ m

$y = 22.5$ cm (3 s.f.)

Problem solving

Start by writing down what you know:

• Arc length $= 2\pi r \times \dfrac{\theta}{360}$

• The radius is 4 cm. You need to work out the value of θ, which is the angle *AOC*.

• The triangle *OAD* has a 90° angle and you know the lengths of two sides, so you can work out the angle *AOB* using trigonometry.

• The angle *AOC* is 2 × *AOB*.

 Problem solving ⚙ ✓

1 **Do I understand the problem?**
The question is asking you to apply trigonometry to right-angled triangles.

2 **What information do I need?**
You need to know that you are dealing with triangles.

3 **What maths do I know?**
• To work out the legal requirement you need to apply trigonometry to the triangle.
• You need to realise that the diagram is a series of similar triangles.

4 **Is my solution correct?**
The answers are sensible considering the diagram given.

5 **Have I completed everything?**
Reread the question. You need to show whether the ramp meets the legal requirement and that the length in part **(b)** is correct.

Always label the sides of the triangle and then write down what you know and what you are looking for.

Write down SOH CAH TOA and then choose the correct ratio.

To work out an angle you need to use $\sin^{-1}$ or $\cos^{-1}$ or $\tan^{-1}$.

Once you know the angle *AOC*, substitute the value for θ into the formula for arc length.

 Exam-style practice | **Grade 5** ✓

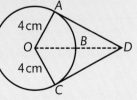

A, B and C are points on a circle of radius 4 cm, centre O.

DA and DC are tangents to the circle.

$OAD = OCD = 90°$
$DO = 7$ cm

Work out the length of arc *ABC*.

Give your answer correct to 3 significant figures.

[5 marks]

Solving algebraic problems

Algebraic skills are often tested in particular contexts, such as problems with volume.

⏱10 Worked example — Grade 5 ✓

The diagram shows a box in the shape of a cuboid. The volume of the box is $36\,cm^3$.

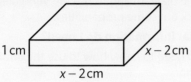

1 cm $x - 2$ cm
$x - 2$ cm

(a) Show that $x^2 - 4x - 32 = 0$

$$\text{Volume} = 1(x - 2)(x - 2)$$
$$= 1(x^2 - 2x - 2x + 4)$$
$$= x^2 - 4x + 4$$
$$x^2 - 4x + 4 = 36$$
$$x^2 - 4x + 4 - 36 = 0$$
$$x^2 - 4x - 32 = 0$$

(b) Hence, or otherwise, work out the surface area of the box.

$$x^2 - 4x - 32 = 0$$
$$(x - 8)(x + 4) = 0$$
$$x = 8 \text{ or } x = -4$$

The length cannot be negative, so reject $x = -4$

So $x = 8\,cm$

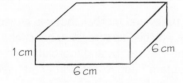

1 cm   6 cm
6 cm

$$\text{Surface area} = 2(6 \times 6) + 4(6 \times 1)$$
$$= 72 + 24$$
$$= 96\,cm^2$$

⑤ Problem solving ⚙ ✓

① **Do I understand the problem?**

The question is asking you to use algebraic skills to work out the dimensions and surface area.

② **What information do I need?**

You need to know the dimensions of the box. This means you need to find the value of x. You can find it by writing an equation and solving it.

③ **What maths do I know?**

- To find the value of x you need to know how to expand brackets and rearrange equations. Then you need to know how to solve a quadratic equation.
- You need to know how to find the volume and surface area of a cuboid:
  volume = length × width × height
  surface area = sum of areas of faces

④ **Is my solution correct?**

The diagram is not to scale but the dimensions of the box should look reasonable. Lengths cannot be negative numbers.

⑤ **Have I completed everything?**

The final line of your working in part (a) should show the equation. The final line of your working in part (b) should be the surface area of the box.

Multiply out the double brackets first and **then** multiply by the number outside.

Solve your quadratic equation to find x. You need to factorise the left-hand side so look for numbers that add up to -4 and multiply to give -32.

⏱10 Exam-style practice — Grade 5

The diagram shows a rectangle $ABCD$.

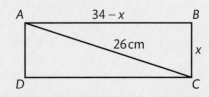

A $34 - x$ B
26 cm
    x
D   C

The perimeter of the rectangle is 68 cm.
The length of the diagonal AC is 26 cm.

(a) Show that $x^2 - 34x + 240 = 0$ **[4 marks]**

(b) Work out the length of the rectangle.   **[3 marks]**

Solving statistical problems

You may need to use statistical skills in particular contexts, such as to solve problems with Venn diagrams and probabilities.

(10) Worked example | Grade 5

80 people were asked which sports they watched on television. Here are the results.

38 people watched cricket.

29 people watched rugby.

35 people watched football.

17 people watched both cricket and rugby

18 people watched both cricket and football.

16 people watched both rugby and football.

11 people watched all three sports.

(a) Draw a Venn diagram to show this information.

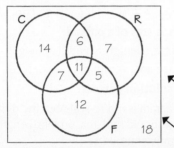

One of the 80 people is selected at random.

(b) Work out the probability that this person does not watch any of these three sports.

$$P(\text{no sport}) = \frac{18}{80} = \frac{9}{40}$$

(c) Work out the probability that this person only watches one of these three sports.

$$P(\text{only 1 sport}) = \frac{14}{80} + \frac{12}{80} + \frac{7}{80} = \frac{33}{80}$$

(5) Problem solving ⚙

1 **Do I understand the problem?**

The question is asking you to draw and fill in the Venn diagram and to use the Venn diagram to work out some probabilities.

2 **What information do I need?**

You need to know how to use the information given.

3 **What maths do I know?**

- Drawing and filling in a Venn diagram.
- Working out probability from a Venn diagram.

4 **Is my solution correct?**

The answers are a sensible proportion of the total number of people.

5 **Have I completed everything?**

Reread the question. You need to draw and complete a Venn diagram and work out probabilities from it. Parts **(b)** and **(c)** ask for probabilities. You can write these probabilities as fractions, decimals or percentages.

> Always fill in the numbers on the Venn diagram by starting from the overlap and then working outwards.

> 16 watched rugby and football, but you already have 11 who have watched all three. You only need another 5 who watched just rugby and football. Repeat this method to obtain 7 and 6 in the other intersections.

> Write down the probabilities for watching only one sport and then add them up.

(10) Exam-style practice | Grade 5

Brian wants to buy a car. He finds out the age and the selling price of each of nine cars of the same type.

The scatter graph shows this information.

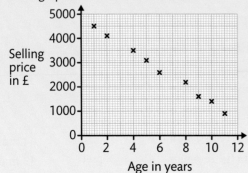

A tenth car is 7 years old and the selling price is £2400

(a) Show this information on the scatter graph. **[1 mark]**

(b) Draw a line of best fit on the scatter graph. **[1 mark]**

(c) What type of correlation does the scatter graph show? **[1 mark]**

(d) Describe the relationship between the selling price of a car and its age. **[1 mark]**

(e) Estimate the selling price of a car that is 3 years old. **[1 mark]**

✓ Made a start | ✓ Feeling confident | ✓ Exam ready

Answers

Page vi Assessment objective 1

1. $-1 < x \leqslant 4$
2. **(a)** trapezium **(b)** parallelogram
3. $x = -2, y = 4$

Page 1 Place value

1. **(a)** Nine thousand, five hundred and twenty
   (b) 800 or 8 hundreds
2. £50 058 (B), £50 142 (A), £50 241 (E), £51 042 (C), £52 014 (D)

Page 2 Negative numbers

1. **(a)** 15 **(b)** 6 **(c)** 32 **(d)** -6
2. $-10, -8, -2, 7, 8$
3. 22 degrees

Page 3 Adding and subtracting

1. **(a)** 113 **(b)** 79
2. **(a)** 5524 miles
   (b) 792 miles
3. The United States, by 54

Page 4 Multiplying and dividing

1. **(a)** 864 **(b)** 653
2. £686
3. 98

Page 5 Order of operations

1. **(a)** 34 **(b)** 4 **(c)** 12 **(d)** 10
2. $8 - 3 \times 1.75$

Page 6 Decimals

1. **(a)** $\frac{3}{100}$
   (b) 9 ten-thousandths
2. **(a)** 0.5, 0.502, 0.505, 0.52, 0.55
   (b) 0.8, 0.814, 0.82, 0.869, 0.87

Page 7 Operations with decimals

1. **(a)** 14.118 **(b)** 5.373
   (c) 36.942 **(d)** 12.1
2. £203.40
3. £2.16
4. £30.80

Page 8 Rounding

1. **(a)** 5460
   (b) 5500
   (c) 5000
2. **(a)** 653.0
   (b) 653.015
3. **(a)** 10
   (b) 0.0056
   (c) 218 000

Page 9 Fractions

1. **(a)** e.g.
   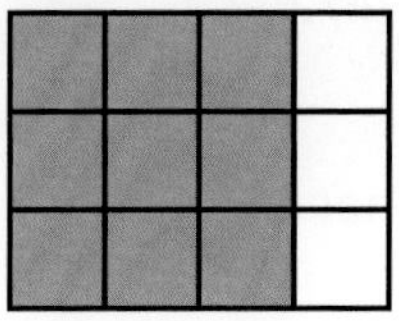
   (b) $\frac{3}{4}$
2. 240

Page 10 Operations with fractions

1. **(a)** $\frac{11}{15}$ **(b)** $\frac{11}{20}$ **(c)** $\frac{9}{20}$ **(d)** $\frac{27}{50}$
2. 54

Page 11 Mixed numbers and improper fractions

1. **(a)** $1\frac{1}{25}$ **(b)** 5 **(c)** $2\frac{1}{3}$ **(d)** $3\frac{7}{15}$
2. 6

Page 12 Factors, multiples and prime numbers

1. **(a)** 60 or 100 **(b)** 5 or 15 **(c)** 5 or 17
2. **(a)** 72 **(b)** 5 **(c)** 5 or 31
3. 23

Page 13 Prime factors, HCF and LCM

1. **(a)** $2^2 \times 3^3$ **(b)** 12 **(c)** 216
2. **(a)** $2^3 \times 7$ **(b)** 14 **(c)** 392

Page 14 Estimation and outcomes

1. **(a)** 20 **(b)** 3600 **(c)** 1000
2. H1, T1, H2, T2, H3, T3, H4, T4, H5, T5, H6, T6

Page 15 Indices and roots

1. 12
2. 3^5
3. 33
4. 25 and 27
5. 29

Page 16 Standard form

(a) 4.5×10^7 km **(b)** 3.4×10^4 km

Page 17 Error intervals

1. $38.5 \leqslant V < 39.5$
2. $45.55 \leqslant w < 45.65$
3. $54.855 \leqslant l < 54.865$
4. $83.575 \leqslant h < 83.585$

Page 18 Exam skills: Number

1. **(a) (i)** 5 degrees **(ii)** 7 degrees
   (b) -2°C
2. 8.57 a.m.

3 (a) (i) $4\frac{11}{20}$　(ii) £24

　　(b) 6000

4 £111.58

5 No, she does not

6 (a) (i) $2^2 \times 3 \times 5$　(ii) $2^5 \times 3$

　　(b) 12　(c) 480

Page 19 Function machines

1

x	y
3	4
4	11
5	20
2	−1

2 ×2, +7

Page 20 Algebraic substitution

1 −20.8

2 83

Page 21 Collecting like terms

1 (a) $3m$　(b) $9x - 5y$

2 (a) $7c^2$　(b) $3x - 10y$

3 $4 - 2t$

4 $5a - 4b$

Page 22 Simplifying expressions

1 $5cd$

2 $6w$

3 $15gh$

4 $4x$

5 $6x$

Page 23 Writing expressions

1 $4x + 2$

2 $8p + 27b$

Page 24 Algebraic formulae

1 $\frac{13}{2}$

2 (a) $12x + 10y = 200$, $10y = 200 - 12x$, $y = 20 - 1.2x$

　　(b) $A = 4x \times 2y = 4x \times 2(20 - 1.2x) = 4x(40 - 2.4x)$

　　　　　　　　$= 160x - 9.6x^2$

Page 25 Algebraic indices

1 (a) p^{11}　(b) x^8　(c) $12x^3y^5$

2 (a) m^6　(b) m^{15}　(c) $12w^8y^4$

　　(d) $8x^4y^7$

3 $n = 7$

4 $(10^3)^a \times (10^2)^b = 10^x$, so $10^{3a} \times 10^{2b} = 10^x$, so $3a + 2b = x$

Page 26 Expanding brackets

1 (a) $5m + 10$　(b) $-3n - 18$　(c) $x^2 - 5x$

　　(d) $3x^2 - 6x$　(e) $4x - 4x^2$

2 (a) $11a - 8b$　(b) $22 + 2g$

　　(c) $12r + 13pr + 24p$　(d) $9t^2 + 13t$

3 $x^2 - 5x$

Page 27 Expanding double brackets

1 (a) $x^2 + 6x + 9$

　　(b) $x^2 - 8x + 16$

　　(c) $x^2 - 2x + 1$

2 (a) $x^2 - 4$

　　(b) $x^2 + 3x - 28$

　　(c) $x^2 - 6x + 5$

　　(d) $x^2 - 12x + 27$

Page 28 Factorising

(a) $5(x + 4)$　(b) $4a(2a + 3)$

(c) $x(x - 6)$　(d) $3ab(a + 2b)$

(e) $3y(2y - 3x)$　(f) $4x(2x + y)$

Page 29 Linear equations

1 $x = \frac{3}{4}$　**2** (a) $x = \frac{3}{2} = 1.5$　(b) $x = 4$

3 Ann is 24 years old, Ben is 48 years old and Carl is 20 years old.

Page 30 Rearranging formulae

1 $n = \dfrac{m - 8}{3}$

2 $g = \dfrac{10t}{h}$

3 $a = \dfrac{v^2 - u^2}{2s}$

4 $x = 2(y - 1)$

Page 31 Inequalities

1 $-1 < x \leqslant 4$

2 $-1, 0, 1, 2, 3$

Page 32 Solving inequalities

1 $x < 9$

2 $x \geqslant 3$

3 $x \leqslant 3.5$

4 $-1.5 < x \leqslant 3$

5 (a) $-1 < x \leqslant 3$　(b) 0, 1, 2, 3

Page 33 Solving sequence problems

1 2, 14, 34

2 **(a)** Fourth term $= 4 + (a + 4) = a + 8$

Fifth term $= (a + 4) + (a + 8) = 2a + 12$

Sixth term $= (a + 8) + (2a + 12) = 3a + 20$

(b) $a = 5$

3 **(a)** 3, 7, 23, 87   **(b)** no

Page 34 Arithmetic sequences

1 **(a)** $5n - 9$

(b) No, because n would need to be 31.4 which is not an integer.

2 **(a)** because it does not end in 3 or 8

(b) $5n - 2$

Page 35 Factorising quadratics

1 **(a)** $x(x + 9)$

(b) $x(x - 15)$

(c) $x(x - 1)$

2 **(a)** $(x + 8)(x - 8)$

(b) $(x + 3)(x - 3)$

(c) $(x + 1)(x - 1)$

3 **(a)** $(x + 7)(x + 2)$

(b) $(x - 4)(x - 12)$

(c) $(x + 7)(x - 8)$

4 **(a)** $(x - 3)(x - 4)$

(b) $(x - 9)(x + 8)$

(c) $(x - 6)(x - 7)$

Page 36 Solving quadratic equations

1 **(a)** $x = 5, x = -5$ **(b)** $x = -1, x = 5$

2 **(a)** $(x + 3) \times (x - 4) = 44$

$x^2 + 3x - 4x - 12 = 44$

$x^2 - x - 56 = 0$

(b) Solutions are $x = -7$ and $x = 8$, so $x = 8$ because x must be positive

Page 37 Simultaneous equations

1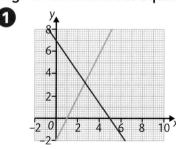

$x = 2.6, y = 3.3$

2 $x = \frac{2}{3}, y = -\frac{3}{2}$

3 Adult £7.50 and child £3.00

Page 38 Gradients of lines

1 $\frac{1}{2}$

2 $-\frac{8}{5}$

Page 39 Drawing straight-line graphs

1 **(a)**

x	−1	0	1	2	3	4
y	10	8	6	4	2	0

(b)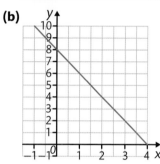

2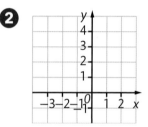

Page 40 Equations of straight lines

1 $y = -3x + 11$

2 $y = \frac{1}{2}x - 2$

Page 41 Parallel lines

1 $y = 3x - 1$

2 Line L_1 has gradient 3, and line L_2 has gradient 3, so they are parallel.

3 Line **A**: $2y = 3x + 8, y = \frac{3}{2}x + 4$, gradient $= \frac{3}{2}$

Line **B**: gradient $= \frac{8 - 2}{2 - (-1)} = \frac{6}{3} = 2$

The gradients of lines **A** and **B** are different, therefore they will intersect.

Page 42 Real-life graphs

(a) -0.625 **(b) A**, because its volume falls to 0 in a shorter time.

Page 43 Quadratic graphs

(a)

x	−1	0	1	2	3	4
y	6	2	0	0	2	6

(b)

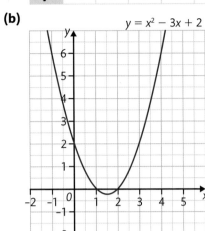

$y = x^2 - 3x + 2$

(c) $(1.5, -0.25)$

Page 44 Using quadratic graphs

(a)

x	−2	−1	0	1	2	3	4
y	6	1	−2	−3	−2	1	6

(b)

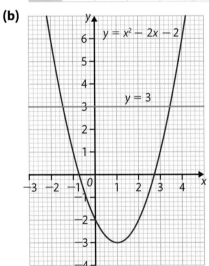

$y = x^2 - 2x - 2$

$y = 3$

(c) $x = 3.4$ and $x = -1.4$

(d) $x = 2.7$ and $x = -0.7$

Page 45 Cubic and reciprocal graphs

1 (a)

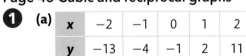

x	−2	−1	0	1	2
y	−13	−4	−1	2	11

(b)

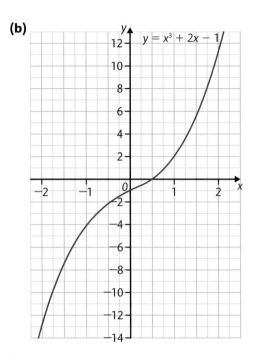

$y = x^3 + 2x - 1$

(c) $x = 0.5$

2 (a)

x	0.125	0.25	0.5	1	2	4
y	8	4	2	1	0.5	0.25

(b)

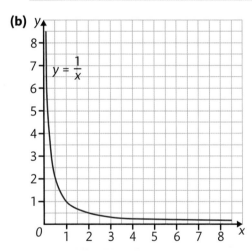

$y = \dfrac{1}{x}$

Page 46 Recognising graphs

(a) B **(b)** E **(c)** A

Page 47 Algebraic reasoning

1

$7x + 3x$	Expression
$9a - 5a \equiv 4a$	Identity
$A = 0.5(a+b)h$	Formula
$5x + 7 = 2x$	Equation

2 LHS $= (x-2)^2 = (x-2)(x-2) = x(x-2) - 2(x-2)$
$= x^2 - 2x - 2x + 4 = x^2 - 4x + 4 =$ RHS

3 $(n+1)^2 - n(n+2) = n^2 + 2n + 1 - n^2 - 2n = 1$

4 Two consecutive odd numbers can be represented by $2n+1$ and $2n+3$ where n is a whole number.

$2n + 1 + 2n + 3 = 4n + 4 = 4(n+1)$

Since n is a whole number then $4(n+1)$ is a multiple of 4.

Page 48 Exam skills: Algebra

1 (a) $20x + 8$ (b) $5x + 2$

2 $x = -2, y = 4$

3 (a) $6n - 1$

(b) Yes, if $6n - 1 = 119$ then $6n = 120$ and $n = 20$
119 is the 20th term in the sequence.

Page 49 Ratio

1 (a) $1:2$ (b) $1:6$ (c) $1:4$ (d) $5:3$

2 (a) $\frac{7}{10}$ (b) $\frac{3}{10}$

3 Angela: £200

Brenda: £160

4 Mia receives £160 more than Niamh.

5 16

Page 50 Direct proportion

1 7.5 kg

2 It is more expensive in the UK: petrol costs $1.53 per litre in the UK and $0.78 in the US.

Page 51 Inverse proportion

1 4.8 hours or 4 hours 48 minutes

2 84 days

3 (a) 20 cm (b) 2.5 cm

Page 52 Percentages

1 (a) £23 800 (b) 2%

2 (a) $\frac{2}{5}$ (b) 20%

3 (a) 77 (b) 29.4% (c) 170

Page 53 Fractions, decimals and percentages

1

Fraction	Decimal	Percentage
$\frac{1}{8}$	0.125	12.5%
$\frac{3}{20}$	0.15	15%
$\frac{2}{5}$	0.4	40%

2 66.7% **3** £900

Page 54 Percentage change

1 £132.60

2 £1242.52

Page 55 Reverse percentages

1 2.5 kg

2 Last year, Jack earned £32 163.46 and Zoe earned £31 940.37 so Jack's salary was greater last year.

Page 56 Growth and decay

1 £1663.08

2 £4913

3 $n = 4$

Page 57 Compound measures

1 3.3 m²

2 5 minutes

Page 58 Speed

1 50 mph

2 12.5 miles

3 She is correct, because her average speed will be 85.7 mph.

4 12 mph

Page 59 Density

1 (a) 1870 cm³ (b) 0.479 g/cm³

2 1.03 g/cm³

Page 60 Proportion and graphs

1 $A = 6B$, because it goes through the origin.

2 $y = 67.2$

Page 61 Exam skills: Ratio and proportion

1 Yasmin got the highest mark. Yasmin got 88 marks, Lexie got 78 marks and Amaya got 75 marks.

2 No, he doesn't have enough cement.

Page 62 Angle properties

(a) acute

(b) 52°, alternate angles are equal.

(c) 46°, corresponding angles are equal.

(d) 46°, vertically opposite angles are equal.

Page 63 Solving angle problems

(a) 133°, angles on a straight line sum to 180°.

(b) 47°, alternate angles are equal.

(c) 86°, triangle *BCD* is isosceles so angle *BDC* = angle *BCD* and all the internal angles sum to 180°.

Page 64 Angles in polygons

36°

Page 65 Constructing perpendiculars

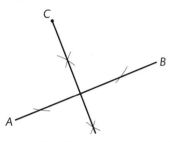

Page 66 Constructions with angles

(a)

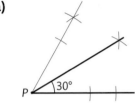

(b)

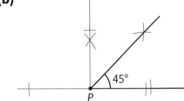

Page 67 Loci

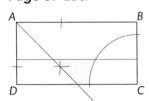

Page 68 Perimeter and area

1 **(a)** 14 cm   **(b)** 9 cm²

2 16 cm²

Page 69 Areas of 2D shapes

1 12 m²

2 45 cm²

Page 70 3D shapes

(a) A: cube; B: cylinder; C: square-based pyramid; D: triangular prism

(b) (i) 5   **(ii)** 8   **(iii)** 5

Page 71 Volumes of 3D shapes

1 37.7 m³

2 96 cm³

Page 72 Surface area

1 **(a)** 340 cm²   **(b)** 400 cm³

2 **(a)** 660 cm²   **(b)** 600 cm³

Page 73 Circles and cylinders

13.0 cm

Page 74 Circles, sectors and arcs

(a) 8.38 cm   **(b)** 40.2 cm²

Page 75 Circle facts

1

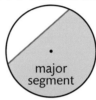

2 20°

Page 76 Transformations

1 $\begin{pmatrix} 5 \\ -4 \end{pmatrix}$

2

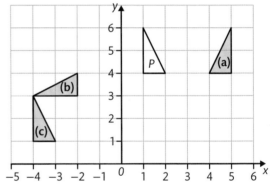

Page 77 Enlargement

An enlargement, scale factor 3, about centre of enlargement (0, 0).

Page 78 Bearings

1 242°

2

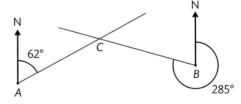

Page 79 Scale drawings and maps

1 45 m

2 **(a)** 3.2 km   **(b)** 1 : 20 000

Page 80 Pythagoras' theorem

1 $11^2 \neq 5^2 + 8^2$, so it is not a right-angled triangle.

2 Yes, because 53.1 m is less than 60 m.

Page 81 Units of length, area and volume

1 40 000 cm²

2 95.7 cm²

3 160 000 mm

4 37.5 s

Page 82 Trigonometry: lengths

1 19.2 cm **2** $\tan 30° = \frac{x}{4}$

Page 83 Trigonometry: angles

1 22.6°

2 23.8°

Page 84 Trigonometry techniques

1 16 cm

2 30°

Page 85 Time and timetables

1 **(a)** 2.18 p.m. **(b)** 16:29

2 11:35

3 **(a)** 10:53 **(b)** 23 minutes

Page 86 Reading scales

1 **(a)** 27

(b)
```
|0    1    2    3    4   ↑5    6|
```

2 150 g

Page 87 Symmetry

1 **(a)** A **(b)** 5

2 **(a)** A **(b)** 2

Page 88 Quadrilaterals

1 **(a)** trapezium **(b)** parallelogram

2 e.g.

Page 89 Plans and elevations

1

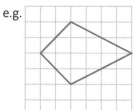

2

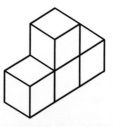

Page 90 Similarity and congruence

1 **(a)** **B** and **G** **(b)** **C**

2 **(a)** **B** and **D** **(b)** **F**

Page 91 Similar shapes

1 **(a)** 8.75 cm **(b)** 12 cm

2 **(a)** 5.2 cm **(b)** 5 cm

Page 92 Congruent triangles

1 $AD = CD$ equal sides
$AB = CB$ equal sides
BD is common
ADB is congruent to CDB (SSS)

Page 93 Line segments

(a) (6, 4)

(b) 10

Page 94 Vectors

(a) **a**

(b) -2**a**

(c) **b** $-$ **a**

(d) $2(\mathbf{a} - \mathbf{b})$

Page 95 Exam skills: Geometry and measures

1 10.5 cm

2 34.9 cm

Page 96 Introduction to probability

1 **(a)** $\frac{1}{6}$

(b) $\frac{1}{3}$

2 **(a)**

		Dice 1					
		1	2	3	4	5	6
Dice 2	1	2	3	4	5	6	7
	2	3	4	5	6	7	8
	3	4	5	6	7	8	9
	4	5	6	7	8	9	10
	5	6	7	8	9	10	11
	6	7	8	9	10	11	12

(b) (i) $\frac{3}{36} = \frac{1}{12}$ **(ii)** $\frac{10}{36} = \frac{5}{18}$ **(iii)** $\frac{18}{36} = \frac{1}{2}$

Page 97 More about probability

1 0.13

2 $(0.3)^3 = 0.027 < 0.1$; Sandeep is correct

Page 98 Relative frequency

1 (a) $\frac{24}{90} = \frac{4}{15}$

(b) $\frac{66}{90} = \frac{11}{15}$

(c) $\frac{69}{90} = \frac{23}{30}$

2 (a) (i) $\frac{2}{15}$ (ii) $\frac{7}{15}$

(b) Sample is too small so they are not accurate estimates.

Page 99 Venn diagrams

1 (a)

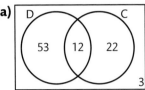

(b) $\frac{3}{90} = \frac{1}{30}$

2 $\frac{37}{60}$

Page 100 Tree diagrams

1 (a)

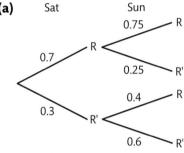

R = rain, R′ = no rain

(b) 0.525 (c) 0.82

2 $\frac{83}{200}$

Page 101 Exam skills: Probability

1 (a) $\frac{14}{25}$ (b) 3

2 (a) 0.0875 (b) 0.575

3 (a) 0.3 (b) 60

Page 102 Averages and range

1 (a) 4 (b) 4.5 (c) 4.7 (d) 4

2 150 cm

3 $x = 11, y = 26$

Page 103 Pictograms

(a)

Thursday	◇◇
Friday	◇◇◁
Saturday	◇◇◇◿
Sunday	◇◇◿

Key ◇ represents 4 radios

(b) 42

Page 104 Line graphs

(a)

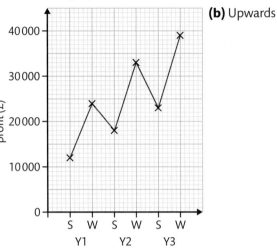

(b) Upwards

Page 105 Pie charts

(a) $\frac{1}{3}$ (b) 2400

Page 106 Stem-and-leaf diagrams

1

5	8
6	3 5 6 6
7	1 2 5 5 6 7 8 9
8	3 9

Key: 7 | 5 represents 75

2 (a)

7	2 2 7
8	2 3 3 7 8
9	2 3 4 5 6 7 7
10	0 2 2 5

Key: 7 | 2 represents 72 cm

(b) 33 cm

Page 107 Scatter graphs

(a)

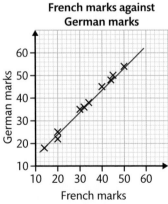

French marks against German marks

(b) There is a positive correlation between French marks and German marks.

(c) (i) 30–32 (ii) 37–39

Page 108 Frequency tables

1 (a) 2 (b) 2.5 (c) 2.7

2 **(a)** $16 \leqslant T < 20$ **(b)** $12 \leqslant T < 16$

(c) 14.4 °C **(d)** The data is grouped.

Page 109 Two-way tables

1 **(a)**

	Mon-day	Tues-day	Wednes-day	Total
Morning	14	26	13	53
Afternoon	21	9	17	47
Total	35	35	30	100

(b) 0.13 **(c)** $\frac{9}{35}$

2 19

Page 110 Sampling

1 Sample size is too small.

The time he chose is from 8.30 a.m.

2 She only asks people in the sports shop.

Page 111 Analysing data

The daytime median is 26 and the daytime range is 39

The daytime median is greater than the night-time median, so people tended to spend more time at the café during the day. The daytime range is greater than the night-time range, so the spread of times people spent at the café was greater during the day.

Page 112 Exam skills: Statistics

(a)

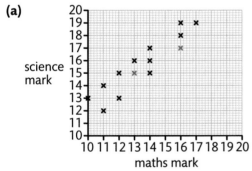

(b) The graph shows positive correlation between maths and science marks.

(c) Jake got 15 in the maths test, so an estimate for his science mark is 17

Page 113 Problem-solving strategies

Problem 1: No, he needs £700

Problem 2: 0.42

Page 114 Solving number problems

She needs to sell the remaining rings at £2.50 each.

Page 115 Solving graphical problems

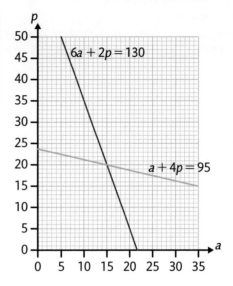

apples = 15p each and pears = 20p each

four apples and seven pears = 60p + 140p = £2.00

Page 116 Solving geometric problems

Length of arc $ABC = 7.70$ cm

Page 117 Solving algebraic problems

(a) $x^2 + (34 - x)^2 = 26^2$, $x^2 + 34^2 - 68x + x^2 = 26^2$, $2x^2 - 68x + 480 = 0$, $x^2 - 34x + 240 = 0$

(b) 24 cm

Page 118 Solving statistical problems

(a) and (b)

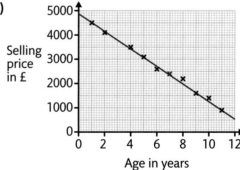

(c) negative

(d) The selling price of a car decreases as its age increases.

(e) £3500–£3800

Published by BBC Active, an imprint of Educational Publishers LLP, part of the Pearson Education Group, 80 Strand, London, WC2R 0RL.

www.pearsonschools.co.uk/BBCBitesize

© Educational Publishers LLP 2019

BBC logo © BBC 1996. BBC and BBC Active are trademarks of the British Broadcasting Corporation.

Edited, typeset and produced by Elektra Media Ltd
Illustrated by Elektra Media Ltd
Cover design by Andrew Magee & Pearson Education Limited 2019
Cover illustration by Darren Lingard / Oxford Designers & Illustrators

The right of Navtej Marwaha to be identified as author of this work has been asserted by him in accordance with the Copyright, Designs and Patents Act 1988.

First published 2019

22 21 20 19

10 9 8 7 6 5 4 3 2 1

British Library Cataloguing in Publication Data

A catalogue record for this book is available from the British Library

ISBN 978 1 406 68608 1

Printed and bound in Slovakia by Neografia.

The Publisher's policy is to use paper manufactured from sustainable forests.

Acknowledgements

BBC: 1-17, 19-47, 49-59, 62-84, 87-94, 96-100, 102-105, 107-111, 113-118 © 2019

Note from the publisher

Pearson has robust editorial processes, including answer and fact checks, to ensure the accuracy of the content in this publication, and every effort is made to ensure this publication is free of errors. We are, however, only human, and occasionally errors do occur. Pearson is not liable for any misunderstandings that arise as a result of errors in this publication, but it is our priority to ensure that the content is accurate. If you spot an error, please do contact us at resourcescorrections@pearson.com so we can make sure it is corrected.

Websites

Pearson Education Limited is not responsible for the content of third-party websites.